FISHING in ICELAND

In the steps of Eiríkur the Red

by Mike Savage

Old Bakehouse Publications

Abertillery

© Mike Savage

First published in March 2003

The rights of the author to this work has
been asserted by him in accordance with the Copyright,
Designs and Patents Act, 1993.

ISBN 1 874538 89 1

Published in the U.K. by
Old Bakehouse Publications
Church Street,
Abertillery, Gwent NP13 1EA
Telephone: 01495 212600 Fax: 01495 216222
http:/www.mediamaster.co.uk/oldbakebooks

Made and printed in the UK
by J.R. Davies (Printers) Ltd.

All rights reserved. No part of this publication may be reproduced, stored in a retrieval
system, or transmitted in any form or by any means, electronic,
mechanical, photocopying, recording or otherwise without the
prior permission of Old Bakehouse Publications.
For the avoidance of doubt, this includes reproduction of any
image in this book on an internet site.

British Library Cataloguing in Publication Data: a catalogue
record for this book is available from the British Library.

I am most grateful for the generosity of the undermentioned kind people who have sponsored this book.

Mike Savage

Nigel Birt-Llewellin, Gloucestershire, UK

Mrs. Charles Brocklebank, Suffolk, UK

Robert L. Constantine, Newton Abbot, UK

Graham G. Ferguson, Rogate, UK

C. Francis & Co. Sporting Agents, USA

William Garfit, Cambridge, UK

Charles R. Godchaux of Abbeville, Louisiana, USA

Frank A. Godchaux of Abbeville, Louisiana, USA

Jean Howman, Ashmere Fisheries, Shepperton, UK

Mr. & Mrs. Edward Money, Woking, UK

Mrs. L.Z. Rowcliffe, Reigate, UK

Derek Strauss, London, UK

Contents

		Page
Preface by Orri Vigfússon		ix
Introduction by Sigurður Helgason		xii
Author's Notes and Acknowledgements		xv
List of Illustrations		xviii
Key to Rivers numbered on the Map		xx
Map		xxi
Chapter One	**The Start of a Love Affair**	1
1958, Introduction to Iceland		1
1964, Back Again	Þverá, Halfralónsá & Hofsá	5
1976, a Holiday of one's dreams	Fróðá, Norðurá & Laxá í Kjós	15
Chapter Two	**Getting to know Iceland**	21
The Country		21
Choosing a River		28
Fishing for Salmon	My training for Iceland	32
	Back to Iceland	
Ethics and Conservation		41
Chapter Three	**The rivers of the South West**	48
Elliðaár		48
Úlfarsá		48
Leirvogsá		48
Varmá		48
Laxá í Kjós		49
Brynjudalsá		64
Laxá í Leirársveit		64
Chapter Four	**The Hvítá í Borgarfjörður**	66
Grímsá		66
Flókadalsá		68
Reykjadalsá		68
Þverá, and Litla Þverá		69-70

v

		Page
Kjarrá		73
Norðurá		79
Gljúfurá		80

Chapter Five — **North to Snæfellsnes** — **81**

Langá		81
Álftá		81
Hítará		81
Haffjarðará		82
Straumfjarðará		89

Chapter Six — **The Rivers of Breiðafjörður** — **91**

Haukadalsá	Description of the river	92
	The Birds	
	A summary of the River and Our Experiences	
The Upper Haukadalsá		103
The Þverá (Tributary)		103
Laxá í Dölum	Description of the River	108
	The Top Beat	
	The Middle Beat	
	The Bottom Beat	
	Mrs. Lilla Rowcliffe	
	A Summary of our time on the Laxá í Dölum	

The Record Week on the Laxá í Dölum, July 1986	137
Fáskrúð	145

Chapter Seven — **The North-West Fjords** — **147**

Reiðá	147
Laugardalsá and Langadalsá	148
Bjarnafjarðará	

Chapter Eight — **The Rivers of the North** — **150**

Hrútafjarðará	150
Miðfjarðará, with its tributaries Vesturá, Núpsá and Austurá	150
Viðidalsá	153
Vatnsdalsá	153

vi

		Page
Laxá á Ásum		153
Blanda and Svartá		155
Fljótaá, Fnjóská and Skjálfandafljót		155
Laxá í Aðaldal		155
Chapter Nine	**The Rivers of the North East**	**157**
Deildará		157
Ormarsá		161
Svalbarðsá	Svalbarðsselhylur Stórifoss Laxahylur	162
Sandá		163
Hölkná		165
Hafralónsá		165
Miðfjarðará í Bakkaflóa		167
Bakkaá		167
Chapter Ten	**The Rivers of the East Coast**	**170**
Selá		170
Vesturdalsá		173
Hofsá		174
The next 150 Kilometres!		179
Breiðdalsá		179
Laxá í Nesjum		180
Chapter Eleven	**The Rivers of the South Coast**	**182**
Rangá		182
Ölfusá		183
Hvitá		183
Tungufljót		183
Stóra Laxá		183
Sog, or Sogið		185
Chapter Twelve	**Sea Trout and Migratory Char**	**186**

		Page
Chapter Thirteen	**Brown Trout and Lake Char**	192
Chapter Fourteen	**Greenland**	196
Statistics	**Tables 1 - 8**	202

List of Tables

Table 1   1860 Farms benefiting with income from salmon.

Table 2   Salmon rivers, with statistics including number of rods allowed to fish, average number of fish per rod per season, facilities provided, etc. etc.

Table 3   Salmon rivers, with 28-year record of annual catches, average catch, maximum & minimum catches.

Table 4   Graphs covering 1974-2001 with the total number of salmon caught by rod, netted & ocean ranching harvest.

Table 5   Salmon rod catch, released, killed, netted, ranch catch, wild salmon percentage 1974-2001.

Table 6   Top 10 Rivers and Lakes for Salmon, Trout & Char (all, both migratory & non-migratory) in 2001.

Table 7   Catch of Trout in some rivers, 1987-2001.

Table 8   Catch of Char in some rivers, 1987-2001.

Index   213

Preface by Orri Vigfússon

I am sure that this book by Mike Savage will be regarded as the third in a series of classic books about salmon fishing in Iceland. The first, A Veteran Sportsman's Diary by Charles H. Akroyd of Duncraggie, Brora, was published in 1926. In 1952 the second, The Rivers of Iceland, by Major General Stewart of Kinlochmoidart near Fort William, found a place on the bookshelves of all serious collectors of great angling literature.

Now, half a century later, an Englishman has joined these two illustrious Scots in penning a superb tribute to Iceland and its wonderful fishing. Mike Savage readily acknowledges his debt to Akroyd who first came to Iceland in 1877 and later brought with him, Stewart in 1912 and then Mike Savage followed in 1958. All three authors fell immediately under Iceland's spell. Indeed, Stewart wrote that this was the place 'where most fish lies come true!'

Two of these authors had no idea when they began their first visits, that Iceland would inspire them to write superb fishing books. Both Stewart and Mike Savage were lured to Iceland by two quite different forms of interest in ducks! Stewart wanted to shoot duck. Mike Savage came with his brother and Christopher Sellick, who had previously visited Iceland with Peter Scott to ring pink-foot geese. The object of the two brothers' visit was to catch Harlequin, Long-tails and Scoters for Peter Scott's Wildfowl Trust.

The two earlier authors were clearly observant about Iceland's birds. Akroyd found there was still an abundance of ptarmigan-eating falcons. Stewart was amazed at the courage, resource and skill of the ring dotterel in shepherding their young ones away from the hooves of wandering ponies.

Once they realised Iceland's fishing possibilities however, both Stewart and Mike Savage became as well hooked on the country as the many salmon they caught. In his time Stewart was the acknowledged authority on Icelandic salmon fishing. I believe it to be beyond doubt that Mike, who has now paid our rivers so many visits, has succeeded him to that title. All who read his book will find ample evidence that he is the present authority.

Akroyd, on the other hand, did not spend many seasons in Iceland though he did take ponies back with him to Scotland because he thought they would make first-class hill ponies. I believe he fished only the Laxá í Aðaldalur. His mode of transport was the S.S. 'Snowdoun' and his companions included Henry Tollemache and Adam Hay Gordon. They set sail for Iceland after a succulent dinner at the New Club in Edinburgh.

Stewart's experience was much more wide-ranging. He fished no less than seventeen Icelandic rivers including the Hrútafjarðará in the North which he rented for a considerable number of years. Mike Savage's experience eclipses even that of Stewart. Mike has fished a total of 36 Icelandic rivers though he is, like Stewart, particularly fond of the Laxá í Dölum.

All three men soon became enthusiastically immersed in the whole range of Iceland's geography and culture. They rejoiced in its clean vital waters, dramatic scenery and natural wonders. They met and mingled with the people who seemed to them to be innocent, pure and greatly interested in literature and those who wrote it.

'Fishing in Iceland - In the steps of Eiríkur rauði, Erik the red' is a very wide-ranging and honest presentation of Iceland because Mike Savage is an honest observer. He takes his readers on a journey through Icelandic history and introduces them to the people, the rivers and the wildlife. He illuminates his narrative with many of his personal reminiscences and anecdotes. In setting down his thoughts and advice on the attractions of Icelandic salmon fishing, he answers many a question.

Icelanders themselves are proud of their history, language and the sagas. Mike's knowledge and experience provides a valuable addition to this culture. In a sense Iceland has developed its own special brand identity as a fishing destination and over the years, Mike has watched the emergence of the angling infrastructure and the way the regulations and the effective management of the fisheries have developed.

The English salmon fishers who have come to Iceland have played a considerable role in promoting the conservation objectives and regulation methods that now exist. They have set strict standards of sportsmanship and encouraged the tackle sterilisation rules that visiting anglers must observe and which now protect the health of Iceland's rivers. They have shown others how to strike consensus deals on angling methods, agree acceptable ways of rotating beats and shown the need to provide visitors with reliable river information.

Accurate fishing records have always been regarded as public property in Iceland but anglers and fishery operators alike continue to make demands for even more sophisticated and robust statistical data with which we can analyse the nature and trends of the fisheries of every river.

The art of fishing for salmon in Iceland can be rather technical and the angler has a range of choices in the way he or she approaches the river, presents the fly and deals with the diverse and complicated currents often to be found in the same pool. The fishing conditions are constantly changing and the range of flies that might succeed is endless. Mike Savage shares his experiences and the choices he has made with fellow fishers throughout Iceland. This is invaluable because there are few Icelandic anglers who have covered as many of their national rivers as he has. He is a genuine and generous fishing partner and this shines through in his everyday life and in the pages of his wonderful book.

Best of all for me, he is giving all his profits to the North Atlantic Salmon Fund. That is a faithful measure of his generosity of spirit because I am sure this new book will be very profitable. It is his way of repaying some of the joy and excitement a lifetime's salmon fishing has given him and it demonstrates his support for the practical action we all should be taking if we are to secure a future for the wild salmon he loves so well.

Orri Vigfússon

Orri Vigfússon.

Introduction by Sigurður Helgason

On one of our many fishing trips together, I suggested to Mike Savage that he write a book on salmon fishing in Iceland. No book has been written in English on this subject since Major General R.N. Stewart's book, 'The Rivers of Iceland', published in 1950. I believed that a genuine need existed for such a book, given the prominence of Iceland as a salmon fisherman's paradise, and notably in view of the decline of salmon fishing elsewhere, except perhaps the Kola area in Russia.

Mike and I became acquainted through my son, Helgi, who shares our common interest in fishing. At that time Helgi was acting as a guide on the Haffjarðará river, aged 17. In Iceland it is common for students to try to find gainful employment during their summer holidays. I introduced salmon fishing to my four children and inspired three of them, Helgi included. Mike was fishing with his son Sandy, and subsequently, the Haffjarðará was to mark the beginning of a family friendship which continues to this day.

Since that time I have fished with Mike on many rivers in Iceland, as well as in Russia, Argentina, Chile and England. Mike is one of the finest fly fishermen that it has been my privilege to know. His skill is absolutely superb and he has that unique ability to fish successfully under almost any circumstance. His knowledge of fishing gear, tackle and all things related to the subject matter is overwhelming, I must confess that I have learned a lot from fishing with Mike and observing his techniques. Dedication to fly fishing is not only a passion - it is an art.

My love affair with fishing goes back to my youth. From about the age of 8, I spent summers with my father's family on a big farm in the Borgarfjörður district. It was a wonderful experience. A boy my age lived on the farm and he introduced me to fishing. There were several streams and rivers that we fished throughout the summer, some smaller, others larger, such as the Urriðaá and Langá, as well as the upper section of the Álftá. We fished for trout and char in all size ranges, from around one up to five pounds.

Our gear was pretty basic at the beginning, a piece of thin string and a hook. Later on we made ourselves rods out of wooden shafts, used for haymaking. We would dig worms out of the vegetable garden for bait. Our duties on the farm were related to looking after the animals, the cows, and the horses, but we used every available opportunity to fish. We would always have a piece of heavier string in our pockets, and we would sometimes catch a horse grazing, put a string through its mouth as a reign, and ride bareback to the river to fish. We caught a lot of trout and char and were extremely popular with the Lady of the House, who was responsible for cooking! I remember that in late summer the bigger rivers would have seen lots of sea trout, a real bonanza!

Salmon fishing came later, and I have consistently fished for salmon almost every year since the age of 18 - 80 years! The Atlantic Salmon is a unique creature, a remarkable species without parallel. This natural wonder keeps those of us who devote ourselves to catching salmon full of admiration.

Sigurður Helgason.

From a painting by Svava Salman.

To my mind, salmon fishing is a unique experience in terms of getting away from it all. I can think of no other activity which has enabled me to distance myself totally from daily life. When on a river I think of nothing except those things directly related to this passion; the river, the water level, the pool, the salmon, my cast, the line, the fly, the equipment that I am using and so forth. Of course the birds get their due attention as they are part and parcel of the beautiful surroundings, as is the weather - the rain, the sunshine and the wind. In reality it becomes a world of its own with no outside interference of any kind. As such, it is totally relaxing and all encompassing.

Iceland is a true angler's utopia. I have fished in many other parts of the world, and the more that I have experienced fishing in other areas, the greater the appeal of Iceland. Salmon fishing here is unique in terms of almost 100 fishable salmon rivers. But so is the tremendous variety in terms of fishing for trout and char; and later in the season for sea trout and sea char. There exists an endless number of rivers, streams and lakes in which these species can be found in abundance.

Mike has fished on more rivers in Iceland for longer than any other foreign fisherman that I know of. Furthermore, he is unique in that he has kept accurate and complete statistics and related details in regard to all his fishing in Iceland. Hence, another reason that I thought that he would be an ideal candidate to write such a book. He simply knows so much about fishing in Iceland; surely a valuable resource to be recorded for us to enjoy - as well as for posterity.

Mike has done a wonderful job in putting this book together and I am convinced that it will appeal to all fishermen - not only to those that have fished in Iceland, but to all who have a genuine interest in the noble art of fishing.

Sigurður Helgason

Author's Notes and Acknowledgements

I have written this book in aid of The North Atlantic Salmon Fund, this is led by Orri Vigfússon. In my opinion Orri is the most distinguished and effective man in the world of Atlantic Salmon Conservation. The money that goes to the NASF is used to the greatest effect. Also Orri is an Icelander! Once it is known that this book is in aid of NASF, all doors have opened!

My first introduction to Iceland was to collect duck for the Wildfowl Trust and I stumbled on some of the best fishing for wild brown trout in Europe. Then I was inspired by 'The Rivers of Iceland', written by Major General Stewart, with a longing to explore the rivers of Iceland for Atlantic salmon, also for sea trout and brown trout. I hope that this book will excite the ambition of other fishermen to sample the delights of Iceland.

Sigurður Helgason, a most distinguished Icelander and a special friend, asked me to write this book. I agreed to do this with his help, which he has given all the way through. The book is profusely illustrated not only with photographs, but also with paintings that are more evocative even than photographs. All artists and photographers have generously donated their pictures for use in this book, for which I am most grateful.

The book is divided, like Gaul, into three parts:-

The first part covers my early visits to Iceland, and also includes information about Iceland and in general about its rivers, my training for Iceland and other issues.

The second part describes rivers, starting in Reykjavík and going round the country clockwise. Naturally the rivers that I know best are covered in the greatest detail, but these illustrate what may be expected elsewhere. I have not only covered the most important rivers but also several of the more minor rivers. Taking into account the number of rods that are permitted to fish individual rivers, the timing of a visit and the facilities that are provided, excellent fishing can be obtained at a much lower price than on the fashionable rivers. These other rivers may be suitable for family parties with the best fishing being during the school holidays. This section of the book also covers fishing for Brown Trout, Sea Trout, Char, both resident and sea run, and a brief section about Greenland, enough to whet the appetite.

The third part consists of tables of statistics; these are very revealing to those readers who are really interested. Much can be learned from them and, to help, I have included some footnotes. I have indicated how many rods are permitted to fish each river, and some indication of the types of river, the average flow (where available) and also the facilities provided. Footnotes explain some of the extreme annual variations.

I wish to thank the three artists Rodger McPhail, Will Garfit and Peter Symonds, who have allowed me to reproduce their wonderful paintings, and to thank Loudie Constantine, who is the owner of one of these paintings. I also wish to thank my wife, Joanna, for her evocative sketch, and my son Sandy, who is the owner of one of the paintings in which he is the fisherman.

Also, I wish to thank:
> Sigurður Helgason for his unfailing help and encouragement. He has tried hard to correct my Icelandic spelling and accents.
> Árni Baldursson for many of the photographs and other help.
> Christopher Robinson for his help and suggestions, at all times.
> My friends and family with whom it has been such a pleasure to fish.
> The Icelandic guides who have found so many fish for us and added to the joy of fishing.
> Páll Jónson who was so kind and generous to me in our early days fishing in Iceland.
> Helgi Jakobsson who helped me so much to obtain fishing on the Laxá í Dölum and continued to help me during the years that I fished it.
> Sigurður Guðjonsson and Árni Ísaksson of the Institute of Freshwater Fisheries, Reykjavík, who allowed me to use statistics from the Institute.
> Landmælingar Islands - Iceland Geodetic Survey for permission to use a map.

I remember with the greatest pleasure almost all those with whom I have fished in Iceland. They have made every meal a party. This house party atmosphere is what we like to achieve fishing with old and new friends. I have met an extraordinarily interesting variety of people on these holidays. Only a few of them could be mentioned in this book.

Every year things change but I have done my best to have everything correct up to the end of 2001. As this book goes to print we know that the 2002 season had a slow start but became a good year on many rivers, most notably the Hofsá, Selá and Norðurá. Both the East and West Rangá were a disappointment but it seems that this is likely to be an aberration.

In this book Icelandic words and names are written in Icelandic in order to give them due emphasis. This is why Eiríkur a Viking does not immediately become Erik! In the Index Icelandic names are listed correctly under their first names, not surnames.

The sport fishing of Iceland has survived the growth and decline of commercial ranching of Salmon, and I do hope that Iceland continues to remain clear of the diseases, chemical pollution and parasites that are associated with commercial Salmon operations and that are doing so much harm elsewhere. I have spent many of the happiest weeks of my life in Iceland.

Mike Savage, Stanners Hill Farm, Chobham.
February, 2003

Mike Savage with a load of salmon on his back!

List of Illustrations

Page No.	Picture
vii	Orri Vigfússon
xi	Sigurður Helgason
xiii	Mike Savage, with a load of salmon on his back!
xviii	Map of Iceland, with many rivers marked that are referred to in the text
xix	Hofsá Valley
6	A salmon under water
7	The lower Þverá Lodge in 1965
9	'Our catch' (29th July 1964) Dettifoss
11	Lower Cambusmore and Hades Mountains, River Hofsá
12	The old school at Hof
13	Hofsá, looking towards the Foss
15	Chateau Brian with Loudie Constantine, Sigurður Helgason and Júlíus Guðjónsson
17	My wife, Joanna in Paradís!
18	3 Savages with Norðurá grilse
19	Norðurá, Snoppuhylur
21	Icelandic stamps 'Discoverers of America 1000 & 1492'
22	Greenland, Brattahlið sheep being loaded from Leifur Eíriksson's rock quay
25	Driftwood
35	Charlie Wright, ghillie, Balmoral Estate
36	Brig O'Dee, Scotland
50	Þórufoss on the Laxá í Kjós
51	Laxá í Kjós - Stekkjarfljót
52	Laxá í Kjós - Króarhamar
56	Laxá í Kjós - Kvíslafoss in a huge spate
	Laxá í Kjós - Kvíslafoss in high water
61	Laxá í Kjós - Ben's car
62	Brynjudalsá
63	Nick Savage guided on the Laxá í Kjós
65	Ferjukotseyrar on the Hvítá
67	Straumar on the Hvítá
68	The 'elephant house'
70	Sigurður Helgason with his son Siggi and son in law Ware Preston
71	Þverá - Þórunnarhylur with Robin playing his big fish
72	Þverá - Robin and Sandy with fish of 19 and 23 lbs
73	Þverá - Dranghylur
74	Kjarrá - My Land Rover fording the river

Page No.	Picture
75	Kjarrá - Robin and Ben Savage on their horses
76	Kjarrá - Keith, Jean and Colin Howman outside the lodge
77	Kjarrá - Árni Baldursson and Tóti Tönn on horses with fly rods
78	The Kjarrá in spate
79	The Middle Kjarrá
83	The Haffjarðará valley and lodge
84	Haffjarðará - Helgi and Sandy
85	Haffjarðará - Outflow
	Haffjarðará - Upper and Lower Luncheon Pools
86	Haffjarðará - Kúla and Cave Pools
87	Haffjarðará - The Foss pool or Kvörn
88	Haffjarðará - Grettir
89	Haffjarðará - Sheep pool
93	The Haukadalsá Lodge
94	Haukadalsá - Torfi Ásgeirsson Golden Plover in full plumage
95	A salmon taking a fly
96	Haukadalsá - Blóti, the junction pool with Þverá, with a raft of Harlequin Duck
97	Haukadalsá - Above the upper bridge Haukadalsá - Kvöruin
98	Graham Ferguson and Robin Savage with a salmon
99	A Wimbrel over mountains
100	Haukadalsá - The pool where this happened
101	Haukadalsá - Three beautiful fresh fish
102	Haukadalsá - Sandy and Caroline Savage playing a 12 lb fish in Símabreiða
	Haukadalsá - Sandy and Caroline Savage with grilse
103	In the Þverá gorge
104	Þverá - Sue Schwerdt with the gosling
105	Þverá - The first foss
106	Þverá - In the 'secret valley'
107	Myself happy on the Þverá
108	Laxá í Dölum, a watercolour sketch by Joanna Savage
109	Helgi Jakobsson
111	Laxá í Dölum Lodge
112	Laxá í Dölum - Our Guides and our party leaving after our first week
113	Ragnar Guðmundsson and Gretar Halldorsson

Page No.	Picture
115	Laxá í Dölum - Sólheimafoss
116	Árni Magnusson with Ragnar
117	Laxá í Dölum - Svartfoss
118	Laxá í Dölum - The Bridge Pool
119	Laxá í Dölum - 'The Pots' or Björnskvörn with Árni
120	Laxá í Dölum - Below Höfðafljót with Jean de Boussac landing a fish
122	Kristján with a big fish
123	Jim Edwards with Kristján and Annatara
124	Laxá í Dölum - Roger Massingbird-Mundy beaching a fish in the 'Home Pool' Laxá í Dölum - Robin with his 22 lb fish
126	Laxá í Dölum - Mjóhylur
127	Laxá í Dölum - Dennis Desmond returning with his fish
128	Laxá í Dölum - Þegjandi, or The Silent Pool
129	Laxá í Dölum - Neðri Kistur
131	Laxá í Dölum - A beautiful fish from Papi
132	Laxá í Dölum - Lilla Rowcliffe with her morning's catch
134	Laxá í Dölum - Michael and Edward Heathcoat-Amory
138	'Charlie's Angels'
139	Frank and Agnes Godchaux
142	The Duke and Duchess of Wellington with Agnes Godchaux
143	The record party fishing 6 rods July 1986
148	Laugardalsá
151	Miðfjarðará - The Austurá
152	Einar Sigfusson and Anna with a fresh fish Myself on the Miðfjarðará with a beautiful salmon
154	The Svartá
158	My wife Joanna and my son Ben and her daughter Angela Temple
159	Edward Temple with his first salmon Deildará - Pool 6
161	Angela with her fish
162	Svarlbadsá - Stórifoss, I beached my fish under the dark cliff
163	Svarlbadsá - My rod!
164	Hafralónsá
166	Robin Savage
167	Miðfjarðará í Bakkaflóa - Outside the 'A' frame

Page No.	Picture
168	Robin with his three fish and Kristján Edwards who is now a part owner of this Miðfjarðará Miðfjarðará í Bakkaflóa - The upper river
169	The Selá Lodge
171	Selá - The Foss with ladder Selá - Fossbreiða
172	Selá - The swimming pool Selá - Árni Baldursson with a salmon
173	A fine salmon from the Selá
174	Garður Svararsson with a salmon of mine from the upper Selá
175	Hofsá - Sigurður Helgason fishing the Wood Pool Graham Ferguson playing a salmon on the Sunnudalsá
176	The Hofsá Lodge Hofsá - On the Top Beat
177	View down Beat One from above the Foss, River Hofsá
178	The Hofsá valley Hofsá - Burstarfell, the old farm house
179	Hofsá - Burstarfell, the old farm house
180	The Breiðdalsá
181	West Rangá
184	Stóra Laxá gorge
185	Mike Savage in a hot pool at Landmannalaugur
186	Brúará with an old sea cliff to the left. This is now some miles from the present coast line
187	Kit Savage on a glacier covered with volcanic ash
188	Eldvatn at dusk
190	Eldvatn Lodge in Winter
192	A Brown Trout fighting
193	Galtalaekur
194	Brown Trout
195	An Arctic Char
197	Migratory Char in Greenland
201	Map of Iceland indicating 1860 farms receiving income from sport fisheries

Key to Rivers numbered on the map

1 Elliðaár
2 Úlfarsá
3 Leirvogsá
4 Varmá
5 Laxá í Kjós
6 Brynjudalsá
7 Laxá í Leirársveit
8 Hvítá í Borgarfjörður
9 Grímsá
10 Flókadalsá
11 Reykjadalsá
12 Þverá
13 Kjarrá
14 Norðurá
15 Gljúfurá
16 Langá
17 Álftá
18 Hítará
19 Haffjarðará

20 Straumfjarðará
20a Fróðá
21 Haukadalsá
24 Laxá í Dölum
25 Fáskrúð
26 Reiðá
27 Laugardalsá
28 Langadalsá
29 Bjarnarfjarðará
30 Hrútafjarðará
31 Miðfjarðará
32 Víðidalsá
33 Vatnsdalsá
34 Laxá á Ásum
35 Blanda & Svartá
36 Laxá í Aðaldal
37 Deildará
38 Ormarsá
39 Svalbarðsá

40 Sandá
41 Hölkná
42 Hafralónsá
43 Miðfjarðará í Bakkaflóa
44 Bakkaá
45 Selá
46 Vesturdalsá
47 Hofsá
48 Breiðdalsá
49 Rangá, East & West
50 Ölfusá
51 Hvítá
52 Tungufljót
53 Stóra Laxá
54 Sog
55 Eldvatn
56 Grænilækur
57 Ólafsfjarðará

xx

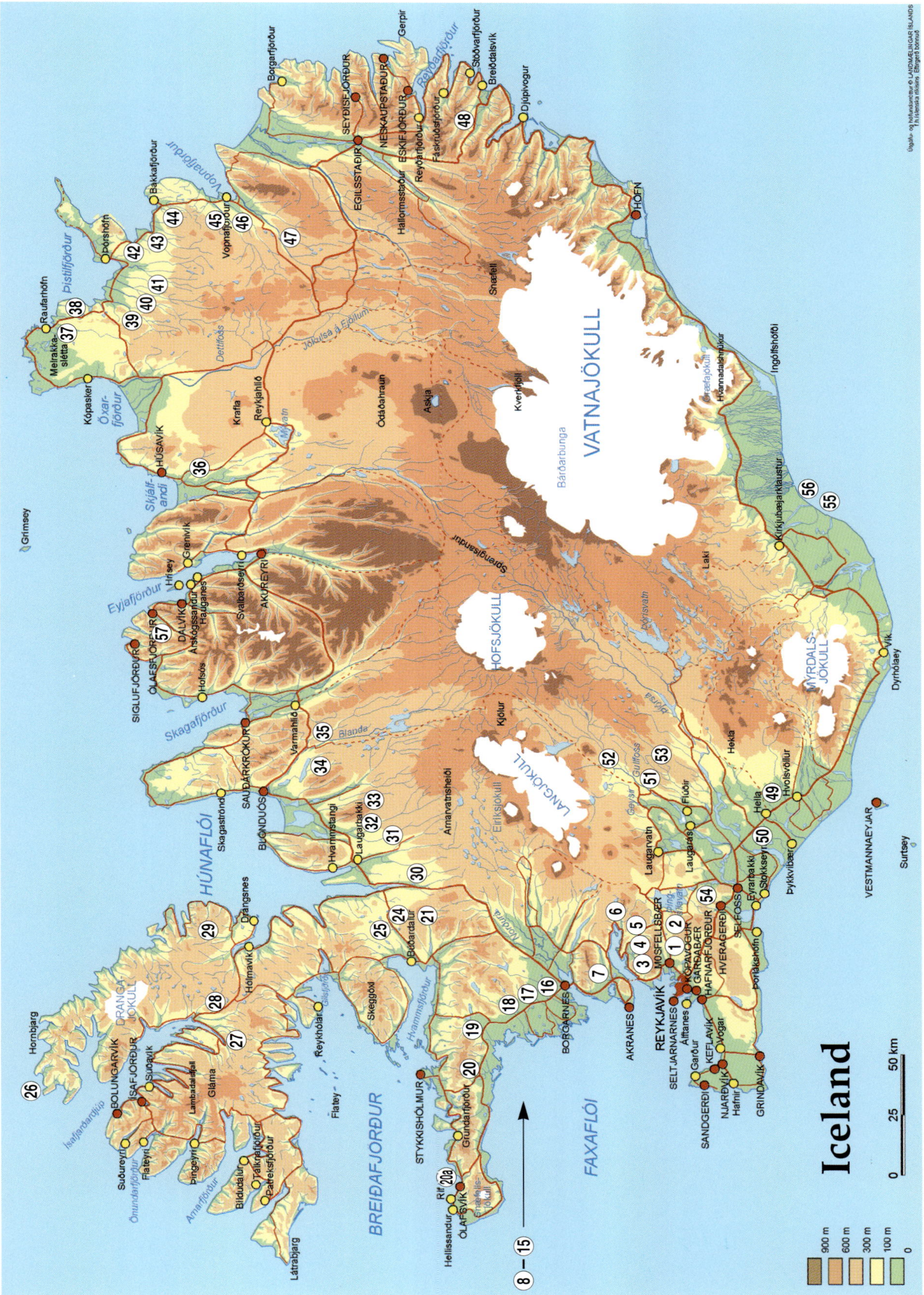
Iceland
0 25 50 km
900 m
600 m
300 m
100 m
0
VATNAJÖKULL
HOFSJÖKULL
LANGJÖKULL
MÝRDALSJÖKULL
DRANGAJÖKULL
BREIÐAFJÖRÐUR
FAXAFLÓI
HÚNAFLÓI
Skagafjörður
Eyjafjörður
Skjálfandi
Öxarfjörður
Þistilfjörður
Vopnafjörður
Reyðarfjörður
REYKJAVÍK
AKUREYRI
AKRANES
BORGARNES
STYKKISHÓLMUR
ÓLAFSVÍK
ÍSAFJÖRÐUR
BOLUNGARVÍK
SAUÐÁRKRÓKUR
BLÖNDUÓS
SIGLUFJÖRÐUR
ÓLAFSFJÖRÐUR
DALVÍK
HÚSAVÍK
SEYÐISFJÖRÐUR
NESKAUPSTAÐUR
ESKIFJÖRÐUR
EGILSSTAÐIR
HÖFN
SELFOSS
HVERAGERÐI
HAFNARFJÖRÐUR
KÓPAVOGUR
GARÐABÆR
MOSFELLSBÆR
SELTJARNARNES
KEFLAVÍK
NJARÐVÍK
SANDGERÐI
GRINDAVÍK
VESTMANNAEYJAR
Surtsey
Grímsey
Hornbjarg
Látrabjarg
Flatey
Vík
Dyrhólaey
Hella
Hvolsvöllur
Kirkjubæjarklaustur
Djúpivogur
Askja
Hekla
Laki
Bárðarbunga
Kverkfjöll
Snæfell
Krafla
Mývatn
Dettifoss
Gullfoss
Geysir
Þingvallavatn
Þórisvatn
Kjölur
Sprengisandur
Ódáðahraun
Ingólfshöfði

Hofsá Valley.

From a painting by William Garfit.

Chapter One
The Start of a Love Affair

1958, Introduction to Iceland

Advice given by a father to a son is sometimes remembered, and may even be passed from one generation to the next. In my family, we were often told 'take your opportunities'. Early in 1958, my wife and I were newly married, when we had the chance to join my brother, Kit, and a mutual friend, Christopher Sellick, on a duck collecting expedition to Iceland. We jumped at our opportunity.

Peter Scott wished to obtain some duck from Iceland, for the Wildfowl Trust. Christopher had been to Iceland twice on Peter Scott's Pink Foot goose expeditions, in 1951 and 1953. In 1953 under Hofsjökull, 9000 geese were ringed in their flightless phase. Wherever Kit went in the world, he had collected duck for the Wildfowl Trust. We were given an order for 10 pairs of Harlequin, 10 pairs of Long Tailed and 5 pairs of Scoters. If successful this would net us £500, which in 1958 would more than cover all our costs.

We set off in late May, with the blessing of Doctor Finnur Guðmundsson, the Director of the Icelandic Natural History Museum. We shipped to Iceland a short wheel based Land Rover, that even then was old, and in it, we took tents, nets, cordage, slotted angle iron (for poles), army 'compo' rations, some crates with individual compartments for the duck, two inflatable boats, fishing tackle, and our personal kit. Our Land Rover was fully loaded, with much tied on outside, leaving only just room for the four of us in the front seat, only just able to see over baggage on the bonnet. The tight fit held us firmly in our seats on the very rough roads.

Our expedition proved to be a wonderful introduction to Iceland, and it started my love affair with this wonderful country. It was my good fortune to go there when young and impressionable.

We flew into the airport in the city centre. Then followed the complicated procedure of obtaining a temporary car licence, car insurance, presenting our bill of lading to the shipping office and clearing customs. We visited Brian Holt, the British Consul, who advised us about the order in which it was necessary to complete these formalities. Nowadays all this is easy, but then it certainly was not. Now it is rare to find anyone that doesn't speak good English, but then it wasn't. In the shipping office after a prolonged struggle, the clerk turned to my wife to explain in Icelandic; he was greatly surprised that the young girl with curly fair hair was not an Icelander!

We fulfilled our order for duck, obtaining the right number, species and sexes; not one died, either while being caught, or on the journey to the Trust at Slimbridge. Altogether this was a remarkable achievement. The Wildfowl Trust couldn't have expected our success, because they didn't send back the empty crates. Consequently we had to persuade a carpenter to make more crates for us, leaving a building site during the short summer construction season. Not surprisingly, these were the most expensive crates that the Wildfowl Trust had ever owned.

On the North Coast, we were shown an Eider colony by the farmer's daughter. There was a mass of Eider nesting on an island. In order to attract the birds to the slightly higher land, where the nests would be safe from flooding, this area was decorated with tinsel and bunting. Among the Eider were some nesting Greylag. In one of their nests there was an egg that was beginning to hatch; the girl picked up the egg, and pulled the chick out, replacing it in the nest. On our return, we showed Peter Scott our film, and he exclaimed with horror when he saw this being done. Eider down is taken from the nests before eggs are laid. This must be done with moderation so that the ducks don't over pluck themselves. Then after the nests have been abandoned, all the remaining down is collected. Both qualities are cleaned and mixed, to make one quality. This eider-down is then used for the very highest quality 'Duvets'. They are extremely expensive, and are treasured in Iceland. Germany and Japan are the biggest export markets. The second best natural down is 'swans down', and is imported from China, where there are no swans! To have an eider colony on a farm is a considerable asset.

On our second night, we arrived late at the upper bridge over the Laxá á Ásum, saw Harlequin duck, and camped beside the bridge. Little did we know then that this small river would become the most expensive salmon fishing in Iceland. It is restricted to being fished by two rods, the average daily catch per rod was the highest in the country at about 6 grilse per day. General Stewart records in his book 'The Rivers of Iceland' that he was invited to fish here, in order to assess whether the river was suitable for foreign fishermen. In his opinion it was not! I have not been lucky enough to fish it myself, but the most prolific fishing is not necessarily the most interesting.

After midnight the farmer visited our camp on his tractor, in order to find out what we were doing; he was reassured by reading a letter given to us by Dr. Finnur Guðmundsson. In the morning we went to the outflow of the upper lake, and I was launched into the water in one of our inflatable boats with a cord attached, the idea being to get the cord across the river. Much to the amusement of the others, I paddled energetically without realising that the cord was too short and the boat had a large leak! I was stationary, paddling hard in a boat that was sinking fast, and they were filming me!

It is the habit of Harlequin duck to fly very low, following every bend in the river, and even to fly under low bridges. When the sun is low, a net set under a bridge or on a sharp bend may not be seen by them. We hung our net under the bridge and walked down from the lake to the bridge, one on each side of the river. Here I saw my first Long Tailed duck, and first Ptarmigan. In Scotland Ptarmigan are birds of the mountain tops; in Iceland they are found down to sea level. The drive was a success, and we caught four Harlequin.

Next day we drove to Akureyri, the capital of the North; this is a most picturesque jewel of a town, set on one side of a sheltered fjord with mountains behind. From the local airport, we dispatched the first crate of duck, and sent a telegram to the Trust. We took up an introduction to Kristján Geirmundsson. He was a brilliant taxidermist. He, and his whole family, gave us a great welcome and were most helpful throughout our visit. One son was a crew member of the gun ship Thor (Þór), which constituted half the Icelandic 'navy'. We laughed together at the absurd notion of him fighting the Royal Navy. However this was not far from reality, as the first Cod War was soon to show. Iceland won!

The road beyond Akureyri had only just been declared open after the winter. In places, it was rutted, with soft sides, and much snow. At one point we stuck and had to unload everything before we could get clear. We drove to Mývatn (midge lake), where we called on Örn Friðriksson, the pastor at Skútustaðir, which is on the South shore of the lake. Örn is a remarkable man. He had a large parish. Communication in the winter was often by riding, or driving across the lake. He worked a large glebe farm (owned by the church and part of his living), his house was the telephone exchange, and, when he had a confirmation class, the children stayed in his house. Altogether he was a busy man. He telephoned to Jónas the farmer at Helluvað, and obtained permission for us to camp on his land, and to catch duck.

Mývatn covers 37 sq. Km., and is one of the tourist centres of Iceland. It is on the main fault line that crosses Iceland and is a most volcanic area. Volcanoes, pseudo craters (caused by explosions of steam), lava flows, and hot springs are all much in evidence. The lake has subterranean sources from a large watershed, and its bottom has huge deposits of diatomite, which is now dredged for export. Iceland has not one single mosquito, very few of the midges bite, but the fly life at Mývatn is varied and phenomenal. Consequently this is the most prolific duck breeding area in Europe. Mink escaped from fur farms and bred, becoming established, living under the lava. They have done immense harm to the nesting duck, and other waterfowl. Only a small stream, Grænilækur flows into Mývatn. This was part of Örn´s glebe farm, and contained some very large trout. A surprisingly large river flows out of Mývatn. This is the Laxá í Aðaldal, commonly called 'the big Laxá'. The average flow of the river is about 42 cu. metres per second, and 33 cu. m. of this is from sources in the lake. The whole catchment area has been calculated at over 2100 square kilometres. From the lake to the sea is about 58 kilometres. Further downstream and below a dam for hydro electricity the river becomes one of the greatest salmon rivers of Iceland, but below Mývatn it has a braided watercourse, creating a paradise for both duck and trout, being so full of food for them.

Our camp at Helluvað was on a hillside, with a wonderful view over the interlocking water-courses and islands of the river. The Harlequin revel in swimming like corks in the white water. This is the main breeding area in Europe for both Harlequin and Barrows Goldeneye. Subsequently I have fished here with a brood of both of these and also a brood of Long Tailed duck swimming in the very pool that I was fishing. The sound of all these duck, Whooper swans, and Greylag is unforgettable. Our timing was perfect. The duck had paired but had not yet nested. We did our netting when the sun dipped below the skyline and the nets were less visible.

We were allowed to fish on payment of 100 krónur per day. When we arrived in Reykjavík the rate of exchange was 45 krónur to the pound, while we were there the official rate changed to 60, but the black market rate remained at 100, or over. Forty years later the rate of exchange is about 135, but two noughts have been taken off the krónur, and the pound is only worth about 1/20th of what it was then. Therefore in Iceland, inflation has been 200,000 % in 40 years, and has been 2,000 % in England. This is a chilling thought, but back to 1958!

Between netting, sleeping, cooking, and dispatching duck from Akureyri, etc, we did as much trout fishing as we could. We gave trout to Jónas, and he gave us milk and eggs. The river below us turned out to be some of the very best wild brown trout fishing in Europe. Now it is highly organised and a substantial fishing hostel has been established, this is run by the farmers. The fishing is still excellent, the growth rate of the fish is unique, for the same reason that the feed is so good for the wildfowl. There is a slight danger of an algae bloom, which can give the lake and the river the appearance of pea soup, making fishing virtually impossible. However this doesn't occur every year, or last long, and goes as quickly as it comes.

The Harlequin were no problem for us to catch when the sun was down. We set our nets across a stream on a bend so that there was a back-ground. We never left a net unattended. Farmers were netting the lake commercially for lake-char; they caught Scoters by mistake, and gave them to us. The Long Tailed duck did prove to be a problem to catch. They were altogether too observant, and intelligent. Several ideas failed, then Kit adapted a technique that he had seen used beside the Caspian Sea. A lake was found in an area where many Long Tailed ducks were resident, and which had a narrows. Across this a net was hung on a slack line between two pylons made with our Dexion (slotted angle iron), and guy ropes. The duck could see this net, got accustomed to it, and flew just above it. With a boat in place and a man on the end of the line, it only required a tweak on the line to raise the net at the last moment, and pull the birds out of the sky. The problem was solved and our quota was soon fulfilled!

We had been trying to take up an introduction in order to get some salmon fishing on the lower river. Our contact was never at work. Finally it was explained to us with some embarrassment that all along, he had been blind drunk, and still was! However we were then offered a day's salmon fishing, but it was too early in the season for many fresh salmon to have come into the river. It was boat fishing without guide or guidance!

On our return to Reykjavík, we were invited to a memorable dinner party given by Mr. Andrew Gilchrist, the British Ambassador. The American Ambassador was a fellow guest. Mr. Gilchrist declared that he was a failure as a diplomat. In his view, to be a success it was necessary to have your windows broken by an angry mob! He believed that his chance might come soon, and it did in the first cod war! It was reported in the press that an angry mob had surrounded the house of the British Ambassador in Reykjavík and thrown stones. Mr. Gilchrist had been entertaining the American Ambassador to dinner and playing Chopin's nocturne on the piano. Mr. Gilchrist was reported as saying that not many windows were broken, and the Icelanders would not make good cricketers. However later in his career, and by now 'Sir Andrew', he was our Ambassador in Djakarta. Again he was surrounded by an angry mob. It was reported that an embassy official, Rory MacEwan, marched round the embassy playing the bag pipes, but stones flew and not one window remained unbroken. Sir Andrew was quoted as saying that the Indonesians would make excellent cricketers! After that his career could only go from strength to strength!

In 1977 I returned to Mývatn. This is how it happened.

I had wanted to try some sea trout fishing in Iceland, and was let fishing on the Ólafsfjarðará, North of Akureyri. We arrived on the last day of August, the wind was from the North East and cold. The river was very exposed as it flowed North East. Snow was falling and lying about 20 feet above us. The river in these conditions didn't look enticing. We were staying in a tiny hotel in the village opposite a fishmeal factory. The smell from this was only rivalled by the smell of burning fat from the café below. Our rooms were the size of very small cabins. There were six of us, including my wife, my eldest brother, Robin, two young sons and another boy. Our Icelandic host gave us a memorable meal of lamb at his home, but after the meal he had to leave for Reykjavík. We were disappointed, after a wonderful week fishing on the Haffjarðará, we were bitterly cold on the river and morale plummeted. I decided on a tactical withdrawal!

We drove to Mývatn and stayed at the hotel in Reykjahlíð. Örn Friðriksson was still pastor of Skútustaðir and remembered us. He telephoned to the farmer at Helluvað. Previously the farmhouse had been made of stark concrete with the former turf house still visible behind it. Now there was a modern bungalow well designed and insulated. We remembered, the present farmer, Ingólfur Jónasson, as a small boy. The fishing on the river had just been closed, so that the farmers could net fish for their winter supply. He reopened the fishing especially for our remaining two days. We caught 40 brown trout, three of over five pounds, and we lost many. They fought like demons frequently 'tail walking' across the pools. We divided our fish between our two Icelandic friends. Örn invited us all to dinner in his house. Very diffidently he mentioned that he had lent Kit a unique photograph of a farmers riot! The outflow of Mývatn had been restricted with a small dam, which the farmers didn't like, so they demolished it! The photograph was found and returned!

I was back there again in 1998 for a week, staying in the fishing hostel, and the fishing was as good as ever, but, sadly, Örn had recently retired.

1964, Back again

My second visit to Iceland was in 1964, with my wife, Graham and Alys Ferguson, and Christopher Sellick. Now we had two children to park with my mother in law, and we could see that it would become increasingly difficult to have such holidays. A seemingly endless future of seaside holidays stretched ahead. I bought a long wheel based diesel engined Land Rover for the trip, which I kept for 18 years. For the benefit of farmers, diesel in Iceland is about 1/4 of the price of petrol, but locally owned diesel cars bear a high annual licence fee. Car hire in Iceland was excessively high, this was because the roads used to be so rough, the tourist season so short and import duty high. Now roads are vastly improved, import duty is much lower, and the cost of hiring a car is greatly reduced.

We planned to fish Þverá, Hafralónsá, and Hofsá. Subsequent changes on all these rivers make conditions at that time seem to be those of another era.

Þverá

The Þverá is a tributary of the Hvítá in Borgarfjörður. Hvítá means White River, it is called this because it is a glacial river, that makes the water milky, and opaque. Its tributaries include the Grímsá, Flókadalsá, Þverá, Kjarrá, Norðurá and Gljúfurá. Together with its tributaries, the Hvítá had by a big margin the greatest natural run of all the rivers of Iceland. In 2001 this has been overtaken by the ranched run of the Rangá system. The Hvítá was heavily netted, but in 1991 these nets were bought off. Þverá and Kjarrá (one river), Norðurá and Grímsá, are all in their own right among the great salmon rivers of Iceland.

The upper half of the Þverá is called the Kjarrá, this as the Thames is to the Isis. Now seven rods fish the Þverá, with its tributary the Litla Þverá, and seven rods fish the Kjarrá. We obtained our fishing on the Þverá from Sigurjón Einarsson. His father Einar Pétursson, who had recently died, was extremely well known and respected, both as a fisherman, and as a businessman. He had particularly loved the Kjarrá. All the way up this river there is no obstacle of any kind to fish with the exception of fosses up the tributaries, Litla Þverá, and Lambá, beyond which fish can't go. In the days of Einar Pétursson, there was no access by road to Kjarrá. The fishermen would ride horses up to the simple lodge, everything else was taken up by pack horse, and the fish they caught had to be brought down in the same way. Two pools are named after Einar, E.P. and Einarsfljót. The latter is the uppermost main holding pool of the river, but more of that in another chapter. Nowadays there is a first class lodge, and an adequate track up to the lodge. This continues for some more miles beyond the lodge and necessitates fording the river many times, which adds to the uncertainty when the river rises. Beyond the end of the track it is still a long ride to Einarsfljót. When Einar's legs gave up, he did all his fishing from his horse. Icelandic horses may be only the size of a pony, but they are incredibly strong, brave and intelligent. It is wise for a rider to accept the advice of his horse! In winter sheep are brought into buildings but the horses remain outside.

A salmon under water.

From a painting by Rodger McPhail.

The Þverá is now fished from one luxurious lodge by seven rods, with reasonable access to most pools by 4WD vehicles. Two other rods, based elsewhere, fish the junction with the Hvítá, where the clear water joins white glacial water; salmon tend to pause at the divide. In 1964 the Þverá was fished as three beats. The lowest we rented this was for two rods, above us was the Norðtunga beat for three rods, and beyond that was the 'mountain beat'. This was given to us as an unexpected and unexplained bonus for us to fish on alternate days; however our limit of two rods remained unchanged. It was explained to us that the lease was very favourable and we must never fish a moment over the permitted hours, or fish more than two rods. In Iceland rod sharing is customary, to share the high cost. Salmon fishing is very much a national sport, and is taken extremely seriously. Traditionally, worm fishing used to be the main method used. On most rivers spinners may be allowed, but are not encouraged. Fishing for salmon with other natural bait, such as shrimp or prawn is not allowed anywhere. Now most rivers restrict all or part of the season to fly-fishing. Icelanders have been innovative with their fly patterns; and during the long winter nights fly-tying is a popular hobby. When worming, it is helpful to have someone to spot fish and watch the take. On some rivers, the most expensive period for fishing, is the first that worming is permitted after exclusive fly-fishing. At that time the rivers should be well stocked with fish that have never seen a worm. This practice is now fading and fly-fishing is increasing, as is the practice of catch and release!

The cost of our Þverá week was £120 in total for the two rods, including a cook, the lodge (at that time it was a tiny hut). We supplied the food, and the fish that we caught were to be left on the roadside to be taken by the milk lorry to the cold store in Borgarnes to be sold for our account. All was planned and arrangements made.

We arrived in Reykjavík, at the city airport, the hotel was overbooked but, as all hotels were full, a pastor was expecting us in his house, arranged for us by the hotel. Graham's luggage and pain relief pills had gone on to New York. Not a good start but we got them back next day, and cleared my car through customs, completing all formalities. We reported to Brian Holt, the British Consul, who seemed surprised at our success in arranging fishing at prime time on such a good river. He then left the room to speak to his Icelandic wife. When he returned he had a look of relief on his face. It appeared that Einar had two sons, Sigurjón, who was honest but drank, and his elder brother Pétur, who was not honest. The year before Pétur had let fishing on the Þverá to two parties for the same week, and took money from them both! Subsequently his record deteriorated.

The lower Þverá Lodge in 1965.

Sigurjón provided a lorry with driver to lead us to Þverá, and to carry the cook and our luggage. Luckily we followed because two suitcases fell off the lorry. The driver showed us the river but he didn't seem to have seen it before and he was no fisherman. We only had a sketch of the river, which was almost indecipherable. The hut had two bunk cabins, six foot by 5 foot. Christopher Sellick slept in the living room under the table, and I presume that the cook slept in the kitchen. (Our hut was still there when I last fished Þverá). Although Sigurjón had pneumonia, he came up to Þverá next day to see us. Before he left, we had whisky with him, sitting in the sun outside our hut. As a present, he pressed on us 100 worms, also leads, worm hooks and bubble floats. He had no faith in flies, and we had only intended to fish fly. He then drove off at speed, in a cloud of dust. It was much later that we learned that, on his way back to Reykjavík, he wrote off his car in a culvert, and he himself suffered an injury. Often, dirt roads have been widened with graders, the sides are soft and the culverts have not been widened. Culverts are identified with warning posts, which sometimes disappear. This combination is lethal. Nowadays the main roads have a hard surface.

Next day it rained heavily, there was a spate, and the river became unfishable. As the river cleared and fell, we began to catch fish. The mountain beat was particularly exciting. Gina beached a 15 lb fish in a cleft of the rocks at Gilbötn, our top pool. Whenever I pointed my cine-camera at Alys while playing a fish, she seemed to lose it! We particularly enjoyed the Viking pool (Skiptaflót), which is a perfect classic salmon pool. In the high water, Klettsfljót was the lowest fishable pool of the mountain beat, below that was a long torrent, the water level was too high, or we were too inexperienced, to recognise pools in the gorge. We fished Klettsfljót from the top of the cliff, casting across to the cliff on the far bank, fish took both there and at the lip of the run out. The problem was to keep them in the pool while we climbed down the cliff, which was only possible at the tail, where we beached them. This was an extremely exciting and difficult performance.

Before breakfast we would fish in Steinahylur, below our hut. At that time, this was an excellent pool, where we had much action, including our best fish, which Graham hooked, landing it 300 yards downstream.

On our fourth day, Wednesday 29th of July, Graham went shopping in Borgarnes, with the wives. I was working my way down the left bank from the very top of the bottom beat. I caught two grilse, and then saw Christopher Sellick squatting like a satisfied otter at the tail of the bank at Gellir. He and I were both throwing a worm out with a fly rod, and letting it come round like a fly. He had caught four salmon each of exactly 15 lbs, and proceeded to catch three more of the same size. I was playing my fourth when the others arrived from Borgarnes. Gina then caught two of 15 lbs, and Alys one of 10 lbs. Graham, to his credit, fished with a Yellow Torrish and caught one of 15 $1/2$ lbs. That gave us a total of thirteen fish of fifteen pounds. In all we caught 43 salmon that week, the biggest was 18 $1/2$ lbs, 13 grilse and 30 salmon. These were my first salmon on a worm, and after this season I never again fished with worm. We ate one salmon and gave three as a thank you to our hosts the farmers; the rest of the fish were collected by the milk lorry.

I believe that progeny of grilse from the Elliðaár were subsequently used for stocking Þverá, and now it would be very surprising to get such a high proportion of salmon to grilse in late July. But I do have a photograph, taken some

'Our catch' (29th July 1964).

years later of my son Sandy and my brother Robin with two fish totalling 42 lbs from Þverá. The proportion of multi-sea winter fish has certainly declined. The mixing of genetic strains is now deplored.

Hafralónsá

We drove to Hafralónsá via Mývatn, and bathed in hot pools in caves under the lava, where we had bathed in 1958. After much volcanic activity in the area, the water temperature was now scalding hot. We were nearly cooked! Driving on, we visited Dettifoss, taking into account height and volume, it is the biggest waterfall in Europe. Near the North Coast we claimed to have seen a Greenland

Dettifoss.

Falcon. This is much whiter than the Icelandic form. We crossed several salmon rivers that looked enticing. At last we arrived at Hafralónsá, where we had been given two days fishing for three rods. The approach track was very rough. One dip was so deep and short that the ground caught the spare wheel, and buckled the back door. The only track was on the left bank, and it ended a short way downstream from the foss. We put up tents, and cooked our supper. Our hosts, who were camping nearby, left in the morning. We had no one to show us the river. We found that it had a good flow, and seemed a lovely river. However much was in a gorge with loose sloping shale and a sheer drop below to the river. I remember seeing Graham spread-eagled on the shale, barely able to move!

The falls pool fascinated me and I learned a lot from it. This pool is a considerable obstacle, but once surmounted, fish can continue a long way upstream. The water was extremely clear and I could see every fish in the pool. I climbed down, (there is a rope there now!), and hid behind a big rock. I tried a fly, which was ignored but the line or its shadow frightened those fish it crossed. They left their lies, and took cover in a hole in the centre of the pool. After about 15 minutes they were back in their lies. I tried a worm using a mono-filament nylon line. The worm was ignored and the fish were undisturbed. I then tried a spoon, and as soon as it touched the water every fish dived for cover into the refuge in the middle of the pool. Fifteen minutes later they were back in their lies. I repeated the sequence and the fish behaved in exactly the same way. I then went below the tail and with fly I caught two arctic char of 2 to 2 $^{1}/_{2}$ lbs, which had been lying in the run out. Then I tried again, and a salmon of 9 $^{1}/_{2}$ lbs took my worm and I succeeded in beaching it. I have never fished with a worm again. The Char were delicious, and a welcome change from our army 'compo'.

At that time the rivers in the North East were considered very remote and were not fashionable. Now the Hafralónsá is leased by Árni Baldursson. There is a comfortable lodge and good access all the way up this river. The fish are of a particularly large average size, and the river has a substantial watershed, providing a strong flow.

Hofsá

Our next and last river was the Hofsá. We rented our fishing from Major Brian Booth, just retired from the Scots Greys. He must have been on the verge of retirement. He was collecting leases of the fishing from individual farms. Most of the river was in the hands of the Akureyri fishing club, and its members seemed to have exclusive confidence in spoons, the bigger the better. This is the only time, or place, in Iceland that I have heard of an 'opposition' fishing the other bank, (with the sole exception of some beats on the large Laxá í Aðaldal). The other fishermen believed us to be Scots, and consequently, brilliant fishermen! Wherever we were seen fishing, they assumed that there must be fish, and spoons came flying to the spot being covered by our flies. When we caught a fish, they would sometimes cross over to see what we were using, which were invariably the tiniest of flies. They were friendly but bewildered! However I have got ahead of myself.

Brian met us, and told us that we needn't put up tents, as he had rented for us the former and disused school at Hof. This was a misleadingly attractive solution. The bare concrete was unforgiving, the W.C. was blocked, and there was a mass of

Lower Cambusmore and Hades Mountains, River Hofsá.

From a painting by William Garfit.

The old school at Hof.

bluebottles, dead and alive. We would have been happier in our tents, particularly Alys, who has never returned to Iceland. I don't think that she believes to this day that things in Iceland have changed. Roads are now surfaced, fishing lodges are warm and comfortable, the catering is usually outstanding, and access to the rivers is good. Excellent fishing guides are normally supplied, or are obtainable. However prices have increased far beyond inflation.

Brian had described to us a perfect river. Gin clear, largely spring fed, so that the flow was steady and reliable, with an endless succession of perfect pools for fly-fishing. In reality this was a fairly accurate description of the Hofsá. It has become the Mecca in Iceland for a large number of British fishermen, as well as some Americans and French. Brian had recently built his hut by the river, this is now known as 'Chateau Brian'. He managed to gather together the fishing rights of the whole river. An excellent lodge was built and the river was well managed and well operated, with a staff of charming 'Sloane Rangers', and cars brought from England.

However personalities changed among the Veiðifélag, (the committee of river owners). The British got less fishing, and the French got more. The Helgason brothers and Loudie Constantine have done much to rebuild friendships and understanding with the owners. Now there is a new lease, and relations with the farmers are excellent. The staff are all Icelandic, and cars are rented from the farmers. There is an enhancement programme, and much 'catch and release'. In 1964 we fished three rods for three days and five rods for four days, fly-fishing only. The cost totalled £140 for fishing twenty-nine rod days. A letter that I received that year, reported that John Ashley-Cooper had taken a lease of the Vatnsdalsá, at a cost reported at that time as £10,000 per year. This caused a huge jump in prices for fishing all Icelandic rivers. The following year the cost of the Þverá had increased three-fold expressed in sterling, and prices continued to spiral. The Vatnsdalsá may be a good river but there are a number that are considered to be better.

We enjoyed fishing the Hofsá enormously although we only caught ten salmon, in those days I didn't record losses, which can be very revealing. The total of caught

Hofsá, looking towards the Foss.

From a painting by William Garfit.

and lost gives a better idea of opportunities. Similarly on a shoot, a count of shots fired is one good measure of sport provided. The number of birds shot depends upon the skill of the guns, which is not the responsibility of the organiser of the shoot, as well as opportunity. At that time for us to get to the top beat, it was necessary to drive beyond the top of the mountain road, before turning off the road and driving down hill for a short distance. From there it was a long way down on foot and a longer climb back when carrying fish. The opposition had an easier approach from the other bank, which was theirs. Our best pool was Long Merlin. Our best pool would normally have been 'Post pool' but a bridge was being built leading to a farm. Naturally it is now called the Bridge pool!

Christopher Sellick was an enthusiastic ornithologist. In a pool that he was fishing there was only one baby Mallard, surviving from a brood. This baby was attacked by a Gyr, or Icelandic falcon, and the duckling took refuge at Christopher's feet. For him this was pure magic!

I have recently been back to Hofsá twice. It is much more beautiful now than I remembered it in 1965. It is fished as a seven rod river, with single rod beats, including the tributary Sunnudalsá. There is much more fishable water than we realised then, but at that time more fishermen were fishing. The Foss is impassable and is 38 km from the mouth. Below this there is a series of rock pools in a gorge, followed by boulder pools. Lower down the river has more gravel and then becomes sandy. When the snow melts, or when there is a very big storm, this mainly spring fed river is overwhelmed and pools can change considerably from year to year.

The present tendency is increasingly towards voluntary catch and release. Many of the bigger fish are placed in cages and are transported above the foss. This extends both the area for spawning and the living space for parr. For these rivers in the North East and the East of Iceland, the sea temperature at the time of smolting is critical, being close to the extreme limit of habitat for salmon. If the sea temperature is too cold, smolt will not leave the river mouth. It is believed that it is for that reason that the runs show greater volatility in these areas. Together with the other rivers in the North East, and East, the Hofsá suffered from a dreadful patch between 1981 and 1985. Now this is only a terrible memory, the river, its management and its salmon are all in good shape. In 2002 40% of the fish were released.

Wherever Loudie fishes there are good stories, but I cannot leave one untold. Júlíus Guðjónsson was coming as a guest for a short visit. For some reason he didn't have his rods with him, perhaps he was visiting Linda Pétursdóttir, a recent Miss World, who lived in Vopnafjörður, the local village, and who was doing publicity for 'Smirnoff Vodka', for which Júlíus was the agent? Anyway, he was told to visit 'Chateau Brian' and borrow a rod and reel. Now Júlíus had lived in the US, and, when there, had been drafted into the US army. As an Icelandic speaker, he was posted to the Keflavík base, there he was appointed driver to the US General, a keen fisherman. So Júlíus, as a Private First Class, had learned to fish. Now he found two rods, one labelled for 'general use' and the other for 'private use'. Being a modest man, and never having been promoted beyond 'private', Júlíus naturally took the 'private' rod. Loudie came looking for his rod, and it had gone! Júlíus, why did you take my private rod?...............!

Chateau Brian with Loudie Constantine, Sigurður Helgason and Júlíus Guðjónsson.

The Hofsá is organised differently from other rivers in Iceland. The rhythm of life is more Scottish. When the British are there, the fishing day is shorter, breakfast is not so early, a picnic is taken to the river, dinner is not so late, and fishermen get more sleep. Changeover is not early in the afternoon, but late in the evening. This enables fishermen to fly in and out, using the same plane, and spend less time in Reykjavík. Beats are for single rods, cars are rented locally, and there are only guides, when required. There are two young men who help: they indicate beats, and pools, deal with the nursery stock and transport fish from cages to the river above the foss; they guard the river, and help in every way that they can.

1976, a Holiday of one's dreams

It was my dream to return as soon as I decently could, together with my family, after serving time with a bucket and spade on the beaches of Cornwall. My three sons and my then wife loved to fish. This seemed to be hopeful.

The boys had started fishing for pike on the Hampshire Avon, over New Year weekends. One year we were so successful that the traffic on the Ringwood bypass stopped to watch four young lads carrying pike. Julian Ferguson was carrying the biggest over his shoulder and it nearly reached the ground. He comes from a family of devout Roman Catholics. When he reached the car, I heard him say to himself, 'I feel as if I have been carrying the Cross of Our Lord!' As there was no great keenness to eat the pike, and as I consider it to be unsporting to kill game, unless it is eaten, I solved my ethical problem by offering to sell the pike for the boys. Next day I returned to the City, and on my way to work, I visited 'Le Poulebot', which was the City restaurant of the Roux Brothers. Michel Roux, the great man himself, was in the kitchen, and proved to be an eager buyer of these magnificent pike. He said that it was most difficult to buy pike in England. The proceeds represented the equivalent of several months' pocket money for the boys. After that they had no doubt that fishing was a good idea!

For the next two years we went, as a family, to the Cape Wrath Hotel in Durness, we took five bicycles on the roof of our Land Rover, and the boys camped outside the hotel. There we caught trout small and large; they touched, played and lost one or two salmon. This was a perfect apprenticeship for fishing in Iceland. They learned to cast in a wind, not fighting the wind but treating it as a friend. Nick, my eldest, lost a rod in Loch Caladail, and Sandy, his younger brother, caught a 5 1/2 lb wild trout of a beautiful golden colour from this limestone loch. On one icy day, Ben, the youngest, then aged 10, returned early to the hotel almost hypothermal. By the time that we returned he had won four gallons of cider from the owner of a brewery, who was betting that he couldn't repeat a card trick! The bet has not yet been paid, nor commuted! In actual fact, it was not a trick at all but relied on the balance of probabilities, so it was a fluke that it came right so many times!

Fróðá

Now that my son Ben would be just eleven, I felt that I could plan our return to Iceland. I had the very good fortune to have met Páll Jónsson. He was wonderfully generous to us, and arranged the whole thing in every detail. The party consisted of myself, my wife, my brother Robin, and my three boys. Páll lent us a huge car, and the plan was for us, to fish Fróðá for three days, fishing three rods. This river is near the North West extremity of the Snæfellsnes peninsula. It is a small, steep, three rod, river that is better known in a Saga than as a salmon river. Páll had arranged for Jakob Hafstein to be our guide, coach and friend, and for us to be based in a small self-catering lodge. Jakob is a brilliant fisherman, his father is famous for a book that he wrote about the Laxá í Aðaldal. For many years, Jakob ran the Elliðaár hatchery. The long term annual average catch from the Fróðá is only about 75. The scenery is dramatic, the river flows down near Snæfell, which is a beautiful ice capped volcano, reminiscent of Mount Fuji, and is famous for being the starting place for H.G. Wells' journey to the centre of the earth. However, on this occasion, it was completely hidden by cloud. We were allowed to fish by any sporting means, so no holds were barred, and the object was for the boys to gain confidence; this they did!

The Fróðá is a charming miniature river to fish with crystal clear pools of great variety, in which we could often see the fish. Between us we caught 13 salmon and six arctic char in the three days. We each caught at least one salmon, and the boys caught eight between them. One lesson learned from Jakob, that we have never forgotten, is not to 'fish the water', but to target fish, changing fly and presentation until a fish takes, and then try for another. The fish that we caught came from seven different pools.

Norðurá

After three days we said a sad goodbye to Jakob, and were ready for our big adventure. We were to fish the Glanni beat of the Norðurá with three rods for eight days, starting on the 28th of July.

The Norðurá is one of the tributaries of the Hvítá, which flows into Borgarfjörður. It flows South West, and has a relatively long, but narrow, watershed. The Hvítá was at that time heavily netted, and the Norðurá has two fosses that are major obstacles; the lower, Laxfoss, had a salmon ladder with a counter, but we believed that many fish surmounted the foss avoiding the counter. The next obstacle is the foss at Glanni. Now this also has a ladder, which is well engineered. In 1976, there was no ladder and the fish mounted the foss with difficulty. An area below the foss was maintained as a refuge where no fishing was allowed. The most fashionable area of the river was the gorge below Laxfoss, where eight rods fished in four rotating pairs. Above Glanni is now heavily fished, but in those days a considerable length of river was lightly fished by two rods. In between, the Glanni beat was magic, and we had it to ourselves as a family beat! We had been asked not to disclose to the other fishermen how good our water was! Now with the Glanni ladder the beat that we were fishing has lost its exceptional magic.

The lodge was full of apparent experts, and the rods on the racks were almost all for worming, but the fishing below Laxfoss was disappointing. Our beat started above Laxfoss, at Ketill and the river there is like a lake for some hundreds of yards. Then there is stretch of attractive water for about 300 yards between old lava flows, called Þrengsli that looked interesting but was quite difficult fishing. Then there is another lake-like stretch, Breiðan. Above that is some of the most perfect fly fishing water that I have ever been privileged to fish, with a series of five runs and pools. At the bottom of this stretch a small stream flows through the Lava that is called Paradís! This is a beautiful area of lava flows, basalt outcrops, and cliffs, with much scrub birch.

My wife, Joanna in Paradís!

Our luck was incredible. The first afternoon we fished in heavy rain on a rising and colouring river. We saw a number of running fish before the river became too coloured. My brother lost one fish, but that was our only contact that day. By next morning the river had fallen five inches and was beginning to clear, conditions were perfect for the next six days. We caught seventy-five fish, many were small grilse but what a thrill nevertheless; they fought like demons. We had a boat so that we could cross the river enabling us to fish both banks. In some places fish were lying in the tails of pools with fins breaking the surface.

In the tail of Réttarholtshylur, Nick hooked a strong fish that sulked. It moved a few yards up or down, but never did more than that. This went on for a long time amid intense excitement. Eventually I waded in below and tried to frighten the fish. What I found was a length of very strong worming nylon fixed between two rocks, about eight yards apart, one above the other. There had never been any salmon, the fly had been going up and down the nylon!

3 Savages with Norðurá grilse.

Sandy hooked a fish in the boat pool (Kýrgrófarhylur), from the left bank. The fish ran down through Grjótin, which is a long sloping stretch with a strong current. We ran, but it stayed well ahead. At the bottom of Grjótin there is a deep inlet where a burn flows in, and below is a bend to the left with a high rock bank above another pool (Snoppuhylur), beyond that is a run, into Breiðan, the upper lake-like stretch. I told Sandy to wade out above the deep inlet, and to stop the fish by tearing thirty yards off the reel, then twenty more, and then another ten! After that we concentrated on getting round and across the burn, climbing a rock face, clearing the line from obstructions, and reeling in. The fish was still on, with a big loop of line below. It was tired and was soon beached. We told the others and the same technique was used successfully twice more! We called it, 'ordeal by salmon'!

Norðurá, Snoppuhylur.

Our most successful fly was the Jeannie. Very little was being caught below Laxfoss, and the counter in the ladder only registered 120 fish going up that week. Back at the lodge we tied Jeannies for the other fishermen, and, outside the lodge, the worming rods progressively disappeared, being replaced with fly rods.

It was here that I met Jim Edwards, for the first time, and his wife Fjóla. They and their children became very close friends. Jim has added colour to my life, and we have had many holidays and much laughter together.

With a day and a half to go, it rained heavily again. Páll came up to see how we were getting on. The river was now very high, and crossing it an adventure. The salmon were taking refuge from the current close to the banks. I was fascinated to watch Páll, fishing with a very short rod. He cast a very short line at the tail of Réttarholtshylur. He was down on his knees, a fish took his fly very close to him, and in that current it was going to be difficult to hold it. He kept down, hidden on the bank, and the fish beached itself on the flooded grass in front of him. It was not frightened, and seemed unaware of danger.

Our total for the 8 days was 75 caught and 28 lost. We only fished fly, and we have never again used anything else in Iceland. As we left, it was still pouring with rain. We were told that this was the biggest summer flood for seven years.

Laxá í Kjós

Páll had given us two days fishing for two rods on the Laxá í Kjós, and its tributary, the Bugða. At that time this river and the Þverá/Kjarrá were the two rivers with the highest catches of salmon in the country. This is only about thirty minutes outside Reykjavík, so is particularly easily accessible. I have had several subsequent weeks fishing here, with many happy memories.

We arrived late from Norðurá, as we had to collect our fish from the deep freeze plant at Borgarnes, and we were also delayed by a puncture. On our arrival the river was a perfect height and clearing although it had missed the heaviest of the rain. We fished beat three, commonly called the gravel pits and caught two fish.

In the morning we were fishing the bottom beat, which must be the nearest thing to a certainty that there is in salmon fishing, but then it was all new and unknown to us. Above us was Laxfoss, and just below us was the bridge that then carried the main road around Iceland. While fishing the Breiða, our top pool we were passed by an excited Spaniard who had played a large fish on a worm. It had come off as he was landing it, and floated down 200 yards through our beat. Sandy waded out and gaffed it, returning it to a grateful fisherman. We caught six between us and had some dramatic fights, before they were landed. After the lunch break, we were on the Bugða, and it had begun to rain again. The river was rising fast and colouring. We lost four and caught two salmon before the river became unfishable.

Next day was our last morning of this incredibly exciting and successful family holiday. The river was still rising, all rocks and pools had disappeared, and the river was like thick chocolate! The river seemed unfishable. We had caught 98 salmon, and Sandy was determined that we should reach 100. We were allocated the top beat, but the only fishermen on the whole river were the two of us, all others had given up. I lost one in the pool below the upper bridge, and I also gave up. The only outside chance was above the uppermost tributary, which was bringing the most coloured water into the river. We were by ourselves. Sandy tried there, while I washed the car, which we would return to Páll next day. Sandy found a pod and he had five pulls from fish, always in the same spot. At last he hooked one, which he landed. He came to me in a paroxysm of excitement, 99, one to go! He almost dragged me to his pool, and showed me what to do. Stand here, this length of line, cast there, and a fish will take you there: it did, and he had caught the last fish! We didn't have another cast, and these were the only two fish that were caught that day. We called the pool '99, 100', more usually, known as Upper Hálshylur. These were caught on a tube fly of $1^{1}/_{2}$ inches called Jakob, as in multicoloured dream-coat. Forty-nine of our fish were caught on the Jeannie.

In those days Icelandair had a unique concession for fishermen, salmon were not counted as part of the baggage limit. We had eighteen cases full of our fish, which was stretching the concession to the limit, but Icelandair made no attempt to charge excess baggage. We had to fly home via Glasgow. The plane arrived late, leaving us little time to make the transfer to the London flight. There was an escalator that we had to negotiate with our luggage. We split our group, and used the escalator as a conveyor belt, then continued the rush to our plane. The baggage doors had closed, and the passenger doors were actually closing. There was a long time before the next flight, and we feared that the fish would defrost. Our advance party persuaded the airline staff to take us, although the doors had just closed. They were astonished to see our baggage, but it was too late for them to change their minds. Some of the other passengers, who were used to normal salmon fishing, were incredulous. Naturally the three boys were on a high!

This holiday set a pattern for several years. It is a joy to go back to a familiar place, as it is also a joy to explore. It is very convenient that the best time to fish in Iceland is during the school holidays. I was also fortunate that this time in my life coincided with a good period for my business, and was before I was struck by various disasters.

Chapter Two
Getting to know Iceland

The Country

Icelandic stamps 'Discoverers of America 1000 & 1492'.

It is interesting for those who have never been to Iceland to learn something about this unique country. Some of this may still be thought provoking to those that have been to Iceland.

It is about 250 miles both from Greenland and from the Faroes, lying just South of the Arctic Circle. It covers 39,600 square miles, which is larger than Ireland, and is about 190 x 300 miles. The coastline is 3700 miles. It is affected, both by the Gulf Stream from the South, and the Greenland current from the North. The high point at 6950 feet is on Vatnajökull, which is much the biggest ice-cap. Iceland forms part of the Mid-Atlantic ridge. It is a young, and highly volcanic country. Much of the centre is a bare wilderness of lava and sand. Even the pollution, is natural, being volcanic ash which colours the water melting from the glaciers.

Iceland is full of surprises, but these are not often as dramatic as was the appearance of the island of Surtsey out of the sea in 1963. A few years later, a farmer was watching an eruption near Mývatn, from about 50 miles away, when he noticed a change on his farm. Land sank close to his house and a lake formed of about 100 acres. In 1997, there was world-wide interest in an eruption under Vatnajökull. As the ice melted deep within the icecap, pressure built up, eventually lifting the ice and releasing the water. The ice burst and the flood carried huge blocks of ice; the flow was greater than the flow of the Indus when in flood, albeit the flood was only for a short time.

In 1783 the ash fall from the Laki eruption led to the death in Iceland of 50% of the cattle, 75% of the horses, 80% of the sheep, and many thousands of the people from famine and sickness. There were even crop failures in other parts of Europe.

The first settlers were Irish monks in the 8th century, they sailed in leather boats from Ireland. Vikings followed as settlers, mostly between 870 to 930. They raided Scotland and Ireland taking slaves to work for them. At that time the Vikings were the greatest boat builders in the world, but they were illiterate. The Norse Sagas were written in Iceland. At that time many Irish were literate, and Christian, their writings being in Latin. There can be no doubt that the Vikings chose the most beautiful girls. Genetically, it has been found that Icelanders are closely related to the British. As a result there are many more brunettes in Iceland than are found elsewhere in Scandanavia. Recent genetic research indicates that, by descent, the ancestry of present day Icelanders is 60% from women of Celtic origin, not of Norse origin, and 30% from men of Celtic origin. One does not need much imagination to understand this discrepancy between the sexes.

Eiríkur the Red was banished from Norway and settled beside the Haukadalsá, in the North-West of Iceland. This is a river that I have fished. Later when Eiríkur made Iceland too hot to hold him, it is claimed that he named Greenland, before creating a settlement. He took with him his Christian wife, Þjóðhildur and many Celts were amongst the Vikings, that sailed with him in about forty ships, most of which were lost on the voyage. This was in the year 1000. It has been said that Eiríkur was the first real estate promoter of the Western world! He established his farm at Brattahlíð, now called Qagssiarssuk. There, I have seen sheep jumping into barges, being driven from the very quay of bed-rock, from which his son Leifur sailed, at the start of the voyage on which they discovered mainland America.

Greenland, Brattahlíð sheep being loaded from Leifur Eíriksson's rock quay.

The surviving Sagas were written in the 13th century. The Icelandic Parliament was established in 930. From 1262 Iceland became formally under Norway, and from 1380 under Denmark. From 1602 until 1854 there was a Danish commercial monopoly. During the Second World War the British invaded Iceland, getting there before the Germans. Iceland dominates the North Atlantic and consequently is of great strategic importance. The Americans took over from the British, extending their Munro doctrine into a part of Europe. They established the huge airbase at Keflavík, which once again was of vital importance during the cold war, and where the international airport is now situated. During the war, the first natural hot water system was constructed for Reykjavík. Prior to the war, this project had been planned by Danish engineers. Iceland has been an independent republic since 1944.

Iceland was converted to Christianity in the year 1000, and the first bishop was consecrated in 1056, soon after that there was a bishop in South-West Greenland at Igaliko in Eiríks Fjord.

In 1700 the population was 50,000, by 1800 it had declined to 47,000. By 1900 the population had increased, but only to 78,000. By 2000, it is likely to have been over 280,000, with a similar number, or more, in Canada, the US, and elsewhere abroad. The birth rate is high but so was emigration, and the death rate is low, thanks to an excellent health service. Nearly two thirds of the population live in, or near, Reykjavík. However politically the parliamentary representation is heavily weighted in favour of the country districts.

The language is still close to the Norse of the old Vikings. The language of the Sagas can still be understood. The lives of foreigners visiting Iceland is now made easy because English is so widely spoken. However it is helpful to have some idea of how to pronounce Icelandic names, even if only of rivers and pools! There are two letters for 'th', hard like the 'th' in 'that' Ð ð, and soft like the 'th' in 'thin' Þ þ. The word for salmon is 'lax' and for river is 'á', pronounced 'ow' as in 'cow'. In Icelandic everrry 'R' is rrrolled. In some words 'LL' is pronounced 'DL', for example, 'pollur' (small pool) is pronounced 'podlurr', as in puddle! Names in a telephone book are listed alphabetically under the first name. The family name of a man, is his father's first name with 'son' added to it or, of a woman, the father's first name with 'dottir' added to it. Only a few families, some with strong Danish connections going far back, have a single family name.

As a consequence of this, family trees are carefully recorded, far back. When someone dies, it is the duty of the pastor to make a funeral oration, about the person's life and family, which is then lodged in the national archives, with his pedigree.

In Iceland one sees geography in the raw. This is a country of dramatic beauty, although it is almost treeless, otherwise it has incredible variety. This variety includes shape, texture and colour of the landscape, as well as detail. Much of the land surface is like a rock garden of alpine plants with beautiful flowers of great variety. Over 10% of the country is under permanent ice. Mixed with the ice are many layers of black volcanic ash, deposited by eruptions. From these ice caps, glaciers flow, and from their feet many big rivers emerge. Because of the ash, these rivers carry down vast quantities of black abrasive silt, particularly if there is heavy rain or a hot spell. This silt is damaging to fish. On the South coast, this silt has created a coastal plain on what was formerly the sea.

For a river not to be glacial, it can only have a relatively small watershed, these are the rivers the salmon prefer. They flow directly into the sea, or are clear water tributaries of two glacial rivers, which do not have a high silt level in their flow. Some of the rivers benefit from glacial water that has gone underground and re-emerge filtered and crystal clear, providing a stable minimum flow. Some rivers are too cold for successful spawning, and some have too much volcanic ash, to have suitable conditions for spawning.

Many big glacial rivers have great waterfalls as they leave the central plateau, such as Dettifoss, Gullfoss, and Goðafoss. The central South and the South-East have very many glacial rivers, and the natural salmon population is minimal. In this area there are some large hydro-electric schemes. Sea trout are a little more tolerant of the glacial silt. There are some excellent sea trout rivers that either flow directly into the sea or are clear water tributaries of glacial rivers. Sea trout come into these rivers when the temperature drops, causing the glacier melt to diminish and silt content to decline. At that time in the early autumn there can be very remarkable sea trout fishing, second only to that of the rivers of the Southern extremity of South America.

Many rivers have waterfalls; in more than forty, salmon ladders have been installed. These extend the river length that can be fished and the territory for salmon to spawn, and parr to live. In most rivers parr grow slowly with the notable exception of the Laxá í Aðaldal, which is so rich in insect life.

Mosquitoes, snakes, frogs, brambles, and thorn trees do not exist in Iceland. The country is very rich in bird life, particularly sea birds, waterfowl of many kinds but with a limited number of species overall. This makes bird watching relatively easy, for example the only raptors are, the White Tailed Sea Eagle, the Gyr Falcon, and the Merlin. Any others that are reported are likely to prove to be skuas! Other birds that are particularly characteristic of the country are Golden plover, Arctic tern, Wimbrel. Sea birds are in great variety and numbers. It is a paradise for bird watchers. There are few wild animals that have not been introduced, except sea mammals.

The sea round Iceland is very rich and is a national treasure. The fishermen and the towns and villages dependent on sea fishing are prosperous, but life for the farmers is very tough. Grass cultivation is widespread for hay and silage, but there is a no arable except for a little in the extreme South. Sheep, and horses are the main livestock to be seen. The cattle are excellent but they are less evident in the open except in places that are sheltered. There are about 4000 farms. These are family enterprises and may have 2, 3, or 4 houses on them for different family members that may be specialising in different enterprises. Often they have small patches growing potatoes, vegetables and rhubarb for family use. Many of the more remote farms have been abandoned, but they are still privately owned. To those that are occupied, the government has supplied a road, built bridges, also supplying electricity and a telephone line. It has been illegal to take a salmon in the sea since 1932, except for five coastal net sites, which have also now been closed. Fishing rights belong to the farmers, and these rights cannot be separated from the farms. A remarkable 1860 farms benefit from the sale of fishing rights. (see Table 1, page 201)

The law regarding these rights is not simple, but as regards salmon it is in essence as follows. The government decrees how many fishermen may fish a river. The season is limited to a maximum of 110 days between the 1st of June and the 20th of September. Fishing is restricted to a maximum of twelve hours per day, these are usually from 07.00, to 21.00, or 22.00, and rivers must be rested for two of the hours between 13.00, and 16.00. If a majority of the owners of the farms within a watershed from the estuary to the source wish to let a river as a unit, the others must accept this, and a 'Veiðifélag', (Fishing Association), is formed. No lease may be for more than ten years. If a farm is offered for sale, a farmer from that municipality had a right of pre-emption over any other buyer. Such a right of pre-emption seems to be against EFTA rules. It has been illegal for land in Iceland to be bought by a foreigner, except with special permission. Now this is also under question due to EFTA rules. All rivers of any significance now have a Veiðifélag, unless owned by one family. The income is divided between the farmers, taking into account the contribution from their farm, length of bank, number of pools and number of fish recorded as caught on their water, water sources etc. The Veiðifélag then works with the tenant in matters regarding the care of the river, stocking, improvements, and also regarding the lodge, which may be owned by the farmers, or by the tenant. In the year 2000, there were an astonishing 170 Veiðifélag, and 20 Angling Clubs.

Salmon rivers are very valuable assets for farmers, whose lives are tough. In addition to their land near the farm house, they are likely to own other assets, such as:- Lakes and rivers with Salmon, Sea trout, Brown trout, and Arctic Char, rough grazing, privately and in common with others, mineral extraction rights, hot springs, eider colonies, the right to take sea birds and their eggs, fish farming rights, even the right to driftwood coming on to their beaches, and, of course, shooting rights. Land and sporting rights are owned privately, however remote a place may be from a farm. It may at first seem strange to include driftwood in this list. But Iceland is a treeless country, so wood is valuable. On certain beaches it arrives in considerable quantity, and is piled on these beaches by the waves. The wood is salt 'cured', and as a result is very resistant to rotting. It is invaluable for fencing, as it is for fuel. Other activities of farmers, now include 'bed & breakfast', horse riding and trekking.

Driftwood.

It seems usually to have been government policy to keep the króna highly valued. Iceland is an expensive country to visit. It is extraordinarily prosperous, with a high standard of living. It has been able to retain control of its sea fishing rights, by being extremely robust, and keeping the European Union at arm's length. Like Norway and Switzerland it has an associated status with the EU. This gives them the advantages of membership of the Common Market that many of us in the United Kingdom would also like to have, while retaining their most precious sovereignty. Of course they do not have the right to influence EU decisions, which would in any case be very marginal. They have an excellent education system and health service. They look after their old people, and have virtually no unemployment of anyone who is employable. During the long summer holidays all children over a certain age are expected to take holiday jobs for work experience.

The biggest town outside the South East is Akureyri in a sheltered fjord on the North Coast. There are many other small towns and villages mostly around the coast, each with its little harbour, and frequently with plants for processing fish, both for human consumption, and industrial use, producing fish meal, and fish oil. Icelandic society is as nearly classless as it is possible to be. A strong work ethic survives in a climate, and an environment that is harsh. Icelanders tend to be full of initiative. Tipping in Iceland is not customary. However foreigners, Americans in particular, have made the tipping of personal guides customary. Tips that are given as a present from a friend are appreciated. Now there is some misuse of drugs, and occasional dishonesty in the towns, but less than almost anywhere else in the world. There is a very active pop culture, and there is also good classical music, opera and theatre. It is claimed that more books are published, relative to the population than in any other country. There is also a greater length of road per head of population than in any other European country. As much of the soil is suitable for use as road material, it has been possible to build the roads raised above the surrounding land, wherever they were likely to be blocked by drifting snow. In this way, the wind sweeps the snow clear of the roads.

There are no railways. The internal and international air services are excellent. Electricity from Hydro Electric plants is inexpensive, and in most towns and villages there is geothermal central heating with hot water to all houses. The largest factory is a huge aluminium plant at Straumsvík beside the road between Keflavík and Reykjavík, which processes imported bauxite ore, utilising cheap electricity.

On one side of this plant there was a salmon hatchery. Once this produced a large number of smolt for Norway, but the order was cancelled at the last minute owing to a change in regulations. It was too late to find any alternative market. On the other side of the plant is a fresh water sea pool, where a strong spring flows out from under the lava. The smolt were released into this. A year later we were taken by a friend to see a huge number of frustrated salmon showing in the sea. There was nowhere for them to go and it was illegal to catch them in salt water. Eventually special permission was obtained to do so. This illustrated the potential for salmon ranching, and showed how quickly smolt can be imprinted with a homing instinct. Salmon ranching is fish farming, without cages, and the fish feeding wild in the sea. The key to viability is the cost of raising the smolt, and the return rate of the mature fish. It has now been realised that the return rate can be high enough for a very profitable sport fishery, but is not high enough to be profitable for food.

The biggest industry is everything related to sea fishing, including the export of fish processing machinery. The tourist industry is seasonally very important, as are farming and related products, which includes woollen products. For many years the American Air Base at Keflavík was extremely important and another big source of income.

Hotels are clean, comfortable, and good within their categories. Iceland gives an excellent training to cooks who benefit from wonderful fish products. The lamb, mutton, and all the dairy products are excellent. In more remote areas there are summer hotels that may double as boarding schools for the remainder of the year. These are called Edda Hotels. There are usually single and double rooms as well as basic youth hostel facilities.

The fishing lodges for the prime rivers are almost always excellent, clean, comfortable, with outstanding catering as well as friendly hard working staff. If a guide is provided he may be a headmaster of a big school, a television presenter, a farmer's son or a boy doing work experience, or anyone else. But he will be a keen fisherman, doing holiday work, often with his friends, and doing all in his power to help the visitor. He should know the river, and usually provides a car. If guides are shared it is better to have a hired car for additional flexibility for fishing. Lodges on the minor rivers are often self-catering, guides may or may not be obtainable. Sometimes a farmer's wife may be willing to come in to cook and/or clean. The changeover between tenants is normally in the middle of the day, and is by its nature very hectic. Rivers are normally let to Icelanders for three days, i.e. two full days and two half days, and to foreigners for 6 days or 7 days. Fishing on the last day usually stops one hour early at midday, and the incoming fishermen are asked not to arrive before 14.00. It is bad manners to leave late or to arrive early, unless to meet friends. Many rivers have part of the season reserved exclusively for fly-fishing. Before booking it is advisable to get as much information as possible, so that it is known what to expect. With luck, some very good fishing is available outside the fashionable prime time.

Not all fishing in Iceland is ruinously expensive, nor is it only the salmon fishing that is of interest. There are many second, and third rate rivers that can provide good fishing, often with self-catering lodges. Brown trout fishing can be exceptional in a few rivers and several lakes. Fishing for sea trout, and migratory Arctic char, can also be outstanding, but it is most important to do home-work before booking. Timing is critical, and is not always pre-ordained. Many Icelanders have their own secret places, which are not commercially available, but if you make a friend, surprises may appear and be offered. An enquiring mind does help, as well as a good supply of maps. These are available with different scales, are frequently revised, and are of a very high standard. The lowest category of route indicated is 'track marked with cairns'! Even a thin blue line on a large scale map may indicate interesting water to fish.

My last word of advice to anyone fishing in Iceland, is to treat everyone as a friend, and to treat everyone as you would like to be treated yourself. Do this and you will get a wonderful response.

Choosing a River

In Iceland, every river has official record books with a standard format. It is a legal requirement to keep detailed records of fish caught. At the end of every season these are then computerized nationally, and the books are returned to the river owners. Not every column in the record is filled in for every fish, but there should be a record as follows:- Date - Name of fisherman - Pool, or name of stretch - Species of fish - Sex - Length - Weight - Spinner, worm, or if fly - Name and size of fly- Killed or released - Comments.

This is an invaluable source of information, and the system is unique to Iceland. These statistics are considered when deciding how many rods are permitted to fish a river. A normal assessment is for one rod to be permitted for every 100, or so of expected salmon catch. When there is a Veiðfélag, these records provide information needed to divide the income from the sale of fishing rights. For fishermen arriving at a river, it is most helpful to know where fish have been caught. The catch is, naturally, a major influence on the rental value of a river. In general the length of river per fisherman is generous, compared with most countries, this restricts over-fishing.

Now in Iceland no fishing for salmon is allowed in salt water, except possibly for a very few, and reducing number of inherited rights. Rights to fishing belong to the owners of the adjoining land, the farmers. River mouths, and lower parts of some glacial rivers were netted. Progressively these have been bought out, the nets in the Hvítá in Bjorgarfjörður have not operated since 1991. River nets were still being operated in 2002, in the South, on the Ölfusá. It is hoped that this will have been their last year of operation. (see page 183). Development of salmon farming and salmon ranching have altered this picture to some extent. In particular if a ranching operation is at a place, where there is not an adequate stream into which the fish can return, netting at the return point is inevitable. This can attract some wild fish which may be caught at the same time. Also some of the ranched fish may find their way to nearby rivers. The extent of this problem is disputed. In particular there was concern about this at a big operation on the North shore of the Snæfellnes peninsular in Breiðafjörður. However this, as well as other commercial ranching operations have now closed. All this should be considered when evaluating statistics. The official estimate in Iceland after taking every factor into consideration, is that the value to the economy of one salmon caught by sport fishing is about US $1000. This is more than 20 times the value of a commercially caught salmon. The return rate experienced ranching was not enough to be viable, but it is not surprising that it is sufficient to be profitable for a sports fishery.

In 2000 there were 170 Veiðifélag, and 20 angling clubs, the most powerful club being The Angling Club of Reykjavík. The Veiðifélag may operate their river, or they may decide to let it to an operator for a few years, upto a maximum of ten. If let, this is usually by tender. The operator will then let the river as a whole by periods, or let individual rods, which may be shared at an agreed and increased fee. Such lettings vary from six hours for one rod to the whole river for one week! The services provided also vary according to the river, and as agreed between the parties. Progressively another factor has entered the chain, the sporting agent, who may act for a commission or trade as a principal, buying the fishing and selling it with all the services that may be required.

When choosing a river, and a time to fish, the most important factor is availability, but let us assume that! The next is affordability, but let us assume that also! To my mind the ideal situation is to rent a whole river for a week, and divide the cost between a group of friends. One then knows with whom one is fishing, and so can avoid an occasional disaster. Then a house party atmosphere is achieved, every meal, and evening is a party. This advice is not confined to Iceland. The bigger the river, and the bigger the camp, the more difficult this is to achieve.

When statistics are given for a week, this is for seven days, and not as fished, which is six days plus two half days.

The earliest rivers are in the South West, and the Blanda in the North. When the season opens there are usually few fish in a river but they may be big. The first two weeks may be the start of the prime time. North of Snæfellsnes, the rivers are two, or more weeks later. The run on the North coast is also about the same, but the North East, and East coast runs are later still. The predominent weather on the West coast is usually the opposite to that in England at the same time. The Weather in the North East is often totally different to the West Coast. The South coast weather is different again, being influenced by the icecaps. The expected rainfall varies in different parts of the country.

When comparing prices it is necessary to compare all elements of a deal. For example a foreign let may include, meeting at the airport, transport to Reykjavík, to the river, and back again, a guide with car for every pair of rods, the guides accommodation and their food, catering at a higher standard than in the locally let periods. The number of rods let can also vary, there may be a reduction in number for a foreign period, and this inflates the cost. Methods of fishing allowed can also affect the price. The first three days of worming after a fly fishing period can be sold at a premium! Sometimes there is an increase in the number of rods permitted by the regulating authority, but not all that are permitted, may be fished for all or part of the season.

When assessing the fishing records there are a number of factors that may not be obvious.

1 The legal season for salmon is 110 days, but not starting before the 1st of June, or ending after the 20th of September.
2 Most rivers are not able to have a fishable season for more than 90 days. In the North East the season may be even shorter.
3 How many rods fish the river. This may be less than the maximum permitted.
4 Is the entire river fished in rotation from one lodge, or if not, how many lodges are there, and how is the river divided. Is this the same for the whole season.
5 The numbers of fish previously caught in a particular week.
6 The average size of fish, and their size at the time proposed. Early fish usually have a heavier average weight.

7   What methods of fishing are employed and when. A river, that does not have inaccessable refuges for fish, can be ruined by excessive worming late in the season, for which one motive may be boosting the statistics, and river value.
8   Are predators controlled, such as seal, mink, and merganser.
9   Is there a limit on the daily catch per rod.
10 Under the proposed deal, to whom do the fish that are caught belong. On one river we left all fish in excess of 15 per rod for the farmers. This is now unlikely. Is catch and release encouraged or obligatory. Farmers are becoming more conservation minded.
11 Is the lodge equiped with cooler, freezer, and a supply of polythene tubing.
12 Do the figures in any year include a flush of escaped farmed fish, possibly of 1 to 3 pounds! In one season, about 1500 of these were caught in one river, and all the rivers of the South West reported record numbers of fish caught that year!
13 Most salmon usually run before the grilse. Some years and some rivers may have a good run of both, or only of one, or of the other. Uncertainty is part of the joy of salmon fishing! (see page 107)

There are other factors to consider. Is there an enhancement policy on the river and if so what is its effect. Such efforts may include salmon ladders on the river, there are well over 40 on the island, are fish transported above a foss in order to extend the nursery area, are parr introduced into areas where salmon cannot penetrate or to supplement the natural spawning, or introduced into the main river as parr or as smolt. How old are parr when they smolt. On many rivers the limiting factor may be insufficient food for parr, in which case stocking those parts would be counter-productive. For example on at least one river some of the parr live six years before smolting. When introduced above the foss in modest numbers, they only took two years to smolt. It can be argued that all enhancement programmes that involve stocking with parr, or smolt are modified sea-ranching. The difference is really a matter of degree.

On one river that I knew well, the Veiðifélag employed the services of a fishery biologist. According to his advice, the number of spawners required was unrealistically low. One common mistake made by biologists, and revealed to me by one of their number, is that they assess the ideal number of spawners taking into account the area of spawning beds and the food rescources of the river, however the salmon are not sent to spawning beds allocated to them by biologists evenly over the suitable spawning beds. They spread out at random, influenced by their particular homing instinct. Therefore a greatly increased number of spawners is required over a theoretical number of spawners. The requirement for regeneration, is a tiny fraction of the number required by fishermen for good sport. Therefore a run that satisfies the biologist, is insufficient to satisfy the fisherman.

Another factor is the return rate of salmon. There have been notable errors in estimates, which were the basis of vital calculations, notably in the UK in the Nickerson report. Some early ranching experiments gave a return rate of over 10%, a costing on that basis would have been disastrous, as actual return rates have more often been between 1%, and 2 $1/2$%.

The ultimate in stocking a river must be the success of the programme on the Rangá, East and West, which join near the mouth. These are attractive looking rivers with a good and stable flow. However they are not suitable for the spawning of salmon, and the annual catch used to average only about 70. As a result of a most sophisticated salmon ranching programme, a big run of salmon has been artificially created. These rivers are now heavily fished, giving great pleasure to many anglers. The grilse returning to the Rangá are of a particularly large average size. Taking the two together, they now have the highest total catch of any Icelandic river. There is an element of propaganda in this presentation. As they join at the mouth, they are included as one river. On that basis Vatnsdalsá, and Laxá á Ásum, could be taken as one river, so also could the Laxá í Kjós and Bugða, and, above all, the Hvítá, in Borgarfjörður, with its many tributaries. The total catch has been increasing with 5400 in 2001. 2002 has been a disaster. Let us hope that this is a rogue year. It seems that the smolts in 2001 were not well grown when they went to sea.

When assessing the characteristics of a river there are many factors to consider. Is it a spate river, how low is the lowest expected summer flow? A spring fed element is a great asset, as are lakes in the watershed, both of which can stabilise the flow. I have fished a drought stricken river in Iceland, and returned one month later for another week, only to find that the drought was still unbroken. Mention is made of this in another chapter. A very few rivers are cursed at times with blanket weed necessitating constant cleaning of one's fly.

Icelandic rivers are wonderfully clear, in fact so clear that frequently it is possible to see the salmon, and be seen by them. However some rivers are much more prone to becoming coloured than others. This is usually only when in spate, but this can also be caused by wind stirring up silt in shallow lakes upstream, or the run off from a clay hill-side close to the river mouth after a shower. In this example, only the bottom mile of the river may become unfishable.

Excellent maps are available for most rivers, marking the pools. Careful analysis will show that some pools are very productive, some occasionally productive, some produce very few fish and some none at all. However fish may also be caught where no pool is marked. Parts of some rivers change considerably from year to year. I have returned to fish a favourite lie, only to find it is no longer part of the river at all. A foss may be a total barrier to fish, or it may hold them up until the temperature is favourable, or until the height is right. Early in the season fish may not run all the way up a river.

In English, we tend to call a piece of water that holds salmon, a pool. In Iceland it is not so simple, but it is more accurate and descriptive. The name of a pool can often give a good indication of that piece of river, for example:-

Hylur	= Pool	Pollur	= Small pool
Fljót	= Flat	Strengur	= Stream
Foss	= Waterfall	Kvörn	= Whirlpool
Breiða	= Broad water	Ármót	= Junction
Hola	= Hole	Brún	= Top, as in Fossbrún
Gljúfur	= Canyon or gorge	Efri	= Upper
		Neðri	= Lower

Most rivers in Iceland now have easy access, 4WD vehicles may be required, but frequently are not necessary. Pools usually have small marker stakes with the pool name and number beside the main lie! In a land with so few trees the main obstacles to casting are wind and rock cliffs. Parts of many rivers run through steep valleys and sometimes, through considerable gorges. Occasionally these can be a major problem, for the less fit angler. An extreme example is the Stóra Laxá much of which runs through a most imposing, and inaccessible gorge.

Accommodation on the leading Icelandic rivers is now very reliable, with catering varying from good to outstanding. The lodges are warm, comfortable, with good plumbing, and friendly efficient staff. On the minor rivers the accommodation is much more variable and is often self-catering. Care needs to be taken in order to be certain as to what is provided, and what should be brought, such as a sleeping bag, towels etc.

When all is said and done, nothing in fishing is certain, and if it was it would be boring! Iceland is a fisherman´s paradise, with many glorious and varied rivers, but it is certainly expensive for the best. Careful choice should achieve 'horses for courses', as far availability does allow.

As one way to keep Iceland free of salmon diseases, all used fishing tackle entering the country must be accompanied with a veterinary certificate of sterilisation, or be sterilised before clearing customs. This used to be paid for by a fee per rod, but there is now no charge, if a veterinary certificate is brought to cover all tackle. This is strongly to be recommended, not only because it saves time, but it avoids the very real risk, of arriving at a river with random rod parts! The regulations provide for soaking for ten minutes in a 4% solution of formaldehyde. This should include waders, rods, lines, flies, nets, and wading staffs. Flies treated like this can be quickly ruined, unless they are carefully rinsed in water after sterilisation.

Fishing for Salmon

A father and son were fishing in Iceland for the first time. They were both experienced and well connected fishermen, who had fished a number of the best beats of big rivers in Scotland. They found Iceland to be something of a culture shock. They described to me the salmon fishing to which they were accustomed, as being somewhat like mathematics. You start at the head of the pool with a long double handed rod. First get your line out to a suitable length, cast at 60 degrees across the river, allow your line to come round until it is below you, take three paces downstream and cast again. With luck, a salmon may take the fly once in 1000 casts.

They were used to good traditional Scottish ghillies, having a deep knowledge of the beat that is being fished, in all heights of water, and work from 9.00 to 5.00. At lunchtime, they would withdraw discretely to eat their 'piece', and supplied with an occasional dram and a modest tip at the end of the day, or week. They used to be armed with a gaff, but now with a net, and another dram is enjoyed after the successful landing of a salmon.

On their river in Iceland, they were faced with an astonishing mileage of fishing, on the main stream and its tributaries, with an enormous number of pools to fish, many of them very small. This was on a very clear river where it was frequently possible to see the fish, and for the fish to see the fishermen. Official fishing hours are from 7.00 a.m. to 1.00 p.m., and, at that time of year, from 4.00 p.m. to 10.00 p.m., fishing a different and equally huge beat in the second period. The fish tend to lie side by side in pods, frequently in very specific lies. The guide, (not ghillie), was a television producer of the most popular current affairs programme in Iceland, who was a keen fisherman, having a holiday, in the place where he came himself to fish later in the season.

I learned in the sauna, after midnight, dinner, wine, and whisky that there did not seem to be much meeting of minds. On the last evening it was described to me how a party of Whooper swans flew down river, low overhead. As they past over the fishermen, they let go 'everything'. Perhaps it was due to the heat of the sauna, but I seemed to detect a slight tone of regret in the voice of the guide as he gave his account of the day, reporting a near miss.

I do not believe that these two fishermen have been back to Iceland!!

When carbon fibre rods, (graphite in American), first came on the market, The reaction in the U.S. was to make rods for salmon fishing that were, single handed, lighter, more powerful, and, often, shorter. Much East Coast America Atlantic salmon fishing is from canoes, so this made very good sense. In Europe the reaction was to make rods that used the greater strength, and lightness of the material, to make double-handed rods that were longer, and more powerful. Many of these early carbon rods snapped like carrots, and in Scotland, a theory was spread that they might be good for casting, but were not good for killing fish. I never understood the reasoning for this belief. Now the manufacturers have made the rods much more robust, and some give a lifetime guarantee to the purchaser against breakage from whatever cause. One even showed a picture of a dog biting a rod! What other product of any kind has such a guarantee? Imagine, for a moment, demanding a free car from a manufacturer because you have crashed yours. It is absurd, but such is the force of competition that such guarantees are given, but in order to pay for this, a high price must compensate those manufacturers for the liability. This gives the retailer a bigger profit per rod, and the purchaser believes that the rod must be good because it is so expensive. Fashion moves on, and now the U.S. has discovered Spey casting, and the joy of using a double-handed rod. This stimulates sales, and demand for more expensive rods, altogether very good business for the manufacturer, and for casting instructors! Some American fishermen that I have met look upon double-handed rods as synonymous with Spey casting, and look at me with incredulity when I admit my inability to Spey cast. I have now been shamed into trying to learn, but fear the worst.

In Iceland, with the exception of a few big rivers, a single-handed rod, or a light double-handed rod, are best, and are all that is needed.

In England when fishing on the Test, if a trout is disturbed, it may be back in its lie feeding within fifteen minutes. In New Zealand, I disturbed a trout, which hid beside a rock with only its nose showing. Five hours later it was still cowering in its refuge. My New Zealand guide had told me, if a trout is disturbed, it will not recover until the next day. After this experience I believed him. Salmon fishermen tend to be very casual about disturbing fish. In Iceland the water is almost as clear as in New Zealand, and the fish are wild. Approaching a pool, care must be taken not to disturb the fish, care is also needed, when playing a fish, to do so in a way that will not disturb the other fish in the lie. In view of present conditions in North America, and in the British Isles it may be difficult to imagine planning the capture of the next fish from the same lie while playing the first.

Pools may be extremely small, and with a big rod, the first cast that many people make already takes their fly below where fish are lying, also with such a rod it is difficult to cover attractively those fish that are lying close to one's own bank. A small rod makes this easier.

My training for Iceland

Early in my fishing, I have been lucky to be influenced by two of the most outstanding Scottish Ghillies. The first was Hugh Campbell, the keeper of the Cape Wrath Hotel, for the river Dionard. He was a brilliant fisherman, and a great character. The river and conditions were very similar to Iceland, so it was a perfect training ground. He advocated fishing with very small flies. If a fish looked at the fly, but did not take, the 'I.A.', (immediate action), was to wait three minutes, change to a smaller fly, and repeat the cast. If he was persuaded to fish, after the head of a pool had already been fished, he would make a short cast at right angles across the run keeping the tip of his rod pointing across, or even a little upstream. This frequently produced a fish that was under the narrow run at the head of the pool. On the outside of a bend in the middle of one slow pool, there was a pile of rocks descending into the river. Above this he would crouch, and using the same technique he would draw fish to his fly. This spot we termed 'Hughie's perch'.

Once close to the road bridge, he watched, what he termed, a 'party' fishing the Rock Pool with a ghillie. This pool had a high bank covered with bracken behind the 'party'. He noticed that there was no fly on the end of the 'party's' cast, (leader). So Hughie went round and had a quiet word with the ghillie, who explained to Hughie, with considerable frustration, that he had been up and down into the bracken many times to recover the fly and cast. Eventually he had not replaced the fly. He said 'Och, he is better withoot!'

Hughie believed in fishing rather square across, achieving fly control, by use of the rod point, only occasionally mending the line. He fished a small fly slowly, and when it was close to his bank, recovering the line carefully before casting again. If the river rose substantially, he would change to a much bigger fly, but come down in size quickly, as the river cleared. On a spate river the fish often take freely as soon as the river begins to fall. When such a river is in spate, it takes a lot of rain to keep it at the highest level. Frequently others would leave the river thinking the conditions were hopeless; we would come in with fish, that began to take as the river began to fall, not so long after others had gone home in the belief that the conditions were hopeless for the rest of that day. All of this experience applies to fishing in Iceland and was wonderful training for Iceland.

Fish were not so common on the Dionard, so risks were not taken when hooking or playing a fish. When a fish took, Hughie would hold it very gently, and go downstream, before tightening firmly. The hook was then set in the corner of the mouth. During that time the fish would remain quiet, or fall back into its lie. When playing a fish he would try to stay downstream of it, so that there was little risk of the hook pulling out.

There, we learned not to be afraid of wind, but to treat it as a friend to aid the casting. It is most important to protect one's eyes with polarised dark glasses, and, when casting, to keep the line down wind of one's head. Also it is necessary to use a relatively heavy line. From him we also learned that a strong wind on the surface of the river caused the fish to behave as if there were six more inches on the gauge.

The second ghillie whose help, and memory I treasure is Charlie Wright of the Balmoral Estate. I was privileged to fish there on the Upper Dee for 25 years, as one of Graham Ferguson's party. Charlie looked after us. He was all that the very best ghillie should be. He knows every inch of the beat, in every possible condition. He knows every lie that might hold a salmon, and the best way to present a fly to that lie, and what fly to choose. He is an interested naturalist, and loved the deer, many of which would come to him in winter, when he was giving them hay to supplement their feed. Above all he is a great companion, fishing with him greatly enhanced the pleasure of a day's fishing.

He knew the Dee when it was full of salmon, together we saw the decline, and in particular the numbers of parr reduce dramatically. Without parr, there could be no run of salmon to return. Our warnings were not heard, until quite suddenly the riparian owners of the whole river woke up to the realisation that they had a crisis. The situation was disguised to some extent by the buying out of the nets at

Charlie Wright, ghillie, Balmoral Estate.

Brig O'Dee, Scotland.

From a painting by Peter Symonds

the mouth of the Dee, and the consequent increase in the run of grilse. This did little to help us, as the Upper Dee relied almost entirely on the multi-sea winter fish. As we got to know the river better we tended to fish more effectively, for a while this disguised the decline where we were fishing. Now at the start of a new century, whilst the numbers of salmon are at a disaster level, we believe that we have detected a marked increase in the number of parr. This gives a glimmer of hope for the future.

For fly-fishing, the Upper Dee is absolute perfection as a river. In spate it colours, and, when the level of the river shown on the gauge reached two feet, we were allowed to spin certain pools, continuing to spin, if we wished, for the rest of the day. Those pools, where spinning was allowed, had a white line on a rock to signify that level. We always had an 'opposition' from the Invercauld Estate fishing the other bank. The opposition would appear on their favourite pool, McLaren, with their ghillies at about 9.15, therefore we would fish it before breakfast, usually disappearing before they arrived, so we were seldom seen on McLaren. However on one memorable occasion after heavy rain, when I arrived with my son, Sandy, the level was clearly over the mark. On arrival of the opposition, an extremely elderly lady went quietly to examine the gauge, the river had fallen and the level was now half an inch below the mark. As she was bending over, reading the gauge, a salmon took Sandy's 'Toby' close to her feet! If looks could kill we would have been dead. We reverted to fly after breakfast. Now only fly-fishing is allowed, and catch and release is encouraged. Personally, I have only ever caught a total of eleven salmon on a spinner and the same number on a worm. I report this as fact, not as virtue.

Much fishing is therapy for the fisherman, sometimes it is little more than therapy. If only the salmon lies were fished, it would not take long or many casts to fish a beat from top to bottom. It is really better not to know too much. When hope is lost, fishing becomes boring.

When interviewed on Television, Charlie was asked what characteristics he liked in a fisherman that he was guiding. He replied 'One that does what he is told!'

Charlie is now enjoying well-earned retirement in the cottage beside Brig O' Dee, always a favourite pool of his. I hope he is still sustained by a small cask of whisky, given to him by us, and inscribed, with his well remembered advice, 'One more, and you will be far enough!' On his mantelpiece was a photograph, taken by my son, Ben. It is a double exposure of Brig O' Dee, with a ghostly image of Charlie presiding over 'his' pool.

Back to Iceland

There is an enormous variety of rivers and conditions in Iceland and it is hard to say anything without generalisation, and consequent inaccuracy. On many rivers a single-handed rod is all that is required. But many people prefer a light double-handed rod. The smaller rod is better for fishing short and narrow places, and for landing a fish without assistance. It is advisable to have an adequate number of spare rods to cope with disasters, which, like other disasters, often don't come singly!

One terrible morning, I had four rods protruding from under the upper door in the rear of my car. As I drove over rocks this door fell on the rods, smashing three, and damaging the fourth. I left my son Sandy to fish with that rod while I returned to the lodge to re-equip. As I drove up to the lodge, I was followed in by a strange car, out of it emerged my brother Robin, who assured me that another son, Ben, was all right. I had no reason to doubt this until then! I learned that Robin had nearly been washed away wading across the river, and he had fallen on his rod against the bank, smashing it. He left Ben fishing, while he also drove back to re-equip. As he turned to cross the bridge, high over the Litla Þverá, his off-side front tyre burst, his suspension gathered up a rock the size of a football, which the car carried across the bridge before Robin could stop. A kindly farmer drove him back to the lodge. The lunchtime damage report was five rods broken and one car written off. Luckily for Sage these were not their rods, or the rods would have been covered by their guarantee! We put up replacement rods, but only had time to collect my sons, and their fish before lunch. A replacement car arrived from Akureyri Car Hire in record time.

Normally a floating line is all that is required. This has the great advantage of enabling the fisherman to see a fish following the fly. Then the cast can be repeated and, if the second cast is ignored, the fly may be changed. In such clear water conditions, I like to use a translucent line. In clear water and sunlight, the shadow of a normal line frightens fish lying in quiet water. This can be avoided by using an exceptionally long leader, but a translucent, (or 'slime') line, is a great help as the shadow is diffused. In very cold conditions, or in white water, a sinking tip, or a leaded fly can be effective, however care needs to be taken to avoid accidental foul hooking.

Personally I don't like tapered casts (leaders), because after a few changes of fly no point (tippet) remains. I prefer to make them from whatever thickness and breaking strain seems suitable, taking into account the size of fish in the river, the number of obstacles, and the size of fly. Some of the 'extra strong' nylon, has proved to be extra shiny, and extra unreliable. The glint has frightened fish, and it has broken in the playing of a fish, at vastly beneath its supposed breaking strain. One season this cost me several memorable fish.

When selecting flies to use, consider why salmon take fly, and what presentation one wishes to achieve. It is well known that, when salmon return to a river, they don't feed in fresh water. This is a wonder of nature; many salmon rivers have little that salmon can eat other than their own young. In some Icelandic rivers it takes four years for the average parr to gain sufficient size to smolt. This is because of the shortage of food for them to eat. Icelandic salmon return to their river having lived off the wealth of the sea, and probably having had a high proportion of shrimp, and caplin in their diet. They don't have far to swim from feeding grounds to reach their river, and often still have their sea-going teeth. The rivers are short so a high proportion of fish are caught with sea lice on them, and many of these have not yet lost their white 'tails', which drop off after about one day in fresh water. I believe that it is for these reasons that Icelandic salmon are so free taking. The season is short, and they advance quickly to sexual maturity, their colouring changes, making them beautiful to the opposite sex, but not to us!

Usually they come in to the rivers in a shoal and frequently remain in shoals, or pods in the rivers. It is not surprising that members of such a group have a tendency to be in the same state of mind as each other. If one takes a fly the others may do likewise.

One can only speculate as to what triggers a salmon to take something into its mouth in a river. Possible stimulants may be:-

Taste, hunger, shape, colour, movement, memory of food recently eaten in the sea, memory of food eaten in the river as a parr, or aggression, irritation, and even playfulness.

Different kinds of fly, and different methods of presentation stimulate different reactions. In Iceland, because of the clarity of the water, and frequently, the abundance of salmon, one can learn so much more about the behaviour of salmon, than in rivers having coloured water and a scarcity of fish.

In Iceland worms are extremely effective but we prefered not to use them. Thankfully fishing with natural prawn, and natural shrimp are not considered to be good form or believed to be illegal. All of these can stimulate fish with their taste, or 'smell'.

The most famous of the Icelandic shrimp fly creations is the Red Francis; also, worth a try are the black, green, blue, pink and yellow versions. Similarly the Krafla series, (pronounced krapla, with a soft 'P'), named after an active volcano, is tied with the same range of colours, also representing shrimp. These use clipped feathers to create the same shape as a Francis, which gives more life to the fly being without a hard body guarding the hook. Flies such as the Ally shrimp and the General Practitioner are equally effective. These can all benefit from being fished with some short hand movements.

The very smallest of flies may act as reminders of little items of food eaten in the sea, or eaten as a parr. Such small flies can be a Stoats tail, (with or without a little silver), a Black and Yellow tied on a hook, (or as a tube fly), a Jeannie, and many others. These are best fished slowly, swinging in the current across, and close to the fish, which will be ready to take them near the surface. Black and yellow is a most effective colour combination that is reflected in many flies.

The Collie-dog, Elver fly, Sheep series, larger tube flies and Waddingtons, may be best fished in heavy water, or stripped, to provide plenty of movement. These are more likely to stimulate aggression, particularly from the bigger fish as they become more sexually mature. They occasionally move quite a distance to attack such a fly.

Most people have their favourite flies, which they often use, and so preferences become self-fulfilling!

In Iceland, as in Russia, if a salmon is seen to move on the surface there is a good chance of catching it, unless it is actually running. Other than in gorges, or below a foss, most pools in Iceland are not very deep, and even in the deep places, undisturbed salmon don't lie deep.

Almost always fish can be tempted to take close to the surface. It is only one small step further to entice them to take a fly that is actually on the surface. This is hugely enjoyed by its devotees, and may take the form of fishing with a 'Bomber', the 'Portland Hitch', or the 'Yellow Dolly'. Basically the technique of surface fishing can be divided in two. The first is fishing with a fly as a true dry fly, floating downstream with little or no movement. To be at all effective, this requires most precise knowledge of the position of fish. The second is much more effective; creating a 'V' on the surface stimulates curiosity, aggression, or even playfulness. Fish may come to the surface and follow the 'V', again and again, or they may strike at it, or even jump out of the water and land on it, or strike at it with its tail. Sometimes the same fish comes several times; at other times different fish from a group may each come only once. The percentage fish hooked to rises seen is usually very low with these methods, but the adrenaline level of the fisherman is high.

To fish the 'Portland Hitch' it is necessary for the leader to be attached to the fly, a little behind the head, and on the flank nearest to the fisherman. This is achieved with a half hitch over a long shank fly, after it has been tied on in a normal way. It is easier with a tube fly. The tube should be previously pierced in readiness, with a heated needle, through its side. The leader can then be threaded through this hole, and tied to the hook in the normal manner. With the rod held a little high, the fly is then fished on the surface, creating the 'V'. It acts on the same principle as a poacher's 'otter', being pulled against the current! It is necessary to have a fly tied on a plastic tube, that is light, and that can be pierced.

This is as exciting as the next presentation is boring! In desperation, sometimes a fish can be made to take by casting the fly to it again and again and again, until it gets so irritated that it bites the damn thing.

I often fish with a dropper, and believe that if a fish sees a minnow chasing a small 'fly', it may join the chase, sometimes even taking both flies! This does increase the risk of loss, when playing a fish, due to 'dropper trouble'. It also increases the risk of wind knots, and the danger of the second fly getting in the way, if netting a fish. Droppers are unpopular with guides!

When playing a fish, if it sulks, it can be effective to persuade it with gentle pressure to leave its pool and then to follow it downstream, where it will soon tire. It is surprising how often a fish isn't lost doing this, however rough the water, or large the rocks, but the danger is greater in low water conditions. If a fish is trying to go downstream, and, it is considered to be a potential disaster if it does, a good way to stop the fish is to give it line so that a belly is formed, and it feels a pull from downstream. In other circumstances it is wise to try to prevent too much of the line from being drowned, so one no longer knows where a fish is in relation to potential obstacles, and so leads to its loss.

It is important, not to over-wade, which spooks fish, and to consider what fish can sense, both in and out of the water. Fish are most sensitive to taste and to vibration. Noise of voices does not disturb them, but heavy footsteps, on a soft bank, create vibrations that alarm the fish. The lateral line on the flank of a fish is a sense organ for detection of vibration. The retina of a fish is particularly sensitive to colour. A rough surface of the river, caused by wind or a fast current, makes it difficult for a fish to see above the surface. If the surface is smooth, there is a cone of vision enabling a fish to see through the surface, but outside that cone the underside of the surface acts as a mirror. This paragraph just touches most superficially on a complicated subject that is well worth studying.

Always remember that fishing in Iceland is more like 'target shooting', than 'fishing the water'. Many fishermen stand at the top of a pool with their double-handed rod and make their first cast. Their fly may be downstream of many of the fish in the pool. Often it is better to fish with a single-handed rod, keeping low and standing well upstream of the pool, starting with a short cast.

If you do have a guide, treat him as a friend, and listen to his advice, before experimenting on your own. Wherever possible I beach my fish. I believe that doing this, fewer fish are lost, fish can be landed sooner and it is less stressful to a fish if it is to be released (but see page 43). Don't be greedy, the bigger the fish the more valuable it is to the river, and fish in accordance with the biological advice as to the needs of the river.

Take all your rubbish, and any nylon that you find, back to the lodge; this can harm birds and sheep. Report any mink or their tracks if seen. Don't fish over the time limit, other than to land a fish already hooked. If sharing a rod, never ever both fish at the same time. This amounts to stealing from the river owners and could cause the cancellation of a lease.

The weather conditions can change very quickly, so it advisable to be prepared with layers of clothes to add, or that can be removed. A wind and waterproof outer garment is particularly important for comfort. In Iceland there are no mosquitoes, and few biting insects. The midges are almost all 'eye flies' which appear when the wind drops. They seldom seem to penetrate behind dark glasses.

A wading staff is most helpful, particularly when a river rises and becomes unexpectedly powerful. At such times a 'third leg' makes all the difference to stability. Also the clarity of the water can be misleading, so that it may be deeper than is apparent. Even for small rivers, breast waders are best as they make it possible to cross a river, or stay in a river through a gorge. Rocks in Iceland are seldom slippery, so felt soles are not so necessary as elsewhere, but if they are worn it is vital to have nails at least in the heels. Without these, felt is dangerously slippery on wet grass. On rivers where there are lava flows, there are additional dangers both on the banks and in the river. There can be concealed holes, so great care is needed. Another potential danger is loose shale above a cliff. It is necessary to be aware of danger, and to take care.

Lastly, always remember that the farmers are your hosts, and that grass is a valuable crop! So be considerate!

Ethics and Conservation

Late one evening in September, after dinner at the Cape Wrath Hotel, an old Rolls Royce drew up, and out of it emerged a huge bearded man in a kilt, with a Bonelli eagle, a Weimaraner dog, and a supply of Glen Livet whisky. This proved to be James Robertson Justice. During the next few days we drank much of his malt whisky, listened to his memorable stories, and discussed how to put the world to rights. In his opinion there were three kinds of naturalist, the 'Sportsman Naturalist', the 'Scientific Naturalist', and 'Old women of both sexes'. It might now be more politically correct to rename the third category, the sentimental naturalist.

Of these the 'Sportsman Naturalist' is the closest to nature in the wild, and has a vast reservoir of knowledge, and common sense. He may well have gained experience, and succeeded in other fields. Nowadays such people are largely ignored and are being squeezed between the scientist and the sentimentalist, hunting with hounds is a case in point. But to turn from the general, to the particular, the salmon situation is a prime example. Orri Vigfússon is driven to exasperation by the way that the British Government, has been willing to spend annually on Salmon research more than the annual value of the UK salmon catch, and yet have no money to close the North-East Drift nets and compensate the commercial fishermen. These nets are indiscriminate and have been a national disgrace. The cost of buying them out would result in much more conservation, at lower cost, than is achieved by the government funded scientific research. Reducing the number of these nets, as is being done, results in the remainder being used with greater effort and there is little change in the total catch from a declining resource. This is similar in its effect to 'set aside' of farmland, in the US, and EU. The least fertile is taken for subsidy, and greater yields obtained from that which is cultivated. In 2001 the government has offered £750,000 for a buy-out of the North East nets provided a like amount is contributed privately. The outcome of this is not yet known.

From a British perspective the picture is disastrous. Sand eels are taken in enormous quantity, with disastrous effects in the higher food chain. Young salmon are being mopped up in the process as an insignificant, and unreported by-catch. The same occurs with the herring catch, post smolts are caught with the herring. Sea birds colonies starve. Quotas for fish result in the death of more fish, for the simple reason that under-sized, and forbidden species are returned dead to the sea. Cormorants come inland in order to find easier pickings, because of reduced availability of fish in their normal habitat. Also because of depleted food in the sea, grilse return, to some rivers in Scotland, visibly undernourished. Fur coats are not politically correct, and baby seals do have beautiful eyes. Seals have hardly any natural enemy other than man, and the killer whale. Now Man is not such great threat, they multiply, in excessive numbers, to predate on a greatly reduced food source. They congregate at the mouths of salmon rivers, and now even follow salmon into rivers. Using published scientific data, it has been calculated that if 1% of the diet of seals at present round the coast of Scotland is salmon, as has been estimated by an official source, they would eat the entire homing run of salmon. A calculation of the other 99% of their food requirements would show their consumption of fish to be a threat to our commercial fishermen.

Animals that are killed commercially must be treated humanely, and killed humanely. It seems odd that this does not apply to fish that are commercially caught. They may be left to die on a long line, or to gasp, or suffocate to death on a fishing boat, yet it is the sportsman who is accused of cruelty. I have yet to hear of the sentimental lobby showing concern about the methods of the commercial fishermen. If animals were treated in ways similar to the way that fish are treated at sea there would be riots in the streets!

The greed of elements of the fish farming industry have led to parasites from the Baltic, where the salmon had a natural tolerance, spreading to the Atlantic, and leading to the destruction of all salmon in whole rivers. The farms are causing massive pollution in the sea and damage to wild fish through sea lice infestation. Escapees damage the genetic integrity of the populations of individual rivers. Fish farming is, in principle, highly desirable, but it needs to be conducted in a much more responsible manner than at present.

There are other factors, both sea and land based. Personally I believe that a good biological report, and monitoring of individual rivers, is the way ahead for salmon conservation in rivers. The catch that should be harvested, and when, should determine the salmon that can be killed, and when catch and release should be made mandatory. Exploitation of wild salmon should only be on that basis, and only within individual rivers and their estuaries. In Russia, the Varzuga salmon run is in such good health, that it can withstand a substantial and sustainable netting operation, and also a hugely successful sport fishery, based on catch and release. Likewise this should be possible on the Ponoi. If netting is to continue, this is an ideal at which to aim. In Iceland there is now no commercial netting of wild salmon except on the Ölfusá. The greater value for sport is appreciated. These last nets may be bought out soon as part of a deal that may lead to another large ranching operation for sport fishing. If this is achieved other salmon rivers that are tributaries will also benefit. Sea fishing is well regulated, and the sport fishery helps the hard-pressed farmers. However this record of success is now being put at risk by proposed huge fish farming operations in the South East Fjords, which may lead to an ecological disaster. (See chapter on South Coast rivers).

'Catch and Release' is a relatively new concept in the British Isles for game fish, as it is also in Iceland. It has been normal practice for 'coarse' fish for a long time. In Canada and the US, it is long established, in countries new to the practice it is not surprising that it is controversial both in principle, and in detail. Opinions on so many things are greatly influenced by perspective. I first practised catch and release on the Restigouche. The camp upstream of us insisted on nets being used to land salmon. Sometimes released fish drifted down into our water, where they were eaten by sea gulls. Our Guides claimed that netting was stressful to fish, so they would not use them, as a result the survival rate for released fish on our beat was close to 100%. Their practice was that, when the leader had been touched, a fish was considered to be a caught fish, because from that moment the effort was concentrated on releasing it alive and strong. This may lead to greater catches being reported, due to 'long range releases', and fish that escape while being landed, being included in reported catches. On the Restigouche, if possible a fish was secured while swimming in the water, and the hook removed without taking it out of the water, except briefly, if required, for a photograph, when it should be held supported with both hands. If it was not possible to release it while still in the water, it was acceptable to beach the fish. As a fish runs up a river, it is perfectly natural for it to run over gravel or rocks with its back out of the water. Fish survive and recover from horrific wounds caused by seals. The loss of some scales is natural, and not a disaster for a fish, whereas serious bleeding from the gills is fatal. Catch and release is not compatible with fishing with worm, prawn or shrimp, because these are taken too far down for release to be successful. With catch and release the size as reported of caught fish often increases by at least 10%, unless they are actually weighed!

To lift a grilse out of the water by its tail may not always harm it, but to do this to a salmon of any size will cause serious injury. To kick a salmon up a bank, may cause outrage, however to flick a salmon up a beach with ones toe, may do no harm at all! Frequently, one Icelandic guide did this, and to my astonishment I noticed that the fish lay quiet, for a few seconds, possibly from shock. I have found the same, when I have done this. If the fly can be removed with minimal struggle, the fish may not even require any time to recover. In Southern Argentina, sea trout, now averaging 9 to 10 pounds, have benefited enormously from catch and release. It is very rare to see one fail to recover. In my own experience one in twelve weeks of fishing by six rods! With all fish, it is sometimes necessary to have great patience to make certain that they do recover. It may be necessary to hold a fish upright in a gentle current, some times moving it backwards and forwards in the water. It may also help to tip it vertically or to stroke its belly to extract air that has become trapped. Occasionally it can help to tap the fish with one's hand on its nose to wake it, but, first, do get out all air.

When practising catch and release, it is sporting to adjust ones fishing technique. One should try to land a fish as soon as possible, and therefore it is better not to use nylon that is finer than conditions demand. Personally it gives me great pleasure to see a fine fish swim away. Depending on the state of a river, I am happy to catch and kill, or to catch and release. I would like a ban on the sale of all rod caught fish; if that could be enforced, it might reduce occasional excesses.

Now from general considerations of conservation, let us return to Iceland, and to a particular example. From the description that I give of the Laxá í Dölum, it will be obvious that each beat provides an enormous amount of choice for two rods to fish in a six hour, half day fishing period. What is not immediately apparent, is that the fish have no refuge whatsoever where they can escape the attention of fishermen. The Laxá í Dölum is somewhat in the rain shadow of the Snæfellsnes peninsula that shields it from the prevailing rain bearing wind. The watershed is small and the river bed is large enough to cope with the spring run off. As a result, the salmon are exposed and vulnerable to over fishing. Being near the Northern extremity of the West Coast Salmon fishery, fish enter the river in large numbers later than the more Southern rivers. The earliest fish usually include most of the bigger multi-sea-winter fish. These are the most valuable, and bear the genes to produce more of their own kind. Yet these salmon are fished for all the season. Those that come into the river after the end of the season, are not fished for at all. It is not surprising that the run tends to get later and later, and the proportion of two sea winter fish decline. The greatest fishing effort is on those fish that are the most valuable. There is no fishing effort on those of the least value.

For the first few days after the fly fishing period, the rental to the farmers has been highest, because worms are taken freely by fish that have not seen a worm for some weeks, if ever. Towards the end of the season, the river is let to expert Icelanders fishing chiefly with worms. The daily limit per rod on the river was ten fish, but, according to what I have been told, when this limit is reached further fish go into the back of the cars, and are not recorded. In our record year, we were actually asked to fish without daily limit, because the Biological advice was that there were too many fish for the spawning needs of the river. As I explain elsewhere we placed on ourselves a limit that we increased from 10 to 15 fish per rod per day. Now with greater experience, I am convinced that the scientific advice was flawed. I doubted it even then.

As I seem to remember, we were told the advice was that the river only required twenty spawning pairs of salmon, and the limiting factor was the availability of food for the parr, which were taking an average of four years to smolt. Recently talking to a distinguished salmon biologist, I was told that it is not uncommon for experts to underestimate the number of salmon that are needed for spawning. With variation in hatching conditions, in particular the river temperature after hatching is critical, the survival rate can have considerable fluctuation. The rate of predation in rivers is also easy to underestimate. Divers, saw-billed duck and the Arctic terns, take a huge number, as is obvious to every fisherman.

Without any refuge, combined with the scientific advice, and the fishing policy, I believe this river was increasingly over fished, after the extemely light fishing during the period that the river was leased by Pepsi, from this the river benefited considerably.

Many years ago, eyed ova were released in Sutherland on the very North West of Scotland, which still echoes the name given to it by the Vikings. This was done on the river Dionard, which river has a close resemblance to an Icelandic river, and is the perfect training ground for fishing in Iceland. On that river the salmon used to run through the bottom reaches, rarely pausing. They ran up to the loch, and the few miles below. In the autumn, the keepers of the two estates on that river, netted one holding pool, two miles below the loch and stripped the salmon. On their own property, they each had a hut beside a small burn which was equiped with trays for the eggs with water trickling through. They hand-carried back the fertilised eggs from the strath, and placed them in the trays. Once these had hatched, and the egg sacks were being absorbed, the eyed ova were planted in every little burn from the sea pools up the river. No food had to be bought, the casualties must have been high, but sufficient survived to smolt and to return in due course to the pool below their home burn.

The result was that almost every pool on the river became a holding pool. These resident fish had the effect of attracting the others that were running to their homes further up the river. As a result, it seemed that fish ran up the river much more slowly. This provided good fishing from the sea pool to the loch. These keepers, Hughie Campbell and Bob McLeod were not scientists, and the cost of this stocking method was minimal, but highly successful. The fish that were taken for stripping could be spared, and reduced the over cutting of redds in the river below the loch. The river's own genetic strain were being used, so there was no negative to their method, provided there were sufficient salmon left in the area from which the brood stock were taken. When they retired, and proprietors aged and changed; what had been done, and the benefits derived from it were forgotten. If they had had the benefit of biological degrees, and had written papers in scientific journals, their experience would have become a part of 'knowledge' and might not have been overlooked.

I am reminded of a piece of doggerel about Lord Jowitt, when Master of Trinity College Cambridge:-

> Here stand I,
> my name is Jowitt.
> If its knowledge
> then I know it.
> What I don't know,
> isn't knowledge.

This method of stocking, is clearly not suitable for everywhere but it is suitable for many places. Another good idea that is even less expensive, is to have some floating boxes, so that salmon, when caught, can be placed in them, then transported above an impassable foss, in order that the salmon can spawn naturally in a previously unpopulated area. Although this idea is excellent, it is a little more work, and the potential spawning area must be suitable for spawning. If the Dionard method was applied the survival rate might be increased tenfold of the spawn from those fish that are stripped.

The experience of the East and West Rangá shows a return rate of between 1% and 2%. This is sufficient for profitability for a sport fishery, but not for a commercial fishery, for which a return of about 5% is needed. The cost of feeding the young salmon from fry to smolt is high. Depending on circumstances, this cost can be greatly reduced, if the river, or parts of it are not fully populated by wild salmon parr. It is then possible to release eyed ova, or small fry into unpopulated places, in order that they can grow up eating the natural food. As we have seen it is also possible to transport brood stock above obstacles, enabling them to spawn naturally in unutilised water. However it is known that Salmon move downstream, as well as upstream to a surprising extent, From experiments on one river in Scotland, it seems that a high proportion of mature salmon caught and transported above a large obstacle, returned to their natal area downstream. This can be overcome by putting the fish in a cage in the river for one or two days in order for them to acclimatise to the new area. Parr, introduced above an obstacle accept this adopted natal area; they are likely to stay in that area if transported as salmon.

When considering ethics it is always important to consider perspective, and to avoid greed, which is the root cause of many problems. When considering conservation, it is important to consider all relevant factors, and then act decisively. Expensive research may be unnecessary and cause delay. Common sense is too often underestimated or ignored. No one 'solution' is going to save the salmon, but a host of different initiatives must be put into action. This is a matter of great urgency.

From an Icelandic point of view, it is difficult to understand why the British would wish to shoot Snipe, Woodcock or Golden plover. If the British knew Icelandic practice, it would be equally difficult to understand why Icelanders eat Puffins, Razor bills and Guillemots. In Iceland country sports are most important, but not long ago this was related to survival in a harsh environment. Eiders are not eaten, because of the importance of the down, which relates to keeping warm in winter in a country with little natural fuel. For Christmas dinner Ptarmigan is the preferred delicacy, and should be shot by the men of the family, and not bought.

For Salmon fishing the preferred method was the worm, and fish were preserved for the winter months either smoked or as 'Gravlaks'. Icelanders know that their Gravlaks is best, every Scandinavian country has their own similar belief. Trout were often caught on strips of herring, now trout fishing is also a major sport.

In the last fifty years the standard of living in Iceland has increased enormously, until now it has one of the highest standards of living in the world; Icelanders travel widely, and have winter holidays in warmer climates, and in places where the days are longer. In Asia with prosperity, less rice is eaten, whereas in Europe for the same reason, more rice is eaten. Both are looking for more variety, while still attached to tradition. In Iceland, with prosperity the emphasis in fishing is now much more on sport, and fish to eat is an important by-product of sport, but sport is of the greater importance. Fly-fishing is now the rage, and fly-tying is an important hobby. Sport-fishing in Iceland is a world market, with visiting fishermen drawn almost equally from North America, and from Europe, North, South and West. They also come from much further away but in small numbers. The cost of the best fishing is high, but Icelanders compete for the best, and not only the wealthy. On a major salmon river at prime time, I have met bakers fishing, who were on strike!

In view of the importance of fishing, and salmon fishing in particular, it is not surprising that the most respected figure in the world of salmon conservation is Orri Vigfússon, an Icelander!

Chapter Three
The rivers of the South West

Nearly 13% of the rod caught salmon are caught in the seven rivers South of Borgarfjörður. In addition, there were in this area two salmon ranching operations. One was beside the aluminium smelter, where a strong spring flows out of the lava, and the other was at the head of Kollafjörður, where the returning fish run under the road up an insignificant stream, into a trap. Both of these are now closed.

Elliðaár

Starting from the South, and working round Iceland clockwise, the first Salmon river is Elliðaár. This runs through Reykjavík, and has been controlled by the Reykjavík Angling Club since 1937. In 2000 the number of rods was reduced from 6 to 4, and in future only fly-fishing will be allowed above the foss. The club allots fishing to members for half a day at a time. It is a small, but productive grilse river, flowing out of a lake. The annual catch over 28 years has varied from over 2000, to under 500, but has averaged about 1400. There is a salmon ladder, and a counter. There has been a hatchery beside the river since 1932, and stock from this river was introduced into other rivers before it was realised that genetic strains should not be deliberately mixed.

The success story of this river has recently been marred by disease, and it is not yet clear whether this is related in any way to pollution. In the last five years to 2001 the average annual catch is down to only 483. There has also been a similar problem at Kollafjörður, where all the fish have been killed as a preventive measure. Hopefully the problem can be contained, and eliminated.

Úlfarsá

This river runs through the outskirts of Reykjavík. It suffers from common problems of clashing sports in suburbs, riders following the river bank, riding through pools, and also bombardment by golf balls. One fisherman bagged over 90 balls in one day! The catch by the two rods that are permitted has varied from 110 to 709 in 1988, but this figure included a large number of farm escapees. However the average over 26 years has averaged a little over 320. Early in the season fish are mostly caught on worm, but later when they have reached further up river, it is more suitable for fly, which is widely used.

Leirvogsá

This is another small river not far from Reykjavík, it is fishable for 12 km, and is susceptable to drought. It is fished on a daily basis by two rods. The catch has varied from 136 to a remarkable 1057, which, surprise, surprise, was in 1988; the run being vastly swollen by farm escapees. The average catch has been 458, which gives an extremely high annual catch per rod. Although it is mainly fished with worm, it can provide very good fly-fishing.

Varmá is the next river which has a good run of sea trout, but is not a salmon river.

Laxá í Kjós (see also page 19)

Driving North out of Reykjavík most traffic now uses the tunnel under Hvalfjörður to Akranes. But if driving on the coast road, fishermen cannot fail to notice the Laxá í Kjós. What was the main road to the North, crosses it about half an hour's drive after leaving Reykjavík. Fishermen stopped, as did coach loads of tourists. The bridge is about 400 yards from the mouth, and a further 100 yards upstream is a wide foss. Usually there is someone fishing below the foss on the left bank. This is not surprising because that place is one of the nearest things that there is to a certainty in fishing! About 400 yards further upstream is Laxfoss. Between Laxfoss and the road bridge is also phenomenal fishing. This part of the river being so visible, the fishermen used to feel like goldfish in a bowl, with every passer-by watching, however, now most traffic goes through the tunnel that shortens the journey North.

It has been said that this is a one beat river, which I consider to be absolute nonsense. The Laxá í Kjós, and its tributary the Bugða are fished together, and form a productive and interesting fishery. The Achilles heel is that it can be very subject to drought, but the South West of Iceland usually has a reasonably high rainfall. However it is a small river when not in spate.

This fishery is always listed amongst those with the ten highest catches, and has on occasion headed the list. The average catch over 28 years to 2001 is 1522. The highest catch was 3811 in 1988.

Fish can be seen in many pools. There is no doubt that it is a lovely river for fly fishing but is very vulnerable to worming. Salmon tend to congregate in large numbers in a few places, causing these fish to be easy to foul hook, in fact in low water conditions it is difficult to avoid foul hooking. From time to time there has been too much emphasis on numbers of fish caught, and the placing in the annual statistics. There was one rogue year, 1988, when there was an enormous influx of extremely small escaped farmed fish that could only be called grilse by courtesy. This almost doubled the catch statistics for that year.

I have fished the Laxá í Kjós seven times, for a total of 35 days, in varying times of the season, in very different conditions, and I have many happy memories of it. My son, Nick, has guided here for two seasons using my long wheel based Land Rover for the rods that he was guiding. He was even occasionally the top guide of the week. He was once guiding two men, one could fish well and the other could not and he was disturbing the pools. Nick took him fishing where he could do no harm, until he was fit to fish where there actually were salmon. That man ended the week on a high with a good catch!

The lodge consisted of a range of bedrooms, each with washing facilities, and, 100 yards away, a school that was used as a 'mess' with dining room, reception room, and living quarters for the staff etc. The catering was outstanding with cooking by good chefs who were on holiday. Eleven rods were permitted, now increased to twelve, but it is normally fished by ten rods in pairs with a guide if required for each pair. Rods may be shared between two fishermen. Throughout Iceland this is common practice, most particularly by specialist worm fishermen using the rod sharer to spot the fish. There was usually a fly only period at the prime time. The

Þórufoss on the Laxá í Kjós.

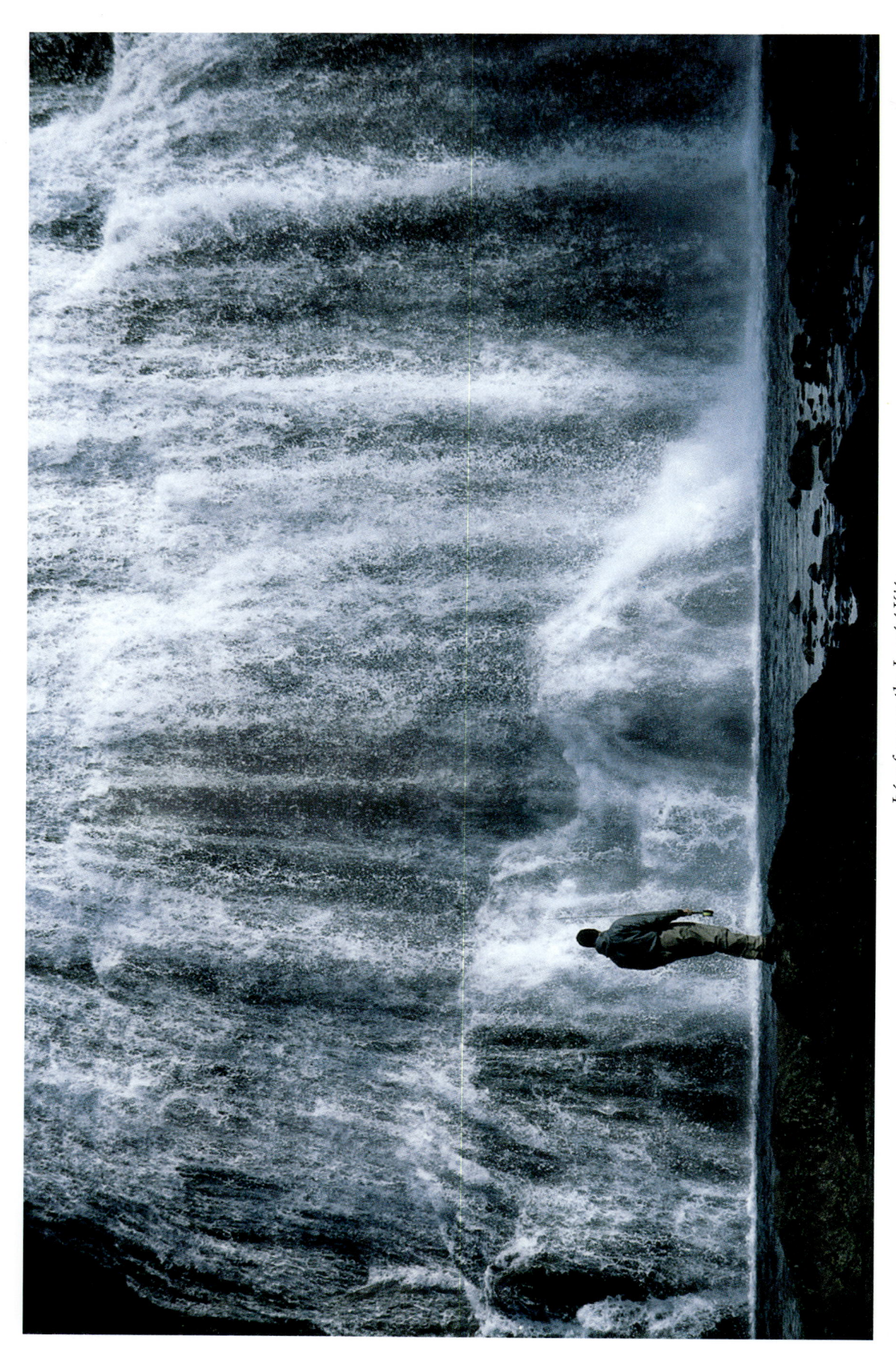

From a photograph by Hákon Steulund.

division of the river into beats varied to some extent according to the state of the river and the fish. Early in the season there was more emphasis on the lower water and later more emphasis on the upper water. From the Bugða junction up the main river, there is a long stretch that is not normally in the beat roster, where anyone bored with his beat, or wishing to try that part of the river, may fish. This is commonly known as 'The Meadows', and it repays getting to know it. The lodge manager was allowed to fish there, using the eleventh rod, without upsetting anyone. This part of the river also has some very good sea trout. It has recently been altered by gravel extraction.

From the sea to the upper barrier to salmon migration on the Laxá í Kjós is 21 kilometres, and the length of the Bugða, from the junction, to its lake is 4 kilometres. There are now 79 'pools' on the Kjós, and 13 on the Bugða, making a total of 92. For salmon the barrier is Þórufoss, where the river falls vertically 30 feet over a width of 30 yards. Below this, there is a short pool with fish lying on both sides, and some in the middle. In spite of the sheer drop some optimistic fish try to jump the foss, but naturally don't get very far. It can be fun to cast upstream and work a small fly on a floating line. Below the river runs through a gorge with easy walking. Late in the season there are a few runs that hold fish. Near the bottom of the gorge there is a corner with a rock shelf on the left bank shaped like a whale. Here, there is a pool where we have caught some fish, but immediately above there is a good run, easily overlooked, in which fish took freely.

The river nears the road at Hálshylur, where a stream enters the river from the left bank, in spate this becomes extremely dirty. Above that there are four possible small pools, including the one we called 99/100. Hálshylur may hold some fish, but the next important pool is one of the main holding pools of the river, Stekkjarfljót. This is usually fished from the left bank. At the head of the pool the run enters the pool bearing to the left against a long rock shelf, which stands some

Laxá í Kjós - Stekkjarfljót.

feet out of the water. All of this can be good, and should be fished carefully, again and again. Below there is a wide, and rather featureless pool. The bottom here can be covered with an incredible number of fish. If this is fished slowly, with small flies on a long leader and a floating line, some most exciting fishing is possible. Another fisherman may return to the lodge with an account of fishing with two tubes fished as one fly, stripped fast, and having his fly attacked by an angry cock fish! I prefer the more delicate approach!

Below an occasional fish can be caught, but the next excitement is in the pool where a road to a farm crosses over the river, at Króarhamar. The run in under the bridge can be good from the left bank, but in some seasons the bottom of the main pool below can be blue-black with salmon. An occasional fish may be tempted to take a fly. Below that there are shallow runs over gravel. There is one small pool

Laxá í Kjós - Króarhamar.

on a corner where the river bends to the right, and there is a rock shelf on the left bank. This looks inviting, and may hold some fish. The river bears left and runs through more gravel until it speeds up as it enters another gorge. The first time we fished this stretch was in the last week of August, we were not guided, therefore we were fishing without the benefit of local knowledge. As we emerged from the gorge we saw a fish jump 100 yards ahead against the right bank. Fishing there we immediately got into fish. We took several from that spot in that week, I have not heard of fish stopping there again, but it does now have a name, Klapparstrengur.

This illustrates two things that I will mention again. Places in a river that are attractive to fish vary to some extent from year to year. Some places can be outstanding, possibly for only one year, possibly for several years, and then fade, for no apparent reason. On the other hand the reason can be very apparent, the lie may even become dry land! The second factor is that in Iceland salmon frequently move as a 'pod'. These fish are likely to have swum the ocean together, entered the river together, and are lying side by side. It is not surprising, if they think, and act, alike. If one takes a fly, the others, if they are not frightened, are likely to do the same. Fishing with a small fly, on a floating line, and with a long fine leader, one fish may take. If that is coaxed gently from its lie, and not allowed to return there, the next fish may then be caught, and so on. With free taking fish like this, it is important not to be greedy, attitudes are changing and not before time. I have discussed 'Catch and release' elsewhere. A skilled worm fisherman, can guide his worm almost into a fish's mouth, and when it takes, he can pull it straight out of the river, and then repeat this process, again and again. There is one fisherman who is particularly famous, (or infamous), for this; he is a dentist, so he is known as Tóti Tönn (tooth)! (see photograph page 77)

Now we enter the gorge. About one third of the way down is Pokafoss. Before reaching that there are some interesting places to fish. Half way to Pokafoss is the Mirror Pool, which is a holding pool. This can only be fished from the left bank, and rewards fishing with care. There is a narrow fast and deep run above the foss, which is an exciting place to catch a fish, as it is likely to go downstream. The foss is narrow, and is not normally an obstacle to fish. This is a beautiful and interesting area. Below the foss is a narrow gully, with a left bend, and then the channel widens gradually. Fish lie all down this, and, if they can be tempted to take a fly, will give a thrilling fight. The river then widens, and winds its way down through the lower gorge. Fish can often be spotted from the cliff top, and then stalked while wading. Here, fishing is difficult, but it is a favourite area for those people who know it well. At the end of the gorge is a bridge carrying the main valley road over the river. This bridge usually marks the bottom of the top beat.

Soon, the river changes character. The valley opens out, and the river meanders through large areas of gravel. Below the bridge is a pool that looks attractive, and I have found it to be so in high water. The river bends to the right, and runs into Réttarhylur. This is a good pool. At the next left bend there is another pool worth a try, as is the stretch below. The river bottom is now less stable from year to year, but there are some corners and rock shelves, where fish lie. On this river the fisherman is spoilt for choice. In all there are 92 named, and numbered places, and others that are not named. In two consecutive seasons, for which I checked the records, not one single fish was caught in twenty-nine of the named places. To some extent this is self-fulfilling. It is natural that guides will wish to take fishermen to the best places, and those that are not guided will either rely on experience, or study the record book. The result is that many places, on the longer beats, are seldom visited.

There is a series of particularly interesting and good pools in the lower half of this beat, including Helgaholtskvörn, Berghylur 1 & 2, Túnhylur, Gaflhylur, Lambhagahylur, and Sjálfkvíar. When I fished it, the tail of Berghylur I had unstable gravel, and was not liked by fish. The very best of this exciting beat is from here down. All these pools on their day are memorable. I have seen the bottom of Túnhylur black with salmon. From time to time one would circle and jump. It was most tantalising; Túnhylur is a wonderful pool. Tún means meadow, or hay field, hylur being pool. One day I was sharing this beat with a good fisherman, and our guide was with him. He was to fish this area and we were to swap when he finished. At intervals I observed from afar, but he was much too busy to move. Eventually with 30 minutes to go I saw him packing up. Soon I appeared and fished just the very tail of the Túnhylur pool, and beached three fish in the time left. He hadn't fished far enough into the tail, and had caught only one fish all morning. Below this is a narrow run against the cliff on the right bank. Fish lie within a few inches of the rock face. The only way that I found to fish this was with a fairly long line from directly above, and play my fly backwards and forwards across the noses of the fish.

The next pool on the left hand corner can be good, but not as good as the pool below, known in English as the Barrel Pool. However it wasn't kind to me. The last main pool on this beat made up for that and is magic, in spite of its name, Sjalfkvíar, which is both difficult to remember and to pronounce.

We have now reached 'The Meadows', which stretch for the next seven and a half kilometres, and were not included in any beat, ending at the junction with the Bugða. Some of the river course is shifting gravel, but most flows gently, meandering through hay fields. Some spots are usually good for salmon, whereas others may be good only occasionally, or may hold good sea trout. In drought conditions, or if the river is in spate, it is very useful to have the flexibility that is given by the availability of the meadows. Access is easy from the Bugða, and is used by more fishermen from that beat than from elsewhere. New and occasional fishermen on the Laxá í Kjós cannot know how good this fishing can be, often it is little fished, and as a consequence it doesn't stand out in the statistics. This makes it increasingly likely that it will be only lightly fished, so this is self-fulfilling to the benefit of those who do know even a part of it well. When I was there the best pool was Hrosshólmi. Pieces of fallen bank formed attractive lies in a run on a long gradual bend. There was also good fishing in the pool above, and fish were visible in the two pools below.

In the lodge, after dinner, while having a 'night-cap' before going to bed, we sometimes saw bow waves caused by salmon running up the main river, or turning up the Bugða. 1980 was a drought year. We arrived on the first of July, and the river was already very low. Fish when seen were running fast. We returned on the 31st of July, and it had not rained since we had left the river on our first visit. Although the Bugða was exceedingly low, I noted that twice as much water was coming down the little Bugða, as down the main river. The Bugða was supported by a lake, out of which it flows, and by a burn flowing from the hill entering into the river just below 'Bugða Foss'. In these conditions the fish congregated in a few places, notably, on the main river at Þórufoss, Stekkjarflót, Mirror Pool, Lower Berghylur, Túnhylur, the Meadows, and Laxfoss, and, on the Bugða, Bakkahylur and Foss. In these conditions fish were very vulnerable to foulhooking, both deliberately and accidentally. We were scrupulous, and as careful as possible.

In 1982 the Bugða, had a box trap, just below the lake, in order to count fish entering the lake. Not far below this, an artificial pool, Bakkahylur, had been dug. In the years 1977, and 1978, not one fish had been caught here in either season, yet by 1982 a flood had undermined the left bank and this pool became most exciting.

It is best fished from the right bank. Below that there are a few hundred yards between two road bridges. Here there are two outstanding pools, The first, Bugavað, is another artificial pool, with two rock groins from opposite banks, and a big central rock, just downstream of the narrows. This rock forms a very taking lie, and the pool has a succulent tail. The second corner below that is Foss. There is no foss at all, but a strong entry run, which continues bending to the right. Here the burn joins near the tail, and the river runs down a fast run for 100 yards to the second road bridge, with another pool below it. This is only an outside chance, whereas Foss is often stacked with fish, which sometimes take freely. Below the bridge to the junction is hardly fished. There are two pools that are worth a try, Einbúinn, and Símastrengur. The latter means telegraph run, and it is remarkable how many rivers have telegraph pools, where fish tend to pause when running. I have gone out before breakfast, waded the main river, and walked up the Bugða to fish these two pools. Once on my way back, I lost a fish in another run. It ran downstream through shallows with its back out of the water. My nylon touched a stone that was little more than a pebble, and the fish swam free.

From the Bugða junction down to the main road bridge is less than one kilometre but in high season this is fished as two beats, both are memorable. The upper part is usually fished from the left bank. The junction is not good but only a short way below there are rocks under water forming possible lies. Then there is a deep run close to the left bank, which is a little higher at that point. This is called Klingenberg, and as the run broadens below, it is called Klingenbergbreiða. It is important to keep low and not to spook the fish, while fishing the upper part. This is a favourite first resting point for fish after mounting Laxfoss, which is the only major obstacle on the lower river. Laxfoss has a ladder in the centre, which isn't the only way for fish to negotiate the foss. Fishing close to the ladder at the top is forbidden.

Laxfoss is wide and can be fished simultaneously by two rods on opposite banks, with the obvious danger of trouble when two fish are being played at the same time. Half way up the foss is a small hole into which a hand net was occasionally dipped when a fish was wanted for the kitchen, and enough had not been donated. Fishing immediately below the foss is naturally exciting, with fish jumping frequently, close to the fishermen, and also showing elsewhere in the pool. This place is the site of many stories and adventures. The left side is much the best. This pool forms the bottom of that beat.

Then the river has a slight left bend, which conceals the fisherman at the foss. Fossbreiða, is immediately below, and is best fished from the left bank. When fish are running, fish are showing here in many places, and can lie and take freely all the way down to its very tail, where the river narrows at Holan, with Strengir immediately below. These are best in lower water. Meanwhile the main current has been crossing the river towards the right bank. Now it descends the lower falls. While starting to do this, there is a strange small narrow pool crossing the top of the foss called Skáfoss. This is a very exciting place to hook a salmon. Below is Kvíslafoss; in low water the fishing is all on the left side, and a procession of fish pause in this pool. The same cast can catch fish after fish. There are two very short runs below before the main road bridge is reached, where fish may also be taken.

Laxá í Kjós - Kvíslafoss in a huge spate.

If the river is falling, but is still high, the bottom of the foss on the right bank can also be good. Here it is helpful to have a skilfull guide, when the fish go round a corner close to the bank, they are difficult to follow quickly enough, but can be netted at that point. Still on the right bank, fish take well just above, and under the bridge. Here I was once fishing with great expectations, having risen a fish several times, when a party of Japanese appeared, and photographed me. One dropped his Pentax into the river. I took mercy on him, and waded in deep into fast water where the fish were lying. I recovered his camera but got wet in the process. I had done my good deed but it rankled!

Laxá í Kjós - Kvíslafoss in high water.

Below this bridge it is about 400 yards to the mouth of the river. Here the river is not included in any beat, and can be fished by anyone from any beat. At the right time of the tide it can be a good place to try. There are rapids all the way down to the sea pool, but fishing in salt water is illegal. A skilfull guide is required to get the timing right.

Several guides on this river were memorable and had all the skills and experience that one could wish for in guides. People who have fished here may remember, amongst others, Kalli, Tóti, Stefán, Óli, and Nonni, (Jón Pálsson, the son of Páll Jónsson, who had the lease for many years). All of these knew the river well, were experienced and good guides. Stefán owned a cabin close to the Bugða Foss Pool. There was one arctic tern which became very tame and which returned to this same place for several years. Stefán had only two weaknesses, drink and a temper. He was once sorely tried by the fisherman that he was guiding. Sadly, after that incident he was banished. He was not only a good guide and schoolmaster, but also an interesting naturalist. In his early twenties, Nonni was camp manager. Once during the fly-only period he found a guest of his father fishing with a worm, forthwith the culprit was sent back to Reykjavík. This showed great courage on his part.

I become anxious when a guide likes to use a tailer, as I have found this to be a potential disaster. I remember a guide that tried to tail a fish of mine but passed the lasso beyond the fish, and caught my line! However Nonni was a wizard with his tailer. Now he is a lawyer and too busy to guide.

I have always kept a detailed fishing diary, and this brings many memories back to life. Here are some extracts from notes of a week in July 1982, slightly amplified, which paint a vivid picture.

Wednesday P.M.
Bad reports from all over Iceland, there is a shortage of fish and rivers are low. Strong upstream wind. Much concern about Faroese long lining. However fish are running fast all the way up the river, and not pausing in Fossbreiða. I lost one in Kvíslafoss, and lost two more in Laxfoss before catching one there. It ran out of the pool on the far side, round a rock and ran on and on.

Thursday A.M.
Jim Edwards caught seven on beat one straight out of the sea, and three others caught one each. Simon hooked himself above his eye. Three rods broken. The fish are now beginning to run well and Laxfoss is full of fish.

Thursday P.M.
I fished beat five, blank, except for one pull in Stekkjarfjót, which was full of fish. I fell asleep while tying on a fly.

Friday A.M.
Scattered clouds. I fished Bugða, and caught four, one each in successive pools down to Foss. I also lost one on the beach. Larry Lindler, the other rod sharing the beat with me, hooked a fish of twelve pounds in the mouth in Bakkakvörn, his leader broke but he was still attached to the fish. When he landed it he found his

line knot jammed between the double hooks of someone else´s fly, still firmly in the fishes back. This fly was recognised as having been lost by Paul Boote the previous day.

(Graham Ferguson once had a similar experience. The story of this was told by a stranger in a book to illustrate the tall stories some fishermen tell. The author had arrogance and ignorance in equal measure, but no personal experience of the incident. For me this spoilt an otherwise good book.)

Simon and Paul each caught 3 on beat 1, and, Jim and Robbi caught 2 in the canyon. On beat five, Mark Payne caught his first three salmon, including one of 15 lb, which he played for two hours.

Saturday P.M.
I lost one in Klingenberg, lost one and caught one below on the Breiða, and then, I hooked one in Laxfoss, on a small fly with a floating line. After five seconds, it took off across the pool, then turned downstream and went on and on until my backing had nearly gone. Nonni went out into the river to clear the line from rocks, and Tóti netted it in Strengir in record time.

Sigurður Helgason, who had joined us for the day, lost a fish on beat five in the Farm Bridge Pool, Króarhamar, after playing it for four and a half hours. It was a monster fish hooked in the back even though he was fishing with a tiny fly and a floating line.

On the Bugða, Mark Payne hooked a fish in Bakkahylur, while fishing from the left bank. The fish took refuge under the bank. Mark Birkbeck was near by and came to help. When all else had failed Mark Birkbeck, lay with his legs held on the bank, he was below the water from his head to his waist in the river. He tailed a fish, and hurled it up to the bank. The fish cart-wheeled in the air and landed back in the river. It was the wrong fish! Mark tried again. This time he followed the leader down with his hand until he reached the fish. Again he got his hand round the fish, and this time it flew up and onto the bank while this performance was going on. They saw about 30 other fish come out from under the bank.

Monday P.M.
I caught three, one each in Strengir, Kvíslafoss, and in Lækjarbreiða. My fish in Strengir was hooked in the mouth on the dropper but, after a wild fight, was landed on the tail fly attached to the fish's tail. My fish in Kvíslafoss swam up, under the foss, and collected about 50 yards of nylon and two worm hooks, plus a huge Francis fly. I treated it roughly, in order not to lose it with all the clobber.

Two days before, two new people arrived in the lodge. They demanded by name two guides, who were allocated to them from us. They were very inexperienced fishermen. They fished Bugða and the top beat and they were out only part time. Seventeen fish were carried back from the river. They were caught in pools where there was a such a concentration of fish that it was difficult to avoid foul hooking. To have caught such a number, in such low water, many more must have been hooked and lost. It seems that it was not they who were fishing, but their guides. I understand that they have now become good and respected anglers.

Tuesday A.M.
This was our last morning, finishing at noon. I was fishing the Bugða, and I caught two in Bakkahylur, fishing very fine and light from the left bank, keeping well away from the edge of the water. Larry caught one in Bugavað, and failed in Bugða Foss, where the fish were very nervous of fly, after their trauma the day before. When I started to fish Foss, I tried from the right bank, because it is the unfashionable side. The river by now was so low, and so many fish were in this pool, which is shallow, that it was not possible to fish without touching fish. I crossed to the other side, and sat at the head of the pool feeling rather sad. Again the concentration of fish was too vulnerable for it to be possible to fish without touching them. Then I saw a leviathan show in very the tail of the pool. It showed several times in the same place. I didn't think that I could reach it, but I cast further and further just for the joy of casting as time ran out. Then it rose again, and my fly was further downstream than I realised, the rise was to me! A very strong fight ensued. The fish coming up into the middle of the pool where it did a great leap, arching its body to the full, and stretching out. Nonni had appeared on the far bank to call me to the car, and was watching. The fish then became uncontrollable, and ran under the main run into the pool where it sulked. Eventually pulling as hard as I dared from near the tail of the pool, I persuaded it to come back into the pool. When I got it near me Nonni realised that the fish was now hooked in the tail. He was armed with his tailer. We were in borrowed time, and it was getting embarrassingly late. He came up with the solution, and went down the run below the pool towards the bridge. I encouraged the fish to run out of the pool, only allowing it to go slowly. As a result it had difficulty in breathing and continued downstream head first. Nonni 'tailed' it over its head at the first attempt as it was passing him. The fish weighed in at 19 lbs. I had been fishing with two flies, a tiny stoats tail tube fly with a size 16 hook, this hook was in its mouth, and a thunder and lightning size 14 that was in its tail!! The dropper had become attached to the tail of the fish, and when the salmon made its great jump, as it straighten out from its jump, it had snapped the nylon leading to the tail fly, that was in its mouth.

This week on the Laxá í Kjós in 1982 was a seminal week for me, Some of the other things that happened are better left unrecorded. Suffice it to say, it marked a watershed in my Icelandic fishing. I determined, whenever possible to fish with a homogenous party, with interlocking friendships. Such a party should have a leader, accepted by the others, have an exclusive private lodge, or camp, and preferably, have the fishing rights to a whole river. Since then I have put together a large number of parties, which have been very happy together. There should be a house party atmosphere with drinking, and socialising, in the mess and not in the bedrooms. I have also fished in many similar parties that were equally enjoyable that were led by others, including Graham Ferguson, Sigurður Helgason, Bo Ivanovich, Loudie Constantine and Frank Godchaux.

Three out of my last four weeks on the Kjós had been in severe drought conditions, which had been far from ideal. Each year the price was increased. I reported to Páll in detail about the events of the week, and said that I would not return, the following year if the price was increased, and unless I knew with whom I would be fishing. He was, and is, a very good friend, but I stuck to my guns only returning once, thanks to Páll's generosity when we were in trouble elsewhere.

This was in early September 1983. It had been an unfulfilled ambition to catch big sea trout in Iceland. Our experiences are mentioned in the sea trout chapter. Suffice it to say here, that because of weather conditions it was not a success. Therefore I telephoned to Páll, calling for 'Help!', and he gave it. He invited us to stay at the Laxá í Kjós for a basic accommodation fee, and fish as many rods as available, at US $100 per day, unguided. There were six of us in my long wheel based Land Rover, and one hired Lada. My brothers Robin, Kit and I, my youngest son Ben, aged 18, and my godson Hugh, of a similar age.

All except Hugh knew the river and were glad to be back. Although it was September, fresh fish were pouring into the mouth of the river. It had been a good season, by 5th September 1470 had been caught on the main river and 430 on the Bugða. There was keen competition with the Þverá / Kjarrá, which had caught the same number! I have never seen so many fish in the lower part, from Laxfoss to the sea. Up river the main holding pools were stuffed with fish.

Saturday a.m.
We fished four rods and the Savages caught twelve salmon up to twelve pounds, four from the Bugða, and 8 from four pools on the top beat.
p.m. We had only one rod, and caught two from the bottom of the middle beat, including Hugh´s first fish.

Sunday
We had only one rod again, all day, between the five of us. We each fished for one hour in the morning on the top beat. We left Ben and Hugh with the Lada. They did not appear for lunch, so we settled down without them. When we were halfway through, a blood stained Hugh came into the dining room to say that Ben was all right! Naturally that meant that he was in a worse state than Hugh!

They had been coming back for lunch, when Ben had realised that he had left a fly box on the bank. They drove back for it, turned round to drive down the valley again. By now they were late and Ben was driving faster. Not long after crossing the bridge Ben drifted slightly onto the side of the road, which was soft, he skidded, left the road, went down the bank, turned over, and the car came to rest on its side facing backwards. Somewhat stunned Ben climbed out of the front window, before remembering, poor Hugh, on whom he had trodden. Hugh regained consciousness and also climbed out. They started walking to a farmhouse, forgetting that there was a river in the way. A car stopped, and the driver collected them, and most kindly drove them to the lodge to tell us, before taking them to hospital in Reykjavík. I followed them in the Land Rover. Once in hospital they were each tidied up in two operating theatres, and released. I informed the car hire company which brought a replacement to the lodge and collected the wreck. Before they got there I visited the car and recovered all personal possessions. The rods had been on the roof, one with a Bogdan reel that was considerably distorted.

Laxá í Kjós - Ben's car.

Monday
We fished three rods in the morning, and four in the afternoon. Ben fished with one arm, and caught a salmon and a sea trout. In all we caught 8 that day. Ben lost two more in Fossbreiða. From Laxfoss to Hólar, the river was stacked with fish, many lying, and showing in the most extraordinary places, but they were reluctant to be caught. Hugh lost one, and just for fun he tried to net one in the kitchen pot with his landing net. He succeeded at the first attempt, and it was returned! Catching salmon like this when we had a disaster elsewhere made an unexpected and good end to our holiday.

Three of us flew back, leaving Hugh to sail with Robin and the Land Rover. Their adventures were far from over. The ferry to Newcastle was caught in a big storm off the South coast of Iceland. For a day and a half it could make no headway against the storm. One great wave broke the windows of a cabin facing the bows. Sea water came in and streamed down the passage between the cabins causing alarm.

Robin drove South from Newcastle, and found the steering difficult. On the off side two shackle pins had snapped, that should have held the springs to the chassis. No lasting harm was done except to the rods, and Bogdan reel. I sent this for repair to Stan Bogdan in Nasshua, New Hampshire. He had never seen one of his reels so maltreated. He keeps it to this day as an ornament in his living room, and swears that he could never forget the Savages!!

Over twenty-eight years between 1974 and 2001 the lowest and highest catches on the Laxá í Kjós were 629 & 1901 and on the Bugða 190 & 461. I have omitted the 1988 when the catch on the Kjós was 3442, because that catch was inflated by the huge number of tiny farm escapees. In the period that I was fishing this river, apart from the first and last two weeks of the season, the weekly catch that could

Brynjudalsá.

From a photograph by Árni Baldursson.

be anticipated was well over 100 fish between 10 rods, and one week totalled 299. To give an indication of the size distribution, in 1983 the total catch was 1995, when I had left the river on the 4th of September, there were only five more days left of the season, and the catch was 1904. Of these 1602 were under 10 lbs, the weight of the others were, 94 of 10 lbs, 65 of 11 lbs, 70 of 12 lbs, 28 of 13 lbs, 23 of 14 lbs, 10 of 15 lbs, 4 of 16 lbs, 4 of 17 lbs, 3 of 18 lbs, none of 19 lbs, and one of 20 lbs.

To fish this river is fascinating for an experienced fisherman, it is also a wonderful place for a novice, or an elderly fisherman with easy access, and easy wading. Once, we even had someone fishing with us and catching fish, who was paralysed from the waist down. One novice was an Icelandic ballet dancer, who had never cast a fly before. As a result of training, his co-ordination was perfect, with the result that almost from the first cast after being shown what to do, he cast beautifully. He was Helgi Tómasson, and is now the director of the San Francisco ballet, which is one of the best ballet companies in the world.

Nick Savage guided on the Laxá í Kjós.

Brynjudalsá

This is another small stream fished by two rods over a length of, only, 2 km with an average catch of 163. One year ranched fish were stocked above the foss, and these were fished by an additional two rods. It was a successful experiment, but was not repeated because of risk of disease.

Laxá í Leirársveit

I have not fished this river. Driving across its estuary, a misleading impression is given that it must be dull. It has a strong, and loyal, following of both American, and British fishermen who come back year after year. It is an excellent river for fly-fishing, with an interesting variety of pools. There is no impassable obstruction to fish that can run up to two interconnected lakes. There is one foss that the fish mount, and above that the nature of the river changes, becoming slower running. Late in the season, fish fall back from the lower lake in preparation for spawning. Two more rods fish between the lakes, which is let separately.

The river is let to a party of six rods, usually each rod is shared between two. The fishermen stay in a lodge that is fully staffed. The catch has varied from 545, to 1887, which was, of course, in 1988, the year of the great escape! This is the most Northern of the rivers that was affected by this event. The average annual catch over 28 years to 2001 has been a respectable 1021. During the most recent five years the average weekly catch over the 90 day season has been about 67. The length of the river that is fishable is 14 km.

Ferjukotseyrar on the Hvítá.

From a photograph by Árni Baldursson.

Chapter Four
The Hvítá í Borgarfjörður

On average, an astonishing 6200, or over 20% of all the rod caught salmon of Iceland run under the bridge that joins the causeway carrying the 'A 1' road from Reykjavík into Borgarnes. A few fish turn South into the **Andakílsá**, which is a two rod river with an average catch of 150 salmon per year. It is very short before an impassible barrier is reached. It was used in 1974 for a successful experiment of smolt release into a holding pond for acclimatisation. After 8 km, all other fish enter the mouth of the **Hvítá**, (pronounced kveetow). This means 'white river', and it is glacial, flowing from the icecap, Langjökull. There must be less volcanic ash in this icecap, because the water flowing from its glaciers is white, not the colour of chocolate. Therefore it can be tolerated by salmon. Swimming up this river they no longer have to run the gauntlet of numerous short gill nets that used to line the banks, these were bought off in 1990. The catch in these nets used to be considerable, and shortly before they were closed there was a large quantity of fish in the deep freeze in Borgarnes that were frozen together, and therefore almost unsaleable. In an earlier year I have seen some huge salmon hanging in this freezer.

About 5 km from the mouth, the Grimsá flows in from the South. Then almost immediately, the **Norðurá** from the north, which in turn had been joined by the **Gljúfurá**, that is even more Northerly. After about 9 km further the **Þverá** joins the **Hvítá**, also from the North, then the **Flókadalsá** and the **Reykjadalsá**, both from the South.

Where the fresh water meets the glacial water they flow side by side, for a while before they mix. This provides good fishing where the salmon pause before going up the clear river, or swimming on to their particular home river. There are three fishing beats on the **Hvítá** with their own small self-catering lodges, between them they averaged over 450 salmon per year. The first for two rods is called **Straumarnir**; this is at the junction of the **Hvítá** to the North with the **Norðurá**. The **Grímsá** junction is on the South side a short way below. Here the salmon can lie all the way down for about 600 metres on the line where the two colours meet. This is called svarthödi.

After another 9 Km, there is the junction pool where the **Þverá** flows in also from the North. This is also fished by two rods, and is called **Brennan**. The fishing here is similar to **Straumarnir**, and there is little to choose between them. The time to fish these pools is when most fish are running, and they pause briefly.

Above **Brennan** is a stretch with its own self-catering lodge for three rods, at Snæfoksstaðir near Langholt, and the junction with the **Flókadalsá.** This is fished from the 23rd of June, until the 19th of September, but is not fly fishing water, by any stretch of the imagination.

Grímsá

This is a river of national importance, which is now run by the Veiðifélag of the river. To help with the economics, for a many years, July has been let for a month

Straumar on the Hvítá.

From a photograph by Árni Baldursson.

of exclusive fly-fishing to Gardner L. Grant, from White Plains, New York State. He has brought many distinguished American Salmon fishermen here, including Nathaniel Reed, a great conservationist and 'White Knight', also Ernest Schwiebert, the well known author of fishing literature and a brilliant fisherman. Ernie is also an architect, and he designed a unique and controversial two storey lodge overlooking Laxfoss, which has ten double bedrooms for the fishermen and is very well equipped. This is sometimes referred to as the elephant house. Foreigners have been fishing this river since 1862.

The 'elephant house'.

Catch and release has been partially practised here since 1960. In 1978/9, when over 600 were released, over 100 were tagged, only one dead salmon was seen, and that was not a tagged fish. This is strong evidence of the lack of damage to salmon of catch and release when properly conducted.

Nathaniel Reed caught a salmon of 28 lbs in 1984, the record on fly. Ernest Schwiebert caught one of 27 lbs in 1974, but the biggest on record was 34 lbs caught in 1917 by Halldór Vilhjálmsson in Strengir.

The Grímsá source is Reiðarvatn, near Ok, which is a mountain crowned by the remains of an icecap. Below the lake, the river flows over a series of waterfalls that form a barrier to fish. The fishable length is 30 km, and has over 60 pools. From the barrier the river flows gently through farmland. It is joined by the Tunguá, which has been barred to fishing since 1978, but for 10 km it is a most important spawning stream. For the next 30 km, Grímsá is fishable to the junction with the Hvítá. The first 20 km flows through meadows, then for 4 km it changes character, speeding up with rock pools, and waterfalls. It then slows down, until Hvítá is reached. The bottom section is good for sea trout.

This river continues to be a leader in conservation in Iceland, and it has its own hatchery, many of the bigger fish that are caught are retained in cages as breeding stock. Since 1991 the annual catch has not dropped below 1000, the average for the last five years to 2001 has been 1438, but the record in the last 26 years was 1975 with 2116 salmon, many of these were caught in Tunguá, so it is not a true comparison.

Flókadalsá

This river is 31 km long but salmon can only penetrate 14 km. It is fished with three rods from a self-catering lodge. In 28 years the catch has not dropped below 181, and in the best year 1975, 613 were caught. The average catch in the last five years has been 354. This gives a decent annual rod average. It is an attractive self-catering river with good fly-fishing water, but it can be sensitive to drought.

Reykjadalsá

The Reykjadalsá is utterly different from Grimsá. It flows through a valley with many hot springs, particularly in the neighbourhood of Reykholt, where there are a number of agricultural enterprises using the heat. An insulated hot water main runs from here to Borgarnes, and to Akranes. Salmon do not favour this river which is fished by two rods with an average catch in the last five years to 2001 of only 74 salmon!

Þverá and Litla Þverá (see also pages 5-9)

The story of my first visit to the Þverá is recorded in Chapter Two. I returned in 1982 thanks to the kindness of Sigurður Helgason. We flew from The Laxá í Dölum, those of us who were to fish another week were dropped off at Stórikroppur, and the others flew on to Reykjavík. Stórikroppur means big 'tits', the landing strip is named after two small hills near by. We were left there in a total wilderness with our luggage and fishing tackle in the blind confidence that we would be rescued! We sat on our luggage and hoped. Our confidence began to fade, but after an hour the others arrived with many apologies for a delay of the ferry to Akranes; this is now by-passed by the tunnel.

We then drove to the fine lodge which proved to be most comfortable, but it has been improved even more since then. The dining table would have graced any board room. The Þverá is the lower half of this river, which, with its other half, the Kjarrá, are frequently the premier river of Iceland, both are fished as a seven rod rivers. The Þverá, as Julius Ceasar said about Gaul, divides naturally into three parts, but three into seven won't go! As a party of friends we preferred to vary our fishing partners, and I had worked out a rotation taking this into account.

The record season on the whole river was in 1979 when 3559 fish were caught; this was before the nets were taken off, and before escapees from ranching boosted the figures on some rivers. The worst season was in 1984 when only 1082 were caught. The five-year average to 2001 was 1682. This river is unique in Iceland, in that it has no obstruction of any kind to the migration of salmon, all the way from the sea, up the Hvítá, and up the Þverá, and Kjarrá until the river is lost among a

Sigurður Helgason with his son Siggi and son in law Ware Preston.

multitude of small lakes. Some of these lakes are very shallow, with a soft bottom. When there is a spate, or even a strong wind the river can become very coloured for up to three days. If the river has been leased for just three days, and these are the conditions, it is necessary to be reminded that uncertainty is one of the joys of fishing. There are fosses that obstruct the salmon run on the two tributaries, the Litla Þverá, after 15 km, and the Lambá after only one km.

In normal conditions, I cannot imagine a better river for fly fishing. When Vice President, President George Bush came to Iceland, he was flown to the Þverá, as this was the river that was chosen for him to fish, in an area where it runs through good farmland in which big farms predominate. The upper beat is mostly rock pools running through an accessible gorge, stretching from Gilbotn, pool 78 to Múlakvörn, pool 52, just below the lodge. The middle of the beat, it is more open, and this section is from Galti to Klettsfljót, and I have particularly fond memories of these two pools as well as Skiptafljót. For some reason, this was much better known as the Viking pool, and is midway between the other two. Galti should be fished right into the tail as I learned, too late, after my first visit. Viking pool is a classic pool of one's dreams. If the river is high Klettsfljót is a resting place after a tough swim. The fish lie against the cliff on the left bank, and in the run out. If a strong fish decides to run down from here, they are difficult to stop. Below this are a series of pools in a shallow gorge.

From the lodge down, there is a stretch of shallow and braided water course that changes from year to year, until Norðtunga is reached with its church, bridge and farm. This is where President George Bush fished. From here down to the junction with the Litla Þverá there are many classic, and productive pools. The very best are Kirkjustrengur, by the church, and Ármótakvörn. Between is Barði, where I once drove confidently across the river in my diesel Land Rover, in the wrong place, water came over the bonnet, but I had no option but to press on, and all was well. I was more lucky than a party of Japanese, who were carried downstream in their 4WD, and had to be rescued.

Litla Þverá

This is an important spawning river, and it can provide very good fishing, particularly after a spate when it clears, and falls earlier than the main river. Ken Watt was once fortunate to be fishing the Litla Þverá in just these conditions, and he left it as unfishable, and so missed the opportunity of the year on that river. He was a very fine fisherman, but was new to this river. The best areas that I know, are near the road bridge, half way down to the junction, and close to the junction.

At the junction there is the old lodge that served this middle beat when it was let separately. Below it Julian Ferguson beached a fish, he got it up on the bank, and removed the fly, it then jumped back into the river and disappeared. Under 'catch and release' this would have been a caught fish! Julian was fishing soon after completing his service in the cavalry with a short service commission. Map reading was not his strong point. While he should have been fishing the top beat, we received a call on the radio from the Kjarrá lodge, reporting that one of our rods was fishing pool 'M804', over a mile beyond our boundary. The next day after the laughter had subsided, he returned from the bottom beat, and said that he had fished the Sea Pool! Remember that the Þverá is a tributary of the Hvítá!!

Just below the junction with the Litla Þverá is Klapparfljót. When the river is low this can be stacked with fish waiting for conditions to be right for them to go up Litla Þverá. The current impinges on a rock point on the right bank, then it swings round that and there is a magnificent tail. Fish lie both off that rock point, where they can be easily spooked, and all the way down to the tail, near the right bank. This is one of my favourite pools, on any river.

Þverá - Þórunnarhylur with Robin playing his big fish.

Below that are two more good pools, in one of these my line parted from the backing, as I was playing a fish. The last pool on the middle beat is Þórunnarhylur, which would also be on the composite river of my dreams.

Imagine it under perfect conditions. It is mid August 1983, the river is still quite high after a spate, but it has cleared, and is falling. From the left bank I wade into the middle of the river, and wade down a gravel spit, casting to the rock shelf that is the far bank, sometimes also casting to the left bank, as there are fish on both sides of me. Salmon are showing frequently in many places. Below me, from a high rock bank on the left bank, my brother Robin is fishing, and hooks a monster. My fly lands close to the far bank, and a salmon dashes across the surface to attack my fly. I get mine to the beach, land it and go out again. Robin is still in the same place fighting the same fish, and I hook another. I encourage him to get off his pinnacle, and take the fish downstream. He does, and eventually lands his fish, it was 19 lbs, and straight out of the sea. Meanwhile my success from the spit continues. Later I find another lie in the tail of the pool near the left bank. This great pool can be waded across in the middle above the tail, and the right bank fished down from the rock shelf. When playing fish from there it was necessary to go downstream of this shelf and slide on one's bottom down a grass bank to the place to land the fish. Robin had lost a bigger fish the day before, and my son Sandy caught another in Þórunnarhylur, of 23 lbs the next day.

That evening we took a photograph of Robin with his nineteen pounder, and Sandy with his fish of 23 lbs, I believe that this was the biggest salmon caught on a fly in Iceland that year. It is a rare event, to have two such large Icelandic salmon in one photograph.

Þverá - Robin and Sandy with fish of 19 and 23 lbs.

In 1964, fishing 14 rod days we caught 9 salmon of 15 lbs or more. In 1982 to 4th August in 350 rod days only 11 salmon of 15 lbs, or over, were caught. This may, or may not indicate a general decline in the size of salmon in the river, as might be reasonably supposed. Some years grilse predominate, and other years there may be a higher number of the MSW salmon. This is common to all Icelandic rivers. However it is now recognised that mistakes were formerly made stocking with parr from Elliðaár. These were predominately progeny of small grilse. Stocking is now done in all cases with parr bred from the stock of the individual river. But now wanderers from ranching operations, and escapees from cages lead to mixing of genetic stock.

It is a marvel of nature, how salmon protect themselves as a species. Many salmon rivers have little natural food in the rivers, so their young, and their food supply are protected by salmon not eating when they return to the rivers of their birth. A further protection is that they don't smolt according to age but the size that they need to be to survive in the sea. In spite of their remarkable homing instinct, a third protection is that it is in their nature for a small percentage to wander, and to ascend rivers other than their home river, and so blending slightly the genetic strains. Other protections are the variation in time spent in the sea, and that MSW salmon, and also grilse, do not breed exclusively fish of the same characteristics as themselves.

The next and bottom beat has pools numbered from 27 down to 1. One year just before we arrived, Dranghylur, the uppermost pool had a seal in it; this must be over 35 km from the mouth of the Hvítá. The pools in this beat that the salmon favour vary considerably from year to year. I have wonderful memories of some pools, runs and tails, but much has to be re-learned another year. The run of fish up this river is considerable, and if one fish is caught there is a good chance that more can be caught from the same lie.

Þverá - Dranghylur.

Close to the bottom pool there is a farm. The farmer was an extremely good mechanic, and had a well-equipped workshop. For a number of years, other farmers, in trouble, would go to him for help, and he would never accept a single krónur. Finally the other farmers clubbed together and gave him a new Volvo estate car as a present. I think this is a fine illustration of these wonderful people, who own the rivers, that we so greatly enjoy fishing.

Over the last eight years to 1999, the following pools were the most productive;-
Top Beat, Skiptafljót (Viking Pool), Klettsfljót, Myrkhylur Neðri, Snasabreiða, Stekkjarkvörn.
Middle Beat, Klapparfljót (av. 180 per year), Ámótakvörn, Kirkjustrengur, Hólmatagl, Guðnabakkastrengur Efri, Strengur ofan Þórunnarhyls.
Lower Beat, Kaðalstaðahylur, Bakkakotsstrengir, Steinahylur.
This is now fished as seven single rod beats.

In all, these three beats total 25 km, plus 15 km on the Litla Þverá. The Kjarrá amounts to another 45 km of fishing, and on the two, the river falls 380 metres, 1250 feet, without any obstruction. The average flow is 4000 cubic feet per second.

Kjarrá

At Nordtunga a road crosses the Þverá, Close to this bridge, on the South side a small road goes to the East, and this now leads to Kjarrá. In 1964 the only access was by horse from the farm Örnólfsdalur, on the North bank, in the middle of the top beat of the Þverá. When going up the valley, this is the last farm. This part of the river is called the Örnólfsdalsá. The present road is often damaged in the winter, and it is a long drive to the lodge. To continue up river from the Kjarrá lodge is even rougher, and involves fording the river many times. When the river rises it becomes powerful, and this can become distinctly 'hairy', unless one's 4WD is substantial. Once when we were fishing the Þverá we got a radio call for help, the Prime Minister was stuck in the river. Helgi Sigurðsson was asked to come with his 'Helgi-mobile'. This he did immediately, albeit reluctantly, because he was not in sympathy with that Premier's politics.

Kjarrá - My Land Rover fording the river.

The lodge is now every bit as good, and as comfortable, as the Þverá lodge. While fishing here one is extremely remote. Occasionally a light plane flies up the valley and dips its wings to the fishermen. It is patrolling all the rivers of the Hvitá system, in order to make certain that too many rods are not being fished, and that there is no poaching. This is where people can meet and enjoy themselves away from any publicity, or invasion of privacy. Here the Prince of Wales has been able to fish, and paint in peace. He has helped teach a novice to play a fish, acting as the fish himself! At the end of the week when a group photograph was taken, there was no one to take it! What a relief and contrast this must have been for him! Here one is really in the wilds, and there are wonderful views of the ice-caps.

From the road to the lodge takes about 30 minutes to drive, and from the lodge it is a slow drive of about one hour to the furthest point that a car can go. Kristinn Egilsson, the farmer of Örnólfsdalur insisted that Sigurður Helgason, as one of the lessees, should see the top of the river. He brought horses up, stabled them at the road end, and stayed the night with us. Next day we drove up to join the horses at the end of the track. Kristinn, took one horse as a pack horse. He insisted on tying our rods to the metal frame of the pack saddle, which he did with all his considerable strength. Fortunately we had spare rods, and only one was crushed! We left Robin at Einarsfljót, and after a total of three hours riding we reached a junction where two small streams meet, to form the river. They flowed out of a series of lakes. We fished downstream from the junction. Einarsfljót looks a

Kjarrá - Robin and Ben Savage on their horses.

totally uninteresting stretch of water, but for some unknown reason the fish love it, and congregate here. The bottom is very soft where they lie, and very soon when playing fish here the water becomes totally opaque. Here, Sigurður and I were both playing big fish standing ten yards apart. While playing my fish I photographed Sigurður; then, luckily his fish took off downstream, where he landed it. Robin nearly lost his waders in a very sticky bottom, and then got seriously chilled, so left us to ride home. We fished down from there for as long as time would allow. I found an interesting pool, which I fished, leaving my horse grazing. I was shivering so much that my fly must have been moving in a most attractive way, and was taken gently by a salmon. After that I thought that it was time to stop. Luckily the horse was still grazing having not been fed the night before. This had been the idea, and it worked. Another year in Greenland when left our horses, they started for home! (see page 199)

Kristinn estimated that we had ridden for eight hours, and the temperature had been 41F. He could not remember a colder day in August. The horses were incredibly strong, sure-footed and intelligent. At the end of the day my horse was as fresh as at the start, and I am no light weight. Although the size of a pony, being on average about 13.2 hands, they certainly deserve to be called horses, as they are correctly called. The horses may still have been fresh, but we were cold and tired. After a hot bath, plenty of whisky and a good dinner, we slept like logs. In the morning we all overslept. Hrun, whose duty it was to awake us, had been unable to get out of the lavatory, or to attract anyone's attention: it was an hour before the poor girl succeeded in climbing out of the high window.

Kjarrá - Keith, Jean and Colin Howman outside the lodge.

Driving up river from the Lodge, called Vighóll, one can drive for about 15 km in a suitable vehicle. This involves crossing the river about nine times, some of the crossings require driving up the river bed, between rocks. If the river rises during the day, the return journey is with the current, which is encouraging. From the end of the track, one can walk for another 15 km before reaching the top named fishing place, numbered 91. The lowest pool is about 7 km below the lodge. When fishing the upper parts of the river it is better to take a packed lunch, and there is no need to stop fishing for the customary time in the middle of the day. Not far above the end of the 'road', a major tributary, the Lambá joins the Kjarrá. Here the flow of both are about equal. A few salmon are caught up the Lambá, but it is not far to an impassable foss. Walking beside that river can be awkward, with rocks that are most unstable. The Lambá comes out of a series of lakes, one is close to the foss, but the others are a long way further inland.

Kjarrá - Árni Baldursson and Tóti Tönn on horses with fly rods.

From a photograph by Séð og Heirt Magasín.

The fishing records of both the Kjarrá, and the Þverá have been very fully analysed and it is fascinating to see where fish have been caught, and also where they have not been caught. It is important to realise that a popular place is fished harder than a pool that produces few fish, this tends to concentrate the fishing effort, so that the other places may be only little fished. This is well illustrated by the story of a car that broke down on the drive to the lodge. While waiting for help the fishermen cast a fly on an unnamed piece of water, and quickly caught a fish. Then they caught some more. This place has proved to be a good pool, and was named after the number of the car, M804!!

During the last eight years the average annual catch on the Kjarrá has been 858 salmon, a total of 6863 fish. Of these 21 have been caught on the Lambá, and 135 in unidentified places. As is only natural, the upper, and remote places have seldom been fished. The pools where most fish have been caught are Selstrengur, Runki, Langidráttur, Réttarhylur, Neðri Johnson, Gilsbakkaeyrar, and Neðra Rauðaberg. There are many other wonderful pools both for catching fish, and for the joy of fishing. The only gorge on the Kjarrá is close below the lodge, where there are three pools called the Princesses, upper, middle and lower. (Efri, Mið, og Neðri Princessa). These are so called because they are particularly beautiful.

The Kjarrá in spate.

There are several pools that do not rate as highly in the statistics as I would have expected, this may illustrate how pools change. The pools that I listed have been good every year, but Gilsbakkæyrar has only one name but nine numbered places. This is because the actual taking spots vary from year to year.

The season on the Þverá/Kjarrá is from 1 June to 31 August. In 1983 we were catching fish with sea lice 4 km above the Kjarrá lodge on the 27th of August, so the tale end of the season can still be very good.

The Middle Kjarrá.

The numbers of fish that we caught on these rivers, did not compare with the numbers that we sometimes caught on the Laxá í Dölum, but I have the very happiest of memories. It is a bigger river and fish are seldom visible, As a result the fishing is less target shooting than on smaller rivers. My last year here was in 1986, but I hope to return, now that I have satisfied my wanderlust elsewhere.

Norðurá (see also pages 16-19)

In Chapter One, I have described my first visit to this river in 1975, which was a very great success, several times I visited the former Glanni beat when driving North, just to look at it again. I once collected flies from a tree where I had lost my flies, and looked at the very substantial salmon ladder that had been created in order to overcome Glanni Foss. In 1993 I arranged for a mere two days for myself and Robin, Graham and Julian Ferguson: Einar Sigfússon was to fish with us, but he had to cancel at the last moment. This was a disappointment, but worse was to follow.

The lodge accommodates 12 rods, with rod sharers, this may total 24 fishermen. In addition, there may also be guides. The changeover of fishermen is not co-ordinated, so there are people coming and going every day. As a result the atmosphere is that of a big fishing hotel, and not that of a fishing lodge. There had been confusion about our reservation, they thought that there was only one Savage, and one Ferguson, and Einar had been replaced by two others. We were believed, and the management did all that they could to make up for the mistake. But this meant that we were fishing five on a four rod beat, and the other poor unfortunate rod sharers had to be asked if they would agree. They could not have been nicer about it, but it put us into a false position, feeling like interlopers on someone else's beat. Therefore, instead of having a beat of our own, we had to make certain that we did not impinge on them. In any case a four rod beat is difficult to manage, particularly without a guide.

In the three days before we arrived 150 salmon had been caught, 90% on fly, as we arrived they virtually stopped taking, all the way up and down the river.

Above Straumarnir, the Hvítá junction pool, there is a separate, private beat. Above that to Laxfoss was beat three for four rods. It is in a narrow steep-sided valley, running below the lodge with attractive and good fishing, and one small hot spring on the bank beside the river. Laxfoss had an old salmon ladder in the centre, which had recently been replaced. It didn't seem to work well, so it had just been further improved, and was now reported to be satisfactory. Beat two, the middle beat, now stretched twice the length of the old Glanni beat, to Heyvað, which is opposite, where a road turns the North towards Búðardalur. Beat one is all the way above that to an impassable foss.

The fishable length of the river is about 45 km, with 116 named places and the average catch in the five years to 1999 is 1848, which over a 90 day season gives an average catch per rod of 132. The lowest and highest catches have been 856 & 867 in 1984 & 1987, and 2132 in 1976. Catches have improved noticeably since the nets on the Hvítá have ceased to be operated, so that in two of the last six years the catch has again been over 2000, in fact with a new record catch of 2310 in 2002.

Naturally, with the construction of such a good ladder at Glanni, the magic has gone out of the Glanni beat, but we caught a few fish there for 'Auld Lang Syne'.

This is a very good river, and exceedingly expensive in prime time, but there are a number of rivers that appeal to me more. Undoubtedly this is influenced by the lack of a house party atmoshere, and having four rod beats. The scenery is outstandingly beautiful. One of the most photographed views in Iceland is Laxfoss with in the background the peak of Baula volcano.

Gljúfurá

Gljúfurá means 'gorge river'. It shares its source, with the Langá, they separate one mile below Langavatn. This lake has a small dam to control the water flow. From the division, the Gljúfurá flows South to join the Norðurá close to its junction with Hvítá, whereas the Langá flows west. Much of the course of the river is in a gorge that is a geological fault, and is remarkably straight. This is a river that is mostly more suitable for worming than for fly-fishing. It is restricted to two rods, the average catch is 211, over 28 years. It has benefited from the removal of the Hvítá nets, together with all the other tributaries of the Hvítá.

Chapter Five
North to Snæfellsnes

This part of the country has seven salmon rivers producing nearly 10% of the rod caught salmon.

Langá

The first river north of Borgarfjörður is the Langá. Both this river and the Gljúfurá have their source in lake Langavatn. The outflow from the lake is controlled, in order to provide stability of flow in times of drought. From the lake to the sea is 26 km. In the best year in the last 28 the catch was 2319, and the worst was 610 in 1984. The average for the last five years to 2001 has been 1377. This is predominately a small grilse river, but it does also have some good sized salmon.

The best section of the river is the bottom 5 km, this is divided into six beats with 28 pools, it is usually fished by five fishermen. The rods were sometimes rotated twice in the morning and twice in the afternoon. The old lodge, that dates back to 1870, has now been replaced with a lodge for 8 rods, which was built in 1998, and extended to 12 rods in 2002.

The sea pools are dramatic, and the bottom two beats are very short, and very good. There is a foss into the sea pool which salmon can jump at low tide, or swim up at high tide. The river was fished by 10 rods for part of the season, and by 12 rods for the rest. The beats on the upper 20 km are long, and varied with 5 ladders to overcome fosses. The water course of its upper section is fairly straight, and flows through a deep gorge. There is a water regulating dam at Langavatn.

Much of the Langá is particularly suited for fishing with the 'Riffling Hitch', or 'Portland Hitch', whichever name is prefered. (see Chapter 2, page 40) Catch and release is now being practiced partially in some weeks.

Álftá

This is said to be a lovely small river that is fished by only two rods staying at a well set up self-catering lodge. Over 28 years the average catch has been 283, in the best year 485 were caught, and the worst year was in 2000, even that was not too bad with a catch of 130. This looks an interesting river to fish, but may be sensitive to drought. The average catch per rod in prime time is higher than on many famous rivers, and sea trout are an additional bonus. There is 16 km of fishing.

There is a small self-catering lodge built in 1999. This river has very good char fishing and also a run of sea trout. This river would be particularly attractive for a small family group. The best time is from the mid July to the end of August.

Hítará

The Hítará is a six plus rod river with two lodges; one lodge is for four rods. That is an outstandingly lovely place to stay, and the other has two bedrooms each with a private bathroom. The river is run by the Angling club of Reykjavík.

Guides can be provided. The best of the salmon fishing is divided into three two rod beats.

The salmon can penetrate 29 km of the main river, and also run up a tributary, the Grjótá. Another tributary, the Tálmi has an interesting run of Char. There are 50 named salmon pools.

In the early 1980s a ladder was constructed in order to extend the water accessible to the salmon. This proved to be a disaster because the fish were encouraged to an area that was not suitable for successful spawning. This led to a decline in the run of salmon.

This is a good medium sized river but it does seem to be fished by too many rods relative to the average annual catch per rod on most other good rivers. The farmers are trying to up grade the fishing with an enhancement programme. The average catch over 28 years has been 326, but in the last three years to 2001 this has increased to 427. The catch in the worst year was 151 in 1984, which was a terrible year for many rivers. The best year was 1978 with a catch of 649. The enhancement programme does seem to be benefiting the river, but the average catch for one rod over the whole season is only 71 salmon in the last three years.

Haffjarðará

I wanted to try a new river, and to fish with a group of family and friends. Páll Jonsson was able to get me an offer of a week on the Haffjarðará in late August. This river was fished annually by Sir Charles Forte, as he then was, so I telephoned to ask him for advice. He was enthusiastic, but his only concrete advice was to take my own supply of wine!

There were seven of us fishing five rods. We were, myself and my wife, Gina, two of our sons, Sandy and Ben, my brother Robin, Julian Ferguson, and John Jackson, who in these politically correct days, I must describe as my 'business' partner! We had the whole river to fish, except the 'owners beat' in the middle of the river, which consisted of the Foss pool and a stretch below that, with its own house. However we were also given some time on this water. Including the owners beat there were six rods on the river, the permitted number is now 8. It is being fished as fly only and with 6 rods for part of the season.

This river does not stand out in the statistics, yet many of the people that know it well, consider it their favourite river in all Iceland. It flows into the sea at the South Eastern base of the Snæfellsness peninsula, out of a most volcanic area. The main lava flow is from the North, and forms the West bank of the whole upper half of the river, it averages about 12 feet high and is covered with moss and is very rough. A little above the owners beat, there is a small volcano on the East bank, the lava and ash from this reaches the bank, almost meeting the other lava flow, this creates interesting pools, and a small lake above. Not far from the lower river there was a natural hot pot, with an ideal temperature for a hot soak. Beside one tributary there is a natural spring of fizzy water!

As we neared the road bridge we were impressed with the scenery. We turned off towards the lodge, passing a small 4WD car on its side in a ditch, and arrived at

The Haffjarðará valley and lodge.

the lodge a little too early, we were waived away, through a window in a locked door! So we looked at the river which was very low after a six week drought. We returned to the lodge at the correct time, and were given a normal welcome, as if we had not driven up to the lodge earlier in the day. Examining the record book, we learned that the previous party of 12 Americans and South Africans had caught 100 salmon, of which 40 had been caught in the 'Stone pool'. The natural, and erronious, assumption was that this would be our best pool. However, except for one pod of new fresh fish found by Sandy, who caught four in quick succession on the smallest possible tube fly, it proved to be almost dead, producing only one other fish that week. We eventually learned that the 40 fish had been foul hooked, and had been returned to the river. In those days to return a fish was unusual, so this was an odd mixture of the unethical, and the ethical. It was probably imposed by the guides who were placed in a difficult situation. The head guide advised us to fish this pool casting upstream using a line with a sinking tip, and a fairly large fly. Normally it is wise, as well as being good manners, first to do as you are told by your guide. On this occasion we did not do so. I noted in my fishing diary, pompously, 'Listen to advice, but have the courage to ignore it!'

Sandy was just 16, and the owner of the small 4WD car, one guide, was the same age as Sandy. His name was Helgi Sigurðsson, and he proved to be a exceptional guide. He has become a family friend and is now Vascular Consultant Surgeon in Reykjavík. His 4WD vehicles grew and became known as the Helgi-mobiles! Through him the two families have become close friends, and we have had holidays together in many parts of the world. In fact, as explained in the introduction to this book, his father persuaded me to write this book, while we were fishing in Tierra del Fuego.

The Haffjarðará lodge has been rebuilt, and is now, probably, the finest Veiðihuis, (fishing lodge), in the country.

Haffjarðará - Helgi and Sandy.

We were fishing after the best time but fortunate to have the opportunity to be there at all. It was autumn fishing, in drought conditions but there were some fresh fish with sea lice.

The 'Outflow' of a lake, formed by a big lava flow, is the upper-most pool of the river. Here it is a small stream, but an almost certain lie to catch one salmon, but rarely two. This is at the head of the 'mountain beat' of the river. This may be 15 minutes walk from the furthest point to which a car can be driven. It was not too remote to be fished before breakfast by young and active fishermen. This is one of the very few places in Iceland where there used to be a poaching problem. Poachers came across the lava from the road, leaving unmistakeable signs. Two or three more pools below, is, the charmingly named, 'Picturesque'. There may be a hint in this name; I found it to be more beautiful than productive, certainly, it yielded no fish to us. Below that, runs lead into 'Upper Luncheon', which is a

Haffjarðará - Outflow.

corner pool turning right, followed immediately by 'Lower Luncheon'. One day Julian and I had a magic time, fishing these two pools, pulling out fish after fish on the very tiniest of flies. 'Long Pool', and 'Gorge' followed, but never did anything for us. This ends the Mountain beat.

Below on a corner was 'Ófœra', which had many fish below a bank, but for us they were uncooperative. Then there was apparently dead water above the junction with a tributary. I saw a fish move in this dead water. I kept low and tried

Haffjarðará - Upper and Lower Luncheon Pools.

this stretch working my small fly, considerable success followed for two years running fishing that spot. Next was 'Upper Junction', and 'Broken bank', these may be good, but they did not excite me. Below that was 'Aquarium' which sounded hopeful. There seemed to be two holding areas about 150 yards apart with a pond in between. Both these lies were full of fish, and we caught many. To catch these fish it was necessary to fish the hot spot with accuracy, and then to play and land the fish away from that place, so as not to disturb the others. Below was the lake caused by the meeting of the two lava flows.

Haffjarðará - Kúla and Cave Pools.

At the tail of the lake, the channel flows slowly out, and is called 'Kúla', this has another very good lie, that fishes best from the right bank. 'Cave Pool' below, is best fished from the left bank, after wading with care across at the tail of 'Cave'. The next pool 'Cliff' looked good but was shallow with a terrible weed problem, which I don't remember on any other pool on this river. It also fished from the same bank. After that the river divided, both streams being about equal. There are pools in both, one is 'Forte', and 'Hanlon' is in the other. They come together again at 'Junction'.

What was then called the 'owners' beat' has now been reached. We were lucky to be able to fish this. The Foss pool is called the 'Waterfall pool' in English, but it is called 'Kvörn' in Icelandic, this means churn, or whirlpool. It is one of the most memorable pools that I have fished in Iceland. It is extremely complicated, with pods of fish, often visible, in several parts of the pool, and facing in different directions. There are many large rocks, and much is shallow. The way to fish it, is by accurate target shooting, fishing different lies from their appropriate banks. Two more good runs below complete 'the owners beat'. We did not then know of a very good holding pool below that.

Haffjarðará - The Foss pool or Kvörn.

Some way down, is the 'Stone pool', which is a simple classic holding pool. 'Home pool' and 'New bridge', may be very good, but did nothing for us. 'Old bridge' has the old road bridge crossing it. This bridge is very narrow, hump backed, high over the river, a large steel blade of reinforcement protruded in the middle of the carriageway. We drove over it with care, particularly on one occasion, when the gale was so strong that all vehicles had been warned to keep off the roads in the Snæfellsness area, this is where we were! We continued fishing finding it difficult to keep our lines from being blown off the water. Usually many fish could be seen immediately below the bridge, they were teasers that ignored all flies, and were seldom caught. However above the bridge fishing from the left bank a fish frequently takes a fly in the run very close to the right bank.

The nature of the river gradually changes as one goes downstream. The total fishable length is only about eight miles. At 'Outflow' there is only a small volume of water flowing downstream, but once below the old bridge it is a decent sized river. There are many tributaries that bring in more water, and there are also springs bringing water from beneath the lava. The only tributary that any fish can go up is the one below 'Ófœra', and there is no resting place up it until an impassible Foss is reached. Salmon do spawn in this stream and it is probable that the fish holding near its junction may be waiting to go up it.

In the lowest two miles there are two pools, which on their day can be extremely good, also other places to try, plus the sea pools. The first of the exciting pools is 'Grettir'. This is in three parts, all fished from the left bank. The upper is relatively narrow, deep and fast. Here it is most exciting, while fishing from a relatively high bank, to see fish appearing from the depths to take the fly. The middle section fans out with obvious likely lies as it narrows towards the tail.

Haffjarðará - Grettir.

The bottom section only fishes in high water, close to the right bank, where I have seen, and caught fish. The next two are early season pools, where running fish may pause, these are 'Helgi', and 'little Helgi'. The last important pool is 'Sheep Pool'. This starts as a narrow shute with a large rock near the head of the right bank from which side the upper part fished best. There was a lot of water to fish in this pool which can be very productive. I believe that in some recent years this pool has been disappointing, but seems to be improving again. Once, Jim Edwards had damaged his back, falling over when landing a fish. After that he sat on the large rock playing his fly backwards and forwards across the current. It was seized by a big fish which he landed. This was the biggest fish of our week. He then went with Helgi to the natural hot pot in a lava field, with a bottle of whisky, two silver goblets, and Helgi´s rifle. He sat deep in the hot pot drinking the whisky. As the whisky went down, the pain diminished. Helgi placed one of the goblets on a rock 50 yards away. By that time Jim must have been seeing three goblets, he fired at the middle one and knocked it flying. Helgi still has the goblet, and Jim's back was better next day.

Once, driving back from 'Sheep Pool' we had a wonderful view of a White-tailed Sea Eagle, which got up from rocks close to the road, and flew beside us gradually gaining height. There are very few pairs of this bird in the country, a known nesting site is on an island in Breiðafjörður, to the North of the Snæfellsness peninsula. I have also seen this bird in the foot hills of the Himalayas, in Nepal.

On the whole I have given the Haffjarðará pools their English names, by which they were then known. Some of these names may now have been changed. Icelandic names are often not used by the foreign anglers who fish a river, but they are seldom changed.

Haffjarðará - Sheep pool.

I once visited the magnificent lodge after it had been rebuilt with my new wife, Joanna, in order to see Kristján, the son of Jim Edwards, who was then a guide. The cook was the chef of the President of Iceland, and was cooking as a holiday job. The river had been rented by an American couple, who had brought their French chef, to care for them and their guests, including, the Duke of Marlborough. To have the two such high-powered chefs was somewhat excessive, but they got on well together. They said that they learned from each other. Probably only Kristján knew that the house maid for the week was the daughter of an English family, much 'older' than the Churchills, and who was visiting Kristjan! One night the two of them drove ninety miles to have dinner with us on our river, which was most sporting of them and enjoyed by us.

The Haffjarðará was for sixty years owned by one family. This was unique in Iceland, and only possible because they owned all the farms on the part of the river that is fished for salmon. For family reasons, they sold up.

I have only fished the Haffjarðará for two weeks but it remains most vivid in my memory, as an exceptional river, ideal for a house party in comfort in beautiful surroundings. The fish to rod ratio is not as high as it is on some other rivers, but every prospect pleases, and numbers are far from being the only criterion for judging a river.

The average catch in the last five years to 2001 has been 659.

Straumfjarðará

For a number of years this was the favourite river of two great sportsmen, and fine fishermen, from Kenya! Subsequently Jack Block died while fishing in Chile, and James Walker died flighting duck on a lake on his farm in Kenya, both dying, doing what they enjoyed.

Very often they used to fish with the smallest tube flies imaginable, tied on a quarter inch tube and with a treble size 16, or even size 18. We once visited them from the Haffjarðará, together with my brother Robin, who was at that time also a Kenya farmer. James gave us some of his micro tube flies called by us 'James Walker´s blue shrimp'. On the tube there were a few short fibres from blue neck feathers of a vulturine guinea fowl, and, as cheeks, two of the smallest jungle cock feathers. This was on our first visit to Haffjarðará, and it proved to be a good fly on that river also.

The Straumfjarðará is fishable for 7 km, and is fished by three rods, with a chance of a salmon further upstream. There is a conveniently situated farm providing full board.

The river flows out of two lakes that are not far from the North Coast of the peninsula. Above, the course of the river is very steep until the impassable barrier is reached. Below that it is rocky, but with good pools for spawning by the heroes that have surmounted an eighteen-foot foss. Salmon do get up this and so do sea trout. Above this foss a tributary joins the river that is by now of a good medium size. From this foss to the road is a stretch of attractive water. Then the river becomes wide, slow flowing and shallow, passing through boggy land. The second tributary joins in this section, which ends at a low foss about five feet high. Below that are two more pools and 2 Km to the sea, with a few possible places where a running fish might pause.

The five year average catch of the Straumfjarðará to 2001 was 234, the worst year was 1987 and the best was 1975 with catches of 161 and 755 respectively.

Now this river is reserved purely for fly-fishing.

Chapter Six
The Rivers of Breiðafjörður

Fifteen of the 100 salmon rivers, commonly listed in the statistics of Icelandic Salmon Rivers are between Snæfellsnes and the North-West Fjords. On average these account for nearly 7% of the salmon rod catch. Some of the minor rivers can be great fun to fish, and may also have sea trout or char to add to the sporting potential. Some may not be suitable for fly-fishing. The smaller ones may have self-catering accommodation, or it may be possible to stay in a farmhouse. These are usually 'two, or three rod rivers' and provide good sport for Icelandic fishermen, and can be particularly suitable for a family holiday, or as an introduction to Icelandic fishing without excessive expense.

Starting near Snæfellsnes the rivers listed are as follows, with average catch;-

River	Catch
Fróðá	92 salmon, (see also page 15).
Grísholtsá & Bakká	57 salmon.
Setbergsá	124 salmon.
Laxá á Skógarströnd	129 salmon.
Dunká	91 salmon.
Skraumá	11 salmon.
Hörðudalsá	48 salmon.
Miðá í Dölum	113 salmon. This has two tributaries, Hundadalsá, and Tunguá. There is small self-catering accommodation.
Haukadalsá	679 salmon. (See, the next section of this Chapter). It seems that the statistics include only the five rod section, and exclude the river above the lake, the lake, and the Þverá.
Laxá í Dölum	933 salmon. (See, the third and fourth section of this Chapter). 8 rods are allowed, it was 7, and fished by us as 6 rods, now once again it is fished as 6 rods in prime time.
Fáskrúð	225 salmon. (See, the fifth section of this Chapter). Three rods.
Flekkudalsá	239 salmon.
Krossá á Skarðströnd	98 salmon.
Búðardalsá	73 salmon.
Hvolsá & Staðarhólsá	176 salmon. This is an example of a river that not only has salmon but is one of the best char rivers, with a catch of over 1000. These two rivers join just above the estuary. There are about 15 km of fishing, and 86 named pools. It is a 4 rod river. Prime time is August. The 28 year record for salmon was a freak year in 1988 with 768 fish, but from 1997 to 2001 the salmon catch has been a disaster, averaging only 135. However as of 1999, a smolt release programme has started. This is a place to fish with small rods, and flies. The accommodation is modern with one single and five double bedrooms. This can be rented with full board or self-catering, with or without one guide.

This is one of the most prolific char rivers of Iceland.

Haukadalsá

Haukadalsá means, the hawk valley river. Eiríkur the Red will have eaten salmon from this river; this is where he lived, after being banished from Norway, and before establishing his settlement at Brattahlíð in South-West Greenland. He may well have sailed from the mouth of the Laxá í Dölum for Greenland with his settlers, many of whom were Irish or other Celts.

The Haukadalsá, and the Laxá í Dölum are neighbouring, and comparable rivers, as are the Selá, and Hofsá on the East Coast. All four are first class rivers with beautiful water for fly-fishing. The Selá, and Hofsá have a greater average summer flow but the East Coast is a less friendly environment for smolt when they reach the sea. Salmon from that coast have different feeding grounds to the West Coast rivers. The Hofsá, and the Laxá í Dölum, have waterfalls that limit salmon migration, and have no refuge for salmon in the rivers, where they are safe from fishermen. The Selá is a long river, and has benefited hugely from a ladder that was installed in the 1970s, which tripled the length of river available to salmon.

The salmon entering the Haukadalsá have an easy passage through a series of pools that are most inviting to the fisherman, until they reach the old road bridge. Just above that bridge a little tributary enters the river, then about two kilometres above, there is a substantial lake. The Upper Haukadalsá flows in to the lake at its Eastern end. This is a much smaller stream, and about ten kilometres further is the highest point that a salmon can reach. The lake is fished a little by farmers and a few salmon are caught there. The lake does much to stabilise the flow of the river, as well as providing a refuge for the the salmon, and a reservoir of food for the parr.

After having fished the Laxá í Dölum for some years, we were interested in trying the rival river just to the South. At that time the lease was held by the SWICE group of fishermen, from Switzerland. They were helpful, and friendly, so without difficulty we came to an agreement, whereby we could fish the Haukadalsá for a week, before going on to the Laxá í Dölum. This became the first of seven happy weeks on this river. We learned from them that their river was a much earlier river than its neighbour. A possible reason for this could be that the salmon running up this river are relatively safe when they reach the lake or tributary. As a result, on the Haukadalsá a salmon's exposure to a fisherman is very brief. The salmon on the Laxá í Dölum have no such respite. Our first two visits to the Haukadalsá were for the fourth week of June. We were the first British for at least seven years to fish this river.

The Lodge was presided over by Torfi Ásgeirsson, and his wife, Munda, sometimes helped by a cook. This is a much more modest operation than the Lodge at the Laxá í Dölum. There is no provision for guides other than being shown the river by Torfi. The lodge was warm, clean, and comfortable, but very simple in comparison with the other. Until a few years before the accommodation had been self-catering, and extremely basic, being little more than a hut, which can still be seen on the other side of the river.

From the lake to the sea, totalling 12 km, is fished as five single rod beats, which have plenty of pools, but the beats are short. The lake is another 8 kilometres long.

The Haukadalsá Lodge.

The 28-year average catch is 678. In recent years the catch has been low, down to 331 in 1997, but up to 916 in 1998. I hope that this river is now fly-fishing only.

The names of pools are difficult for foreigners to learn, so they tend to call them by their numbers. This causes confusion when numbers are changed. In our first year here, there were 32 pools, then they were increased to 40, even then there was scope to add a few more. It is therefore best to try to learn the names.

It was part of the contract for the party to be driven to and from Reykjavík, and for Torfi to drive the rods daily to and from the lower beats, so strictly speaking, no car was needed. However we preferred to maintain our independence, and in any case we often wanted cars for the Laxá í Dölum the following week, so we always rented two cars. The lodge is well sited overlooking the river, and the old road bridge. Close above is a bridge that carries the valley road over the river and there is a series of bends above, between and below these bridges, with several pools that were usually well stocked with salmon. To fish the top three beats no car is needed.

We only fished with fly, but normally the Swice group was always equiped for both fly and worm fishing. In such exquisite fly-fishing water this did not appeal to us. Torfi strongly favoured the worm, and wished to prove to us how effective this is. We greatly preferred fishing with fly, and that was that, but he kept trying. Torfi was keen on conservation, the river banks were kept clean of all rubbish, and there was no old nylon to be seen. As is customary, on the last day, the tenants leave the river at 12.00, one hour early, in order to help the staff achieve a smooth changeover to the new tenants. On this river, every time that we came off, Torfi could be seen going to his favourite pool with his worming kit, to pull out some fish in that one hour, which we had sacrificed so that he and his wife could prepare the lodge for the new fishermen. Promptly at 1.00, he would return proudly with his catch. I have not seen anything like this on any other river.

Haukadalsá - Torfi Ásgeirsson.

Golden Plover in full plumage.

From a painting by Rodger McPhail.

A salmon taking a fly.

From a painting by Rodger McPhail.

The lower beats had many birds, which he loved, and which were little disturbed. Golden Plover in their glorious full plumage called, and followed us from tussock to tussock. Skuas and Terns frequently mobbed us, when we neared their nests, Andrew Neve, a friend of my son Ben, broke the tip of one of my rods defending himself from a particularly aggressive Skua. This did not matter until later. On the last morning of one week, I was fishing the middle beat, and broke my rod, beaching a fish below a cliff. I hurried back to the lodge to re-equip, seizing a rod, and rushed back to the same pool, where I found that my replacement rod had no tip. For a moment Andrew was not popular! With my knife I shortened the rod further to the top intermediate ring, and quickly caught another fish, by then it was time to stop.

Haukadalsá - Blóti, the junction pool with Þverá, with a raft of Harlequin Duck.

Description of the river

Of the 40 named pools, six are in the top beat, which stretches from the lake down to the Lodge, about two kilometres in all. The first 1 1/2 km, is wide and slow with only one hot spot. The bottom four pools of the beat are outstanding.

From the lodge down the next two and a half beats are in a shallow gorge, with many rock shelves, and the river is reasonably fast running with many pools. Beat 2 is extremely short, in fact it is little more than half a kilometre, comprising 7 pools, starting with Blóti, the pool crossed by the Old Bridge. From the road at the end of that bridge one can often see an accumulation of fish in several lies. One day in our first week it rained, and these fish disappeared, we learned that they had run up the little tributary. This is called Þverá, which was not included in our fishing. Naturally I wanted to learn more about this stream, to which I shall return later.

Haukadalsá - Above the upper bridge.

This pool continues for about 70 metres below the bridge. Initially the lies are close to the right bank, then the current crosses, and fish lie under the left bank, finally the tail can also be excellent. Two more reasonable pools follow before the new bridge is reached. This is another good pool fished from the right bank. Then we would cross the bridge, looking down at the fish that we failed to catch, and continue down the left bank. There are three more pools before the bottom of the beat is reached.

Haukadalsá - Kvöruin.

Beat 3 is longer, but the further that one went downstream the more the pools varied from year to year as to whether they held fish. In general there were few holding pools, but many places where running fish might rest. There are eight pools in beat 3. The best is usually a long pool that now has two names, the entry run, Systrasetur, and Símabreiða, meaning the broad pool with a telephone wire across it. We caught good fish here from the top run down to the tail. The bottom two pools of the beat were exciting, provided runs of fish were pausing there that season.

As the river flows through Beat 4, the gorge, which had never been very deep, gradually disappears. Nine pools are named, all hold fish at times, but none are consistently exciting, my personal favourite was the Long Strong. The name of this is reminiscent of the place where Lord Lamancha caught the salmon in 'John Macnab', by John Buchan. This book is a joy to read and bears little relationship to what is now called a 'Macnab'. It is very odd how this term has become popular amongst sportsmen who have never read the book and got it wrong!

Beat 5 is the longest beat, and a wonderful place to be. The river is now flowing mostly through gravel, periodically meeting bed rock that causes it to bend. If

Graham Ferguson and Robin Savage with a salmon.

A Wimbrel over mountains.

From a painting by Rodger McPhail.

fish are found, they are just out of the sea fighting like demons, and with sea lice still complete with their white tails. One such fish 'carted' me for 500 yards before I beached it. As I did so the fly came free and the fish returned to the river, where it drifted vertically in the water with its tail in the air. I waded in and grabbed the tail, it returned to life, and dashed off. With catch and release this would definitely have been considered to have been a caught fish, as it was, it is recorded as having been lost, and is all the more memorable for that!

Haukadalsá - The pool where this happened.

The Birds

There were frequently about 60 Harlequin duck just below the lodge, and from there up to the lake. The drakes were in full plumage, but there were never any immature, and on inquiry, I was told that Harlequin don't nest on this river. The explanation seemed to be that they don't nest in their second year, and that these were a gathering of yearlings.

Birds seen in the valley and river mouth included;-

Arctic skua	Harlequin duck	Short eared owl
Arctic tern	Icelandic falcon	Slavonian grebe
Black tailed godwit	Icelandic gull	Snipe
Black backed gull	Merganser	Snow bunting
Eider	Merlin	Turnstone
Fulmar	Ptarmigan	White wagtail
Golden plover	Raven	Whooper swan
Greenshank	Red throated diver	Wimbrel
Great northern diver	Red necked phalarope	
Greylag goose	Ringed plover	

A summary of the River and Our Experiences

Fishing for one week a year for seven years with five rods, we caught 337 fish. In our parties we had a total of twenty fishermen and six caught their first salmon. In the years that I made an analysis of the catch of the whole season, about 1% was caught on a spinner, and about 35% were caught on a fly, the rest being caught on a worm. Not more than ten of our total were caught on a worm, this was when Torfi eventually succeeded in 'leading some young astray'!

Haukadalsá - Three beautiful fresh fish.

We fished several different weeks, from the second week of June to the second week of August. Our experience of the beats was as follows:-

Top beat I	Twice was blank. Four times it was very good.
Beat II	In 1988 was poor, but other years was good.
Beat III	Always produced fish.
Beat IV	In 1988 produced 10 fish, but only 3, in the other 6 years!
Bottom Beat V	One year, blank. One year poor. Other years good.

One year we caught fish from 20 pools, otherwise we caught fish in 8 to 14 pools. From these figures, it can be seen that Beats and pools varied very considerably from year to year. As we were always a party of friends, we could fish the river as we liked. Normally a rod could fish his neighbour's beat downstream for the last two hours of each period. But when the bottom beat was bad, rods moved upstream instead. When the bottom beat was the best we combined beat 4 and 5 as a two rod beat. Our overall memory of the Haukadalsá is of a series of most happy weeks fishing, in a lovely river with sufficient fish, much laughter and plentiful food.

Haukadalsá - Sandy and Caroline Savage playing a 12 lb fish in Símabreiða.

Haukadalsá - Sandy and Caroline Savage with grilse.

The Upper Haukadalsá

This is let under a separate contract. The salmon seem to hold in the lake, with few going up until after we were there. We did little more than try it, catching a few char, and only one salmon. The catch of salmon recorded in a season seems to vary between 10 and 20.

The Þverá (Tributary)

This little river is a hidden pearl, and takes a big share of the salmon that run up the Haukadalsá. But at first we did not know that.

1985 had been a low water year, and Blóti, the old bridge pool had been full of fish. 1986 was a high water year. The fish were running fast up the Haukadalsá, and seldom pausing. In our whole week we only caught one fish without sea lice. We didn't catch a single fish above the Þverá junction, and even Blóti was empty of fish. This is the junction pool, but surprisingly the meaning is wet! At last 'the penny dropped', the idea occurred to us that many fish might be going up the Þverá. We then learned that Þverá had been leased by SWICE for the season for 1200 Swiss Francs, with a limit of 75 fish to be caught. We learned that they could run up for 12/15 km, first through a very impressive gorge with many rock pools, and three water falls, into an open valley with a few obvious lies in the stream, before more rock pools, and, eventually an impassable foss.

In the Þverá gorge.

Sue Schwerdt and I got permission the next day to try Þverá, and Torfi came with us. We started up the burn, and soon entered the canyon. We had to cross from side to side several times, and occasionally wade up the burn itself. Almost every pool had fish in it. In one I hooked and played a fish of about 12 pounds. My fly started in its mouth, but then attached itself to the pectoral fin on the far side of the fish. It came free from there and caught on the dorsal fin. It fought like mad, and started to go upstream, it went on and on. Torfi and Sue came to help. Torfi became distracted by a lamb that he thought was stuck on a cliff, he went to its rescue, but the lamb was well able to look after itself! Sue was in mid stream with a gaff, which added to the obstacles! I brought it across the current very gently, because the hook in the dorsal fin looked most insecure. I eventually got its tail onto the bank for about ten seconds before we parted company!

We started at 9.00, passing two ravens nests, and a Greylag, that pretended to have a broken wing, and tried to lead us up a steep incline. We stopped at the first falls pool to have lunch. While we were eating our sandwiches, at least 30 salmon jumped the foss. There was a solitary surviving gosling of the brood, that swam arround the pool, and eventually plucked up courage to investigate us. It even took some of our bread, and was stroked by us. Torfi was by now saying that with a worm he would have caught 45 salmon!

Þverá - Sue Schwerdt with the gosling.

The second foss was quite close, and had a big pool below it with a shallow tail, where we could see three fish, one was large and one was vast, not less than 20 lbs. We fished from all angles for these and others. At one time Sue had been sitting well behind me, and without being aware of it, I had hooked a parr. As I cast, it sailed through the air, and bounced off Sue's cheek. I picked up the parr unharmed, and returned it to the pool. Sue had thought that she had been struck by a pebble falling from the cliff. After she left with Torfi to go upstream, I hooked the smallest of the fish which I landed about 500 yards downstream.

Þverá - The first foss.

We went on up to the third and final foss in the canyon. 100 yards below it there had been a lovely looking pool but we could see nothing in it. The foss pool was long and narrow. Sue rose a large fish four times without a touch. Its head and shoulders would slowly surface each time behind her fly.

It was now 7.15 pm and we had only just reached the bottom of a beautiful open valley. Sue and Torfi started back, Sue fishing as they went. I fished behind them, getting my second fish in the middle foss. Salmon were no longer jumping the first foss, but there were still many there. Sue caught one in a corner pool below the first foss. When going up such a narrow stream, in a steep gorge it was inevitable that fish were disturbed, whereas returning downstream, one can fish over undisturbed fish. Fortunately salmon are not like New Zealand trout, which once disturbed are on guard for the rest of that day! It would have been better if we had walked up over the hill and then fished downstream.

We got back to the lodge at 10 pm, well exercised but feeling ready for more. Sue said that it had been the best day of her life, and it was also one of my most memorable days. We found the others happy and excited, with a possible record fish for the season of 18 $1/2$ lbs, caught on a small silver stoat.

Þverá - In the 'secret valley'.

My plan for the Þverá was, in addition to two rods walking, to try fishing for one day with four rods. The idea was for two, to fish up from the lodge, and for the other two to ride up to the very furthest place that a salmon could reach, and fish down until the others were met. Those that walked up would then fish up to the foss and ride down. Siggi the son of the farmer at Vatn, came with the horses. The plan worked well, and was enjoyed by all. The 'secret valley' was pristine, with this little river running through it, and untouched by man. Salmon were visible in the uppermost pools. We caught 2 in the valley and four in the canyon.

Going up a steep slope the hind legs of the horse that I was riding sank deep into the ground, so I rolled off to relieve it of my weight. The cantle of the saddle was rather high, so the operation was not as elegant as I would have wished. I ended up with a hook in my hand and laughter from the others. I am now experienced at getting hooks out of myself, and also out of others, quickly, and painlessly. I was not then, and cut it out with nail clippers. This was painful, messy and unnecessary.

For anyone who doesn´t know, there is such a simple method of extracting hooks from fishermen. First attach a piece of nylon to the bend of the hook against the place where the hook has penetrated the skin. Then press firmly on the rear of the hook, in order to overcome the barb. While doing this, a sharp pull on the nylon is all that is required. This must be done with total confidence, don´t contemplate failure! The hook pops out without any pain at all. This is best done by someone other than the one with the hook attached. I have twice operated successfully on myself, and also on others.

Myself happy on the Þverá.

An analysis of the size of all fish caught in a river in two years, is of interest; such information from rivers in the British Isles would be virtually impossible to obtain! Here are the Haukadalsá figures:-

		1984	1986
Grilse	2lbs.	7	2
	3lbs.	60	52
	4lbs.	82	190
	5lbs.	49	272
	6lbs.	23	149
	7lbs.	29	51
Salmon	8lbs.	81	27
	9lbs.	84	14
	10lbs.	87	23
	11lbs.	55	9
	12lbs.	32	5
	13lbs.	25	10
	14lbs.	8	2
	15lbs.	6	2
	16lbs.	2	3
	17lbs.	3	3
	Total	**633**	**814**

Weekly Catches 1984		Weekly Catches 1986	
16-23 June	65	15-21 June	17
24- 1 July	91	21-28 June	25
2-8 July	84	28-5 July	103
9-16 July	102	5-12 July	78
17-23 July	78	12-19 July	139
24-30 July	45	19-26 July	126
31-6 Aug	31	26-2 Aug	78
7-13 Aug	65	2-9 Aug	43
14-20 Aug	46	9-16 Aug	87
21-27 Aug	6	16-23 Aug	23
28-3 Sep	12	23-31 Aug	23
4-10 Sep	2	31-8 Sep	58
11-14 Sep	7	8-13 Sep	1

Note : There are so many variables, including:- The weather, the run of salmon, the numbers of grilse, and the number of m.s.w. salmon, fishing methods, skill of the fishermen, and how hard they fish.

Laxá í Dölum

I was tantalised by the description of the Laxá í Dölum, in the book 'The Rivers of Iceland' written by Major General Stewart in 1952, and, I formed an ambition to fish there. The more that I learned about this river, the keener I became. It had been leased for a number of years to Donald Kendall, who was then 'Chairman of the Board' of Pepsico. Páll Jónsson, of Laxá í Kjós fame, was at that time the agent for Pepsi products in Iceland, but Helgi Jakobsson was Don Kendall's representative in Iceland for fishing, so I spoke to him.

Laxá í Dölum, a watercolour sketch by Joanna Savage.

The river had been fished very lightly during the Pepsi lease. It was never let on the open market, and in some weeks it was not fished at all. When it was fished, Don Kendall often had the bosses of Pepsi plants to stay, and to fish. Sometimes, he invited someone famous to stay, perhaps in order to increase the interest of the week for his guests, who were expected to jog before breakfast. These included Neil Armstrong, the first man on the moon, and Jack Nicklaus, the golfer. They really appreciated the fishing, and Nicklaus became addicted to salmon fishing. Obviously many of the guests were novices, but Donald himself was a very keen and good fisherman. I learned that he was about to retire, and had bought a ranch in Wyoming. This sounded hopeful. Particularly as some Pepsi friends had been allowed to take the river for a week.

I telephoned to Pepsi and spoke to the man with responsibility for running the river. He said that he would see what he could do for me, and he soon replied with the offer of a week on very reasonable terms, which I accepted with alacrity. This was to be the start of a great thing in my life, in fact I was to take the river, to fish with friends and family, for a total of eighteen weeks, over eleven years. All local arrangements were made with Helgi Jakobsson, telexes being sent to Coca Cola, Iceland, whose boss was a friend of Helgi's. Considering the bitter rivalry between these two companies, this connection was surprising! I also booked seven weeks in successive years for Billy Dunnavant from the US. It is an extraordinary thought that the reminiscences in one chapter in Major General Stewart's book read by me, led to this river being booked in its entirety for 150 rod weeks! Such is the power of the written word.

Helgi Jakobsson.

I had been convinced that the statistics were misleading, because the river had been so underfished, and that as a result the river was a 'sleeper', being better than was apparent. Other rivers at that time were feeling the impact of the Greenland and Faroese high seas fisheries. Whereas the Laxá í Dölum had 'invisible reserves'. This was good for the river but not so good for the farmers, as the market value of a river is greatly influenced by the record of its catches. In due course we did much to increase the value to our own detriment!

North of Snæfellsnes peninsula, at the inner end is Hvammsfjörður, this has a group of four rivers flowing in to it. The most important of these is the Laxá í Dölum, to the South is the Haukadalsá, South of that, Miðá í Dölum and to the North is the Fáskrúð. The first two of these are rivals, but the Laxá í Dölum has the edge. When one knows this river, it is fascinating to read the Laxdæla Saga which was written about this valley, and its original inhabitants. Several of the farms and the pools are named after these very people, which brings this Saga to life. It was easy to imagine a Viking ship in the basin between the Feeding Pool and the Sea Pool.

In translation I read the Laxdæla Saga, written in about 1250, from the verbal tradition concening events 250 years before. Included in this Saga is the story of Höskuldur, whose farm is still called Höskuldsstaðir, and the top pool of the bottom beat is Höskuldsstaðastrengur.

Höskuldur sails to Norway, leaving behind his young wife with his two sons. He eventually becomes a friend of the king. He wants to buy a slave girl, and asks a Russian trader, who shows him twelve. He picks out one, but is told that her price is three gold marks. He remonstrates claiming that the market value is only one gold mark. The trader agrees and offers him any other girl for one mark, but he insists on three marks for this one particular girl, but he warns Höskuldur that she is dumb. Höskuldur buys her, cleans her up and dresses her in fine clothes. She responds to this treatment, and he has his way with her.

Höskuldur becomes a friend of the king, who is sad when he wants to return to Iceland. The king gives him what he wants most of all, which are roof timbers for his house. He also gives him a gold ring for his wrist, and a sword with gold on the hilt. Höskuldur returns home, bringing his ship into the river mouth, where he beaches it. In due course the slave girl gives birth to a son, Ólafur, who is brought up as a family member.

One day Höskuldur returns home to hear happy voices, one of these he doesn't recognise. It was the slave girl, who had only feigned that she was dumb. He then learns that she was captured when fifteen and was the daughter of an Irish king. And so the story continues….., but we must move forward a thousand years!

Helgi advised that we should not come before the middle of July, by which time sufficient fish would have come in to populate the river, with more salmon entering the river on every tide. Although seven rods were allowed to fish the river; we always kept to six, preferring to fish three beats with two rods and one guide for each rod, rather than divide the river into seven beats with one rod each.

As the good pools varied considerably from, week to week, as well as from year to year, this system resulted in there being no dud beat. If fished as seven beats that would be impossible to achieve.

The Lodge was very comfortable, with six double bedrooms, and a large bathroom between each pair of bedrooms. There was a large and comfortable living room with panoramic views in three directions. The dining-room was separated by an open partition, from the living-room. The kitchen was large and well equipped, and beyond was good accommodation for the guides and staff. Below that end were store rooms with a large cooler, and large deep freeze for the salmon. The American influence was shown by having two ice-making machines. Now the Lodge has been 'improved' after being inspected by an American sporting agent. There was no need for this. The most fastidious of wealthy Americans, used to the very best, liked it just as it was, our only request was for some more shelves in the bedrooms.

Laxá í Dölum Lodge.

The river runs South West down a wide valley through soft scenery and many farms. There is a road up the valley, crossing the hills to join the main road from Reykjavík to Akureyri. This valley road is now good which it was not in the days of Major General Stewart, when to drive on it was an considerable undertaking. The main coast road to Ísafjörður crosses the river near the mouth and less than one mile further on the little village of Búðardalur is reached. This village is famous in Iceland for its cheeses. To the South of the river and on a promontary is the airfield, only ten minutes drive from the lodge. In the late forties all towns and villages, that were able to do so, built a landing strip, and hoped for a scheduled service. Now the roads generally are so good that these communities are not so cut off. In view of the terrain, these airfields are not difficult to make once the site is chosen. One year shortly before we arrived the runway had been regraded, it was soft particularly near the end. That year we arrived in two Cesnas. When turning at the end of the runway, the front wheel of one Cesna stuck in the ground, we man handled the plane round, lifting and pushing, so that it could take off.

Our first year, it was arranged for us to fly up in a Twin Otter and be met by the guides. Sadly, my then wife, Gina, had to cancel at the very last moment because her father had broken his arm, she stayed to help her mother look after him. Nine months later she had left me, and only came to Iceland once again, as in due course I will relate! Two young men came to share her rod. This, my first party of many on this river, consisted of myself, my elder brother, Robin, two of my sons, Sandy and Ben, Jim Edwards, and his wife to be, Belinda Fuchs, Tim Jackson and Dominic Enderby. The Guides were Árni, pronounced Ardni, who was the headmaster of a big school, Ragnar, whose family came from the valley and was

Laxá í Dölum - Our Guides and our party leaving after our first week.

second master of another big school, Grétar, who came to be nicknamed 'the Netter', and Eiríkur, also both schoolmasters, Héðinn, pronounced 'hair thin', a motor mechanic, and, last but not least, Einar, the owner of an import export business. We were looked after exceptionally well by Gunnar the cook and his wife Erla, pronounced 'Erdla'. Gunnar was the chef of the US officers club in the air base at Keflavík. Gunnar's grandfather lived in the uppermost farm of the valley, and was a great age helped by whisky. Five of the guides had eight years experience, with Pepsi, only Eríkur was new to the river. This team, with minor variations was to look after us for all our years on the river.

Fishing started at 3.00 pm on Sunday, but as the previous party had left early, we were invited to fly up immediately on Saturday. Helgi had arranged everything. He flew Jim and Belinda from Reykjavík to meet us at Keflavík, we flew from there and 30 minutes later we were flying low over the lodge to alert the guides as to our arrival. There was little time that evening, so we were taken to two pools which we fished for only 1 1/2 hours. The river was low but many fish were showing. We lost three fish, and caught nothing, but we were installed early, unpacked and ready to start in the morning.

On Monday it rained heavily, the river had risen 9 inches by lunchtime and continued to rise in the afternoon, about 15 inches in all. By the evening the river had cleared at the top, and had begun to fall; we had caught 19 fish, and lost 8. The next day I lost a twenty pounder and remember every detail as if it were yesterday. I had seen it rise, fished for it, it cartwheeled across the pool, and left me hooked on a rock in the deep hole in the pool centre. (Dropper trouble!)

During the previous ten years the best week had been 145 fish and the best individual rod catch had been 24 fish. Excluding our bonus time at the start of the week, we caught 140, and the highest rod catches were 36, 34 and 24. The excitement that we felt shines from my notes made at the time. In all, our total catch was 144 and we lost another 60. Forty were caught on a tube fly with a size 16 hook, and half an inch over all. Thirty-four were caught on flies size 8. The most successful flies were a Stoat's tail, both silver and black, 37 fish; Francis, red, black and green, 30 fish; black and yellow tube, 23 fish (later to be known as a traffic warden); and Jeannie, 14 fish. We caught salmon in 18 different pools. The top beat produced 61, the middle beat 47, and the bottom beat 36. The average weight was 5.8 lbs. This proved to be our smallest average weight for any year on this river.

Here are some of the notes from my diary, which give the flavour, I have retained the old pool numbers;-

'In 7, Mjóhylur, Ben's fish ran through a hole under two rocks and Ragnar tailed it.'. (They celebrated with Campari!)

Ragnar Guðmundsson and Gretar Halldorsson.

'At 21, the Bridge Pool, I fished the runs above, with a floating line and tiny fly, to the horror of Árni. I hooked one, lost it, and got into another beside the biggest rock. After hairy wading in the high river, I got it into the pool below and landed it.'

'I put on a Red Francis, and quickly lost two, then caught two. They might attack the Red Francis, or it might act as a teaser, and swallow the Stoat (on the dropper). I lost one on the dropper when the tail fly caught weed on the bottom. By 6.00 pm Jim had caught his limit of 10, and Belinda also caught one.'

'On the middle beat, a farmer appeared on a horse with news of fish in a new place.'

'I put a Red Francis on the tail, and immediately got life from a dead pool. In Pool 14 we could see every fish in the pool. Two fish came three times to the same cast.'
'Two flies were attached to its body, but they were not our flies!'

'I caught three fish in the new pool, 9 1/2, one followed my fly seven times before it took. River stocked from bottom to top.'

'In 20, with huge rocks standing out of the water everywhere, Sandy hooked a fish that ran up a two foot fall, through more rocks. The tail fly broke away, and he landed it at the second attempt. An epic fight.'

'I hooked a fish 60 yards above pool 20, huge rocks everywhere, it was lucky that the fish was not bigger. I beached it early on the only patch of gravel. The dropper fell out but the fish was lassoed by the tail fly. The fish was greatly surprised, and so was Árni.'

'With twenty minutes to go before 1.00 pm, I reached pool 14, and started just round the corner, ankle deep upstream, in the short time left I had two pulls, one boil, lost two and caught two with sea lice. For the morning I had six fish from five pools, lost two, and several interviews, difficult to beat. Fantastic!'

'A difficult morning, very bright. Jim caught four fish and lost two all from the same place, round Einar's rock, in the Home Pool.'

'Dominic hooked another which he landed with both flies in its mouth, or three, if my James Walker Blue Shrimp fly is included.'

This week could not have been a better introduction for us to the river, and to our 'carers', who became good friends. On the last evening we had our traditional party with the staff, and, as a surprise, gave them seven carbon rods, which were greatly appreciated. After such a week, and an exceptional opportunity to secure it, surely it is not surprising that I 'adopted' this river. It became clear that the farmers also liked the way that we fished. It was a great privilege to be in this position, and Helgi was the greatest help.

Description of the river

The Laxá í Dölum is 25 kilometres from the impassable foss, to the sea. The lodge, or Veiðihús, is near the middle of the middle beat. Access to the upper two beats is particularly easy and, access to the bottom beat has become easier over the years. Twenty-six pools were numbered, from 0 to 25. Other good places in between pools that were unnumbered became known by fractions, such as 22 $^1/_2$. This is now even more confusing because the numbers have been changed! The Icelandic names may be difficult at first but they change little. There are now 31 pools that are numbered, and 4 more designated by a letter, all are named.

In times past this river is said to have had annual catches approaching 2000. The average catch of the previous five years had been only 475, totalling 2374 fish. Of these 921 had been caught in Kristnipollur, the Home Pool. 1772 had come from six pools, and another six pools had produced no fish at all in that period. An analysis of our records gives a very different picture. For the 12 years that we came the average increased to 1240 for the season. After we stopped the average declined to 888 for the next 9 years to 2001. It has become a later river, and there has been more worm fishing, even in the fly only period.

The farmers employed a fishery biologist as a consultant. This led to an enhancement programme under which fish from the river were stripped, for a hatchery. The resultant parr were then planted in the river above the foss and also in other streams inaccessible to salmon for spawning. This had a noticeable effect in subsequent years on the number of fish that ran up to the foss. However, in my opinion, as I have explained in Chapter Two some of the other advice that was given was unfortunate.

The Top Beat

Laxá í Dölum - Sólheimafoss.

At Sólheimafoss the river has a greatly reduced flow. The foss is a total obstacle to migration. Below is a small narrow gorge for about 60 yards. Fish can be caught immediately at the foot of the foss from the right bank. This pool is now numbered 31. A little distance below it is possible to sit behind a rock and cast for fish that are visible, and watch their reaction to different flies and try different presentations. If a fish is hooked here, the way to play it and to beach it, is to go to the end of the narrows, keeping back from the edge of the cliff, and climb down to where there is good beach. From there a fish can be played in the gorge and then coaxed downstream. Also from that beach it is possible to cast upstream to fish lying against the cliff on the far side about 25 yards above. However it is best to fish these places in the reverse order. First start from the beach, keeping well back and low, and if as yet undisturbed, a few fish are usually lying on the far side, only just downstream of the end of the narrows. This lie is very shallow and sensitive to disturbance. Both the fish and fisherman can see everything.

If the river is high, salmon may come down from the foss pool, and lie amongst rocks below. Prominent amongst these, is one that we called Dennis's nose, after a well-formed feature of a good friend and brilliant fisherman, who was particularly successful fishing that lie! These lies are now numbered D, and called Hyljir.

The next numbered pool is 30, Helluhylur, called Flagstone Pool by Billy Dunavant. In high water the entry run is worth most careful fishing. This is quite a big pool, the bay on the left bank was shallow and without fish. If one climbs down quietly into this, and creeps along staying short of the point, the fishing from there down can be dramatic. The main run comes to that point, the first lie is just above that. The current then runs down close to the left bank, where the river is deep beside the rock shelf and fish lie along it, frequently showing on the surface. It is also possible to fish both the entry run, and the main pool from the right bank. To get there one can cross the river well below the pool or above the entry run. Árni taught me how to fish this pool, and having done so, I have happy memories of him asleep in his car on part of the former road above, periodically

Árni Magnusson with Ragnar.

116

being awakened by a shout to help me land a fish. Doing this from the left bank involved crossing the tail to beach it on the other side. It is possible to catch many fish in this pool, provided great care is taken not to spook the pool, both when fishing and when playing a fish.

About 200 yards below is a run that was not named or numbered where I frequently saw fish but never caught one. A short drive below, and down to the river takes one to Helgabakki, wrongly translated as Holy Bank, 29. This is a small and obvious pool, but of no great merit, which I fished religiously, but never even saw a fish in it, however one of our party did catch two particularly big fish in it on the same day, so I went on trying, and failing!

The next, is again a short drive off the road. It had no name that we ever heard, except 22 $1/2$, it is now Hamarsfljót, 28. It is an obviously attractive rock pool. I never did any good here either, although I remember coming here to see Sandy with three fresh fish on the bank. Just below the road here I once saw the appointed mink exterminator waving for help. He had a mink holed up under a fallen bank. He thrust his ancient gun into my hand, and dug at one end of the bank, while his terrier stuck its nose in the other end. As I waited nervously, there was a sudden movement from the dog, and the mink had been decapitated.

Laxá í Dölum - Svartfoss.

Pool 27, Svartfoss, Black falls, is one of the great holding pools of the river. There is no foss, but a fast run down a narrow shute, after twenty-five yards the pool widens, for about another 50 yards. Much of this part is shallow. In high water, below the tail of this pool, are two more pools, immediately following one after the other. Both of these also become exciting fishing. The pool is fished from the left bank, and in normal conditions the entry run repays very careful fishing. It is easy to have passed several lies before the first cast. The hottest spot, is close to the tail of these narrows. I prefer to start standing well above the entry run, then working down carefully, wading under the rock shelf beside the run, sitting down on comfortable rocks as I proceed, keeping out of sight. It is worth trying more than one fly when fishing the hot spot. Dennis Desmond was particularly talented at catching fish under the white water at the heads of pools, probably because he got his fly down to them. I was more successful further down the pools. As the pool widens there are a number of individual lies that gradually give up their secrets. Ragnar was particularly keen to avoid over wading in the wider part of this pool. One lie was rather far down the pool and far across, it was particularly favoured by big fish. There is a place close to where cars are parked for this pool, where the Iceland falcon was often seen. The reason was that a chicken farmer often dumped dead broiler chicks there. Whatever the reason it was wonderful to get such a close view of this handsome bird.

Down the valley again, the next road to the right leads to a bridge over the river. Here there is a most interesting and varied area to fish. Two hundred yards upstream, there is a corner that is only good in high water, close by is a tail above a stretch with huge boulders. In high and medium water this tail is good from the left bank. Then the big boulders start. Amongst them, there are several lies which need to be fished with accuracy. To play a fish amongst them is always an adventure. This area is called Dönustaðagrjót, which may be difficult, but is better than 'Doughnut Rocks', we just called it by its number, which is now 26, and includes the Bridge Pool. This bridge provides access to some farms. It crosses about 10 feet above the river. From the bridge looking down it is easy to see, and to spook, fish both above and below the bridge. Salmon like this pool and there are often many visible. It fishes from both sides, but is better from the left bank. There are also fish higher in the run than are visible. The chief lie is in

Laxá í Dölum - The Bridge Pool.

the main pool just above the bridge. Fish also lie just below the bridge, and again below that in the run out. Below the bridge there are two rocks that 'kiss' below the water; salmon sometimes run between, causing an interesting problem when playing a fish. Once this problem was compounded by Árni who lay on the rock, and passed his tailer not only over the tail, but over the head of the fish. It was an unlucky fish, we beached it. Before being able to do this, the rod had to be passed through the underwater hole, with the tailer still attached to the line. At one minute to 'close of play' I have caught a fish in the pot immediately below the tail of this pool, which doesn't seem to be a likely place for a fish.

The gradient of the river increases and the river descends through a cascade of large rocks, for a considerable distance. This we called 'The Pots', but it should be called Björnskvörn, now 25, again the English translation is unattractive, 'Bear Grinder'. It is best to go down this stretch on the right bank. Some of these pots are the greatest fun and source of adventure, others may have more, but smaller, fish that are more controllable. The first pot, on a corner, is obvious. This can have

Laxá í Dölum - 'The Pots' or Björnskvörn with Árni.

particularly big fish. One that I caught there I nicknamed the troglodyte. It came from a cave and went from hole to hole as I played it. I had to pursue it in the water and kick it out of its holes. Another and even larger fish milled about and then went off downstream. In order to clear my line from rocks, I had to follow in the river. Luckily it went downstream gradually, pot by pot, I must have followed it for 300 yards or more before it gave up very suddenly and completely.

The next important pot has several lies, and is occasionally full of a large number of small grilse. Both playing them and landing them is difficult. Further down and round the next corner is another area with many individual lies. One is again virtually under a rock. Another is in mid stream in front of a big rock, below that again there are several more lies, nearer the left bank.

At last the river flattens out but the great rocks continue a little further. The main current runs more smoothly close to the right bank, where fish lie. The river bends to the left and at last looks more normal. The upper part of this is better from on top of the right bank, and the lower part from the left, fishing from the middle of an almost dry river bed. For two years this was one of the favourite places for fish on the river. From below, I once watched Belinda, beach fish after fish, I believe it was seven that she caught in the same place in quick succession.

Below this the river can be approached with courage from the road down a steep slope, through a small stream, and then across the river. A little below, a high bank rises a few yards away from the river, opposite and below this can be another most productive pool. In our time this was just called 19 $^1/_2$. It is now 24, Höfðafljót. A few fish lay in the run but further down there were more fish. Year by year, they increased here until there was a congregation that blackened the bottom of the centre of the river. They could be tempted to take a small fly. It seemed that they only started to lie here when they stopped lying in the place previously described, which is about 400 yards further upstream.

Below this pool, it is possible to drive across the river on a diagonal line, and continue downstream. The next pool is number 23, Drykkjarhylur, never known by its English name of Drink Pool. It had an undercut right bank where many salmon were sometimes in residence. The run into this pool could be good for a grilse or two, but in the main lie, Dennis could occasionally work his magic, with

Laxá í Dölum - Below Höfðafljót with Jean de Boussac landing a fish.

some minute Irish creation. Below it is necessary to cross the river again. The next two pools are beneath a farm called Gröf. These were called Grave Pool and Grave Bank in English, or Grafarpollur, 22 and Grafarbakki, 21, in Icelandic. Both occasionally gave us a few fish. There is a ford between them, and then the track goes through the farm yard, and past a barking dog, to the road.

Incredibly all of the river described so far formed our beat three. This is some of the most varied and exciting fishing in Iceland, and where we have had many adventures. There is a lot of water to cover in one fishing period of six hours by two rods.

The Middle Beat

Beat two has a very different feel to it. There was extraordinary variation from year to year as to where the fish chose as their favourite haunts.

Pass by Leirmúli, Clay Mound, pool 20, I have never known a fish come out of this. Perhaps it was once good, and may be so again, in our day it seemed to have been named and numbered by an optimistic owner. But just below it there is a place that began to hold some taking fish, then the farmer placed some large boulders nearby, which seemed to encourage them further. Above it is a wire across the river. To get there one drives through a gate and down towards the river. Turn upstream, for a few hundred yards. Perhaps this is now called Leirmúli, but there is no mound or high bank.

Below this is a corner with a pool below, with some interesting looking rock lies. It is pool 19, Dísubakki, or Fairy Bank. Some years this was dead, but occasionally it was so good that I fished it with optimism ever after.

Driving from there alongside the river there are two little ponds, one usually had a pair of great northern divers nesting in it. A little below there is an 'S' bend, to the right then to the left. The first bend is worth trying in a spate, at that corner a backwater comes in from the left with a sticky muddy bottom, I write of this from bitter experience. Care needs to be taken where to drive across, then up a short steep slope, and now there is the fence of a meadow, with barely room to turn right, then beyond is a good place to use as a base for an exceptional holding pool. In general, as the beats are so long, and the choice so great, it is best to use a car as much as possible between pools in order to maximise the fishing, but beware of the track here when it is wet. This is the only place where I have got my car sruck on this river. First my car was bellied on the bank before the slope. I used the jack several times, progressively building a pile of stones under one wheel. Then I drove it with confidence over the bank into the boggy backwater where it sank into the mud. The farmer brought a tractor to rescue me, but my beat sharer arrived in time to witness my disgrace.

After our second year we always hired three cars, so with the guides' cars we had one car for each rod. This made all the difference, and is very strongly to be recommended. As we got to know the river, we did not always have six guides, but it is important to have one car per rod, and not to share a guide between two rods with one car.

The next pool is Svarfhólsgrjót 18, or Red Bank as we called it, on the far side there is a high and sticky clay bank. Some people called it Telegraph Pool, after a pole that actually carried an electric cable! I was taken here on our very first evening with two others, to fish side by side, by the only guide who didn't know the river at all! He was an extremely nice man, and this was the only bit of unfortunate guiding that I ever had on this river. But that evening we were only there by invitation, and four guides were having a evening off before the time that we should have arrived. The corner is an outside chance, then there is a gravel bar across the river, with a lagoon above the far side, in which there was usually a red throated diver nesting. The pool immediately below this bar, down to a 'V' in the clay bank, is often stacked with fish that are showing frequently on the surface. Below that the fish are more spread out, but there are lies for the next 100 yards or more. The main pool, and fish, extend to a little below a big rock near the far bank. About 50 yards below that in mid stream there was sometimes an unexpected pod of good fish. The left bank is a perfect beach for landing fish. Over-wading must be avoided in this pool. At the head, when there is a large number of fish, it is difficult to avoid foul hooking them. When someone new to the river came back from this pool reporting several losses, this was usually the reason. On one occasion a fisherman, who only came once had no idea of this, as his guide had landed his fish. On another, I arrived at this pool to fish, and to my absolute astonishment the fish from all over the pool began to gather and then slowly and very deliberately, they swam past me, like a naval review, until it seemed that they had all gone. I counted them out, as best as I could, and estimated the total at over 130, but they did not come back. After that this pool remained empty until after we had left.

Pool 17, Lambastaðakvörn may be difficult for foreigners to get their tongues arround, but surely it is better than to call it Grinding Hills Rocks. We had some very good fishing there, some were big fish, including ones caught by the young children of Jim Edwards. Then immediately upstream an artificial pool was

Kristján with a big fish.

created with a rock groin from both sides. This attracted more fish to lie there and show on the surface. This also attracted the fishermen, but the fish seemed less than willing to take a fly. The previous hole stopped holding fish.

After passing Kotbakki, 16, on a bend close below the road, turn off through a gate opposite the lodge. This leads to The Home Pool, or more correctly Kristnipollur, number 15. In this pool 921 fish had been caught in the five years before our arrival, very nearly 39% of the total catch from the whole river. It remained a very good pool, but became less exceptional as the years went by.

Jim Edwards with Kristján and Annatara.

Just above the pool the river takes a right bend, with a steep moraine on the right bank. Upstream of this, there were sometimes small pods of fish lying close to small stones in mid stream where the current is very gentle. On one occasion Jim was very successful here. Once round the bend fish lie in pods for about 100 yards. The current remains gentle throughout. It is best fished extremely fine and very slowly, and, in my opinion, with two flies. I have had two fish on at the same time but never landed both. I always have a stronger nylon to the dropper, so that in a crisis the tail fly can break away. Twice in this pool I have caught a fish with both my flies in its mouth.

Near the tail of the pool there is a huge rock. This is known as Einar's rock, after one guide, who believed that the area in which fish lay could be extended by placing a rock in the pool. When work was being done on the road, he persuaded one of the drivers to bring this massive rock to the river and to place it about $1/3$ of the way across. His enterprise has been extremely successful. Fish lie all round and beyond it.

Rivers are always changing, some changes are obvious to us, but other changes that may be imperceptable to us, are important to fish. Below the Home Pool was a lie well across the river where one year Robin caught a cock fish of 22 lbs, his rod broke as he was playing it, and his guide photographed him holding the fish with the broken rod in his mouth. Graham Ferguson had a theory that a big cock would

*Laxá í Dölum -
Roger Massingbird-Mundy
beaching a fish in the 'Home
Pool'.*

*Laxá í Dölum -
Robin with his 22 lb fish.*

be accompanied by a big hen. Next day, in the same place, he hooked but lost, what is now called the 'partner' of the cock, or in the most recent politically correct parlance, what may have been its 'significant other'! I pray that this ridiculous expression is from a phase of political correctness that will soon pass!

Round a slight bend, is the start of Gíslakvörn, pool 14. This improved year after year, there were fish from the head of the run until it petered out. Sometimes many fish were showing on the surface. Below that there was nothing worth fishing for quite a distance, but one week, an excited lad from the farm appeared on his horse to tell Ragnar that a number of fish were jumping in a new place. Ragnar had grown up on this farm as a boy, and knew every inch of this part of the river. Below Pool 10 is another bend to the right with a run down the middle of the river, with rocks and patches of white clay bottom. There were a considerable number of salmon over a length of about 100 yards. We caught many fish here that year, and some the following year. Then its attraction to the salmon faded. It is now called Nesbakki, 13.

The next pool, number 12, is reached by driving down the road from the lodge and turning down a small track. This pool has a historic name being called after the farm which bears the name of the original Viking settler. It is called Leiðólfsstaðakvörn, the English, or more probably, the American name, Scouts Chopper, is totally without merit.

This pool starts as a run on a right hand corner, and then there is a gentle current, with several rocks standing out of the water, over a length of about 150 yards or more. This is all surprisingly shallow, with some channels, and greater depth close to rocks. To fish it all takes a very long time, but some surprisingly large fish lie in unexpected places in this pool. When these are hooked they go like a train through the obstacle course. Close to the bottom of the entry run in a quiet spot, I once saw a slight movement, casting to that precise place, I caught two beautiful fish of 15 lbs, one after the other. The most famous lie in this pool is arround a big rock in the middle of the river just below the place where the approach track reaches the river. About 30 yards below that, there is a relatively deep hole. I believe this hole to be the refuge in the pool for salmon, and from here a few at a time move up to the big rock. Fish also take in the hole. In high water there is another lie on the far side about 50 yards further downstream.

A quarter of a mile below is another obvious place which does sometimes produce a fish, but more often disappoints. This for us marked the end of the fishing on the middle beat. However another artificial pool has been created with large rocks, that is visible from the road. By now, it may well be worth fishing.

In the Laxá í Dölum there is a greater proportion of big fish than appear to be the case from the statistics. The reason for this is that by and large, they are lost. So much of the river is shallow, with big rocks, yet it is advisable in slow currents and gin clear to fish with a fine leader. Salmon in Iceland enter their rivers close to feeding grounds. Unlike salmon entering rivers in Scotland, they have not just swum the Atlantic, when fresh out of the sea they have not lost their sea teeth or their appetite! This is the reason, they take more freely, and fight so well. It is noticeable that Icelandic smoked salmon has more fat than Scottish; the reason is, they are in better condition!

The Bottom Beat

To fish this, one fisherman used to start at the bottom, and the other start at the top. One car was parked by the road bridge, and the other was parked on a bluff above the second pool on the beat. Gradually cars have penetrated further, so to my regret, there is no longer the need to walk, and exchange car keys, when the fishermens' paths crossed. It was a pleasure to sit down, watch each other fishing, and have some coffee or a dram. We often met at Þegjandi, where two rods could fish in the pool at the same time.

Later we drove about 800 yards from the road, and, if ground conditions allowed, up to Pool 11, Höskuldsstaðastrengur, named after Höskuldur of the Laxdæla Saga. The pool was listed, in American, as 'Husky Rapids'. After a long dull stretch between the beats, there is a tail above the rapids where running fish often rest in high, or medium water conditions. There are about four lies there, the last is on the lip. Then there are about 80 yards of rapids with runs, that may be worth a trying for a fish. These end in a two foot drop into the pool, itself. There is even a lie in that drop. Below there are two runs into the pool that are close together, they are best fished separately, further down the pool almost everything can be covered from the rock shelf above the drop, or wading down a few steps. This pool is unpredictable, but good on its day for fresh fish that are pausing.

Laxá í Dölum - Mjóhylur.

Pool 10, Mjóhylur, meaning the Narrow Pool, is well named, and repays the most careful fishing. The river bends slightly left into it, with a fast entry run, then curves a little to the right. The pool is indeed very narrow, and is also deep, with a slightly wider and attractive tail. This leads into a shallow lower small pool, before the flow becomes widely difused. From the top of the bluff some of the fish can be seen. Fresh fish rest frequently in this pool. It can be fished from both sides, but it is advisable to keep low and back, so far as it is possible. This is a pool about which there are many stories to tell, notably by Charles Godchaux, and my brother, Robin. I have etched in my memory one picture. I was fishing from the right bank, and hooked a big fish, it ran across the tail of the pool and leaped high onto the far bank! Naturally the fly came out, and it jumped back into the pool. I was once having a great fight with another very big fish. It left the pool and ran over the shallows below, much of the time, half out of the water. Below, in mid stream I tried to beach it, but the fly came out of that one too. I ran after it trying to hit it on the head with my wading staff! Luckily I wasn´t seen as this must have been an unedifying sight. In this pool Robin once caught four fish one after the other. In such a sensitive small pool, this was a notable achievement.

On the last morning of our first week, Dennis didn´t return for lunch, or to finish his packing. Finally we sent out a search party, and found him playing a big fish from this pool that he had on for nearly two hours. It had spent a long time sulking under the run. Eventually he coaxed it out and after an extended battle landed it 200 yards downstream. As it was being beached our plane flew low overhead calling us to the airfield. Perhaps it was with this memory that the following year, fishing with me, Dennis started at the bottom of the beat, but reached this pool before I came down one pool from the top!

We used to walk, but now there is a steep track used by cars down and across the river, soon there is a short run that is sometimes worth a few casts, and then round another bend pool 9 is reached. There is another ford across the river above it to pool 8 and 7. Care is needed when crossing here, once the car of one of our party was bellied on a rock in mid stream, and had to be jacked off it. This is the area that is described in the chapter about the Laxá í Dölum in General Stewart's book, and which created my ambition to fish this river.

*Laxá í Dölum -
Dennis Desmond returning
with his fish.*

This pool 9, Þegjandakvörn, forms a long bend to the left. The run in, is best fished from the right bank, and then the bottom of this run, and the rest of the pool from the left bank. The lower right side has a high bank, all the way to the tail. For the Laxá í Dölum, this is a big pool. Where fish lie in this pool, and, whether they do so, varies considerably from year to year. It can be a very exciting place to fish or extraordinarily unrewarding, where much time can be wasted. Occasionally there is an unexpected pod, visible, pausing in the run out.

Immediately below, there is a shallow run into pool 8, Þegjandastrengur, the run out of which takes a sharp turn to the right. Fish are taken in the entry run, but the really hot spot is on the lip of the run out. This is fished from the left bank wading out a long way towards the tail, and swinging one's fly across the tail. This catches running fish that are resting, or waiting for their 'mates' after swimming up from the pool below.

A shute leads into pool 7, Þegjandi, or The Silent Pool. This is a most complicated pool, and is a fascinating piece of water to fish. It is also consistently good, and sometimes outstandingly so. At the bottom of the shute the main flow divides, about 1/3 goes to the left around a rock outcrop that stands about seven feet out of the water. Beside this the left stream falls into the pool, to join the main current below. The right stream also divides, part runs down close to the right bank, and the main stream goes half left, beside the rock outcrop, to join the left stream below. Then these two continue down the centre of the pool. Between the right hand run and the centre run is another rock outcrop that is mostly under water, and is soon replaced by a sandbank that continues down the pool. The main stream in the tail exits half right.

The greatest concentration of fish is in the centre run, and down the middle of the pool. This needs to be fished with the utmost care, as it is difficult to present

Laxá í Dölum - Þegjandi, or The Silent Pool.

Laxá í Dölum - Neðri Kistur.

From a photograph by Árni Baldursson.

the fly to the upper lies, which are easily passed before the fly starts to fish. The normal way to fish is down the right side of the centre run, but fishing from behind the central outcrop can be deadly; playing a fish from there is another matter. In high water the right hand run holds fish, and the tail of the pool becomes excellent. The tail is best fished from the left bank, wading down below a rock shelf. This pool is a favourite for the bigger fish but holds plenty of grilse as well.

Below this is the lower half of this beat, which is likely to be approached from below. Normally one tends to fish this from the bottom up, but this may be influenced by the tide. One's car is usually parked near the bridge, and we walked up the right bank to Krókur, the Hook, pool 6. This is basically a left-handed corner pool. Above the run in, there is a rock outcrop in line with the river, the main channel is to the right beside the rock, against which fish lie, and, they also take as the fly swings across the lip. Fish also lie in the narrow shute behind the outcrop, but they are very difficult to catch, and easily spooked. Below, four runs go into the pool, which have to be fished separately, but it is rare to catch a fish in the pool itself!

The river bends again immediately to the left, then to the right flowing close to a high cliff, which forms the left bank. At that point there is a small, and very narrow fall. This is the entry to one of the best worming holes in Iceland, (so I am told!). It also provides good fly-fishing, (as I do know!). There are several lies, most can be fished while sitting down in one place, keeping as low as possible. They range from the tail of the white water to the lip. This place is Efri Kista, which with Neðri Kista forms pool 5 or The Chests, upper and lower. Below the hole is a glide that can also hold fish in low water, then, still against the cliff face there is the run into the main pool. This always seems to hold fish, and depending on the height of the water, the pool can go down about 50 yards from where it widens out. Below that it goes on but is shallow with no fishing in normal conditions. The eventual run out is near the right bank, and we have known this to be full of fish for a length of about 50 yards. Initially we thought that the fish that showed were running, but then I wondered, and had a go, 'hitting the jackpot'. This is now called 'B' Útfallið and 'C' Doddsnef.

From here it is a short walk to the bridge which carries the main road high over the river. Above the bridge the river flows through runs close to the left bank, which can be fished from either side. These are Brúarstrengur, 4, fish can often be seen here from the bridge. The last lie is on the lip. Dennis was deadly here. Then there is a small pot with fish in it that is easily overlooked.

Below is Papi, 3, Old Irish Monk Pool. When the Vikings first came to Iceland they found Irish monks that had jouneyed in their leather skin boats. Did they get as far as here? I do not know. There is no reference to them in the Laxdæla Saga.

The river enters Papi down two small falls. The main current is on the left, and comes into a small upper pool that is forced by bedrock to swing round to the right, where it joins the right stream. The two join forces and run down the centre of the pool. The great feature of the main pool was a massive boulder. One winter this was carried downstream about 100 yards. Seeing this river in summer, it is incredible to imagine the power of the current, and ice in the winter and spring floods, but for this rock to have been carried downstream, gives a vivid impression. The top of the pool can be fished from the left bank all the way down. The right run, and the left run also, can be fished from the rock shelf in the middle, I find fishing from this position to be particularly exciting, it being virtually impossible to follow a fish downstream.

Laxá í Dölum - A beautiful fish from Papi.

About 300 yards below is Pool 2, Matarpollur, or the feeding pool. The time to fish this depends upon the tide, which comes into the pool. When the tide is out, there is in the middle, a small pot, then a shute, which opens out, and is joined by a run descending close to the right bank. All these places provide good fishing at times, frequently many grilse can be seen splashing. After the streams have joined there are some ledges that provide good lies and where fish take. At low tide there are rocky runs going down to another corner where there can be a lot of activity as the tide and fish come in. Occasionally they take here also. This is Efra Sjávarfljót, Pool 1.

From there it is about another 400 yards to the Lower Sea Pool, Pool 0, passing a basin, where I visualise that Höskuldur beached his ship, in about 950 A.D.. I have occasionally seen a fish in the pool but it is really only of interest as a walk when sharing a rod, and not fishing. Below that, the tide goes out 150 yards or so, and the river trickles over the sand on a wide front. On a bright windless sunny day, when the river was low, and the tide was out, I have seen two shoals of grilse swim over the sand with their backs out of the water, going up into the sea pool. We are told that salmon only run into a river at a certain time of the tide, these fish can't have been told how to behave.

Such a detailed description of a whole river may be of interest to anyone that has fished, or will fish, this river. Those that have fished it will no doubt have their own and varying ideas, some of which will coincide with mine, but all such impressions are clouded by personal experiences. I hope that much can be learned from this description, which can also be applied to other rivers, which will not be dealt with in such detail.

Mrs. Lilla Rowcliffe

There are so many stories about our weeks here, which could be told, that it is almost invidious to choose one! But I must!

The theory about fish being attracted by the Pheromones of Ladies fishing can only be nonsense, but if it applied to anyone, it must be Lilla. As a complete novice, she caught the record salmon on the Spey. It is probable that she has caught the biggest Mahseer on a fly from the Ganges, and the story of her performance with Karnatic Carp, on the Cauveri River in South India on a muddler minnow, is often told. They were feeding on floating monkey droppings!

I was fishing the middle beat with Lilla, and it was her turn to have the Home Pool area for the first half of the morning. I started at Leiðólfsstaðakvörn, where the day before Jim Edwards had caught a 22 lb cock fish that was coloured but had sea lice. It was surprising, that it was coloured as it was still early in the season. The scales were read; it was found that it had spent four years in the river as a parr, and then two winters at sea. However today I didn't find a large hen fish, or even anything at all, so at half-time I visited Lilla. I found her to be in a great state of excitement, a fresh run had come in to the pool, and she had caught five or six fish. I withdrew leaving her to enjoy her opportunity, and went to Svarfholtsgrjót, which had been dead, for two days. I found a fresh run of fish were there also! It was now 11.00 so I had two hours of action, in which I caught nine fish, and lost one, these weighed 41 lbs. Lilla arrived back for lunch radiant, she had also caught nine fish, all fresh out of the sea. We caught eighteen between us, but Lilla's weighed 79 1/4 lbs, nearly double the weight of mine!

*Laxá í Dölum -
Lilla Rowcliffe with her
morning's catch.*

A Summary of our time on the Laxá í Dölum

An analysis of our catches and experiences may provide some points of general interest.

I rented the Laxa í Dölum for 18 weeks in 12 years. The first week was mid August, otherwise it was always late July to 5th August at the latest. We always fished 6 rods, except in 1988, when for two weeks we fished 8 rods, but fished 2 of them on the Fáskrúð. Over the period 60 people fished in these parties, including a few that only fished for one day. This totalled 108 rod weeks, on the Dölum, of these 34 were fished by two rods sharing. Such pairs were strictly on their honour never both to fish at the same time.

Our total catch was 2608, equalling 35 per rod per week and after a fight we lost another 884. The average overall weight was 6¾ lbs. In individual years the average varied from 5.6 to 7.4 lbs. The weight breakdown is detailed in a table. My personal catch from 15 weeks as a full rod, and 3 weeks as a shared rod was 530, and I lost a disgraceful 247, well over my share of losses. This was in part because I usually fished with a dropper.

We never used anything other than fly. The patterns and sizes of fly and tube fly recorded are tabulated. How to decide the size of a tube fly is a matter for some debate and varied practice between fishermen. In my opinion it is logical to give an approximate measurement of the length to the bend of the hook. I have tried to do that, not always recording the size that I was told, if it was on a different basis. Some people record the length of tube itself, and some might argue that the length of a fly is the length of the dressing. This can be very long in the case of a 'collie dog' and a 'Sunray shadow'.

I give below a table, listing the pools, giving their Icelandic names, numbers old and new, beats as fished by us, and the number of fish recorded as caught by us in each, as well as a breakdown for the full season of 1990. All these and other figures are as accurate as I can calculate.

The annual comparison of the full years can be taken from the general table of official statistics of the rivers. For three years I have other figures of interest that are from the river record books, and I find thought-provoking, these are:-

Fishing Method	1984	1986	1990
Worm	600	858	554
Fly	269	1029	495
Spinner	8	75	25
Total	877	1962	1074

These totals vary from the official statistics.

The start of the season is slow on this river as is shown by these astonishing figures of the total catch in the 6 ½ weeks between between 15 June and 31 July:-

    1978   44
    1980   98
    1982   242 (176 by us)
    1991   98

In our first 8 seasons, in 13 weeks, our weekly average catch, between 6 rods, was 150 salmon.

In our last 3 seasons, in 5 weeks, our weekly average catch, between 6 rods, was 63 salmon.

In 1986, our record year, we were urged to catch more salmon on biological advice, and we caught an incredible 345 salmon, between our 6 rods, losing after a fight another 146, making a total, of what I call chances, of 511. This was between the 20th to 27th of July. Our catch by 6 rods in one week was 1.6% of the total Icelandic rod catch for that year!!

In our opinion the salmon run on this river after 1988 seemed to be getting progressively later. In fact we felt that we were no longer coming at prime time. In 1990 for example, the first half of the season accounted for under 20% of the catch! Prices continued on their upward course without regard to these perceived changes, which we felt justfied a re-evaluation in our favour; our record year, naturally, resulted in a price rise against us! We had enjoyed our experiences here beyond measure, but taking all things into account, we decided that the time had come to fish elsewhere. It was a particularly great wrench to say goodbye to Gunnar, the chef, his family, and our regular guides. It also meant the break up of the nucleus of our parties. This was an additional cause of sadness. Nevertheless I do still believe that it was the right decision for us to take. It was time to move on.

*Laxá í Dölum -
Michael and Edward
Heathcoat-Amory.*

Our total catch in 19 weeks over 12 years on the Laxa í Dölum

Weight of fish LBS	Caught by us NO.	Weight of fish LBS	Caught by us NO.	Weight of fish LBS	Caught by us NO.
2	10	10	54	18	6
3	54	11	79	19	3
4	280	12	64	20	0
5	643	13	37	21	1
6	490	14	35	22	1
7	260	15	24	23	1
8	100	16	7		2208
9	47	17	12		

FLIES	No. of Fish
From records of 18 weeks.	
Black and Yellow	584
Jeannie	96
Tosh	23
Stinchar	61
Other black and yellow flies	35
Total - Black & Yellow	**= 799**
Red Francis	215
Green Francis	38
Black Francis	39
G P / Ally	43
BC Special	23
Red Krafla	8
Total - Shrimp flies	**= 366**

FLIES	No. of Fish
Silver Stoat / Witch	295
Black Stoat	100
Black Pennel	24
Olin Special	26
Other Dark Flies	29
Total - Black	**= 474**
Hairy Mary	148
Munro Killer / Thunder & L.	89
Tadpole	51
Blue Charm	35
Peter Ross	22
Yellow & Red	30
About 40 other flies	194
Total	**= 569**
TOTAL LISTED	**2208**

Hook sizes		
	4	13
	6	70
	8	362
	10	549
	12	426
	14	80
	16	17
		1517

Tubes		
	4"	2
	3"	10
	2"	86
	1 1/2"	77
	1"	155
	3/4"	34
	1/2"	292
	1/4"	35
Total		= 691
TOTAL LISTED		**2208**

Catch by rod weeks 1990

Week	Fish	Week	Fish
1	39	9	140
2	29	10	188
3	6	11	108
4	17	12	126
5	41	13	78
6	52	14	55
7	62		
8	133	**Total**	**1074**

LAXÁ Í DÖLUM

Numbers Old	New	POOL NAME	The Total of our Recorded Catches	Total Season 1990
BEAT 1		**Bottom beat**		
-1	0	Neðra Sjávarfljót	0	0
0	1	Efra Sjávarfljót	2	4
1	2	Matarpollur	29	19
2	3	Papi ⎫	70	37
	4	Brúarstrengur ⎭		5
	A	Doddsnef ⎫		
	A	Útfallið ⎬	88	0
3	5	Neðri Kista ⎭		17
		Efri Kista	58	64
4	6	Krókur	8	9
5	7	Þegjandi ⎫	126	191
	8	Þegjandastrengur ⎭		4
6	9	Þegjandakvörn	44	34
7	10	Mjóhylur	110	26
8	11	Höskuldsstaðastrengur	72	28
		Beat total	**607**	**438**
BEAT 2		**Middle beat**		
9	12	Leiðólfsstaðakvörn	80	61
9½	13	Nesbakki	22	18
10	14	Gíslakvörn	90	101
11	15	Kristnipollur (Home pool)	340	121
12	16	Kotabakki	0	2
13	17	Lambastaðakvörn	34	2
14	18	Svarfhólsgrjót	261	98
15	19	Dísubakki	21	6
15½		Bakki	15	8
16	20	Leirmúli	0	0
		Beat total	**863**	**417**
BEAT 3		**Top beat**		
17	21	Grafarbakki	0	6
18	22	Grafarpollur	5	32
19	23	Drykkjarhylur	38	13
19½	24	Höfðafljót	48	12
20	25	Björnskvörn	100	4
21	26	Dönustaðagrjót	182	65
22	27	Svartfoss	183	34
22½	28	Hamarsfljót	7	18
23	29	Helgabakki	12	1
24	30	Helluhylur	111	29
	'D'	Hyljir ⎫	52	0
25	31	Sólheimafoss ⎭		5
		Beat total	**738**	**219**
			2208	**1074**

The Record Week on the Laxá í Dölum, July 1986

This was to be my ninth week, and was preceded by Billy Dunnavant, and his party. He is a friend of Frank Godchaux, and at his request I had arranged this for him, through Helgi Jakobsson. The season had started on the 20th of June, and by the time that Billy started, 341 fish had already been caught, 299 on worm and 42 on fly. In his week they caught 157 on fly. They had a wonderful week, but the river was now low with a water temperature of 62F. It was Sunday the 20th of July. Reports from most rivers were very bad, but the Dölum, and, its neighbour the Haukadalsá were the exception.

We were to fish six rods, as usual, but we had four teams of husband, and wife, fishing one rod. Dennis Desmond, from Londonderry, and I, were fishing a full rod each. So, in all, we were a party of ten, with three guides. I paired with Charles Godchaux, and his new wife Patsy, she was also new to salmon fishing, with Ragnar, as their guide. The Godchaux family is from Louisiana, and they represent the ultimate of Southern gentlemen. Dennis paired with Bill Horne, and his wife Caroline, from Kenya. They needed no guide, because they knew the river well. The third pair, were Frank Godchaux, and his wife Agnes, guided by Grétar, fishing with their old friends, the Duke and Duchess of Wellington, who are expert fishermen, but were then new to Iceland, and to be guided by Helgi Jakobsson.

After an enthusiastic welcome we unpacked, and got ready as quickly as we could, in a fever of excitement. It seemed that most fish were on the upper beats, and that it was an early year. We fished until 10 pm, and our first evening was encouraging, with seven of us catching 12 salmon, the biggest 13 lbs and one arctic char. I saw four shoals of grilse in tidal water.

At dinner that night we forgot we were tired, and had much laughter. Charlie didn't want to feel intimidated by his brother's important friends, so, after deep thought, he had prepared himself with five tee shirts printed with a cartoon and 'Charlie's Angel', and a sixth with the cartoon and just 'Charlie'. He proposed a fun competition for the week with him, the four wives, and me, versus the other men. We dutifully put on our tee shirts, feeling faintly ridiculous, and had a team photograph! This may have broken some ice, if there was any, and the shirts were not seen again, nor any competition!

Very kindly, the Wellingtons had brought a Stilton cheese, in the Duchess's luggage. I had given it to Gunnar, the cook, with strict instructions, not to put it in the refrigerator, and to do nothing with it until told what to do. In order to impress him with the importance of what I had told him, I said that it might look like a cheese, but that in England it was almost a religion. At the end of dinner Gunnar was asked to cut one inch off the top as a hat, and to bring in the cheese. He first brought in the hat on a plate, but this was returned to the kitchen, and replaced with the cheese. It was carefully explained that although there are diggers and slicers of stilton, we were definitely to be slicers! However Charlie had been telling a story at the other end of the table, and had not listened, so with his spoon he dug deep! The divot was replaced, and we continued slicing the prime stilton.

'Charlie's Angels'.

Next morning was fine and warm, the water temperature rising to 62F. Dennis and Bill did well on the bottom beat. On the top beat Charles was very successful in Svartfoss with Ragnar, and I had adventures and great success in the pots, we caught 20 salmon before lunch, averaging 7 lbs, and another 7 that evening, all this, in spite of the weather being very warm, and bright, with hardly a breath of wind.

That night, Dennis who had had a very good day was teasing me. I had now been wifeless for five years, he said that I needed a replacement. His proposed solution was that I should put an advertisement in 'Trout and Salmon' for a candidate with a minimum of five miles of good salmon fishing, ten years records required! I looked at the Duchess, and suggested that this was rather close to home, as she had brought the Stinchar into their family!

Tuesday morning was again warm and bright. Dennis hit the jackpot again, this time in the middle beat with seven fish all weighing six pounds, for Caroline this must be rather like playing racing demon with an expert! In all we caught 15 that morning. Frank found a fish that was dying with a worm hook from at least nine days before, and put it out of its misery. That afternoon there was a change in the weather. The gentle wind had been downstream, but now it became overcast, and the wind went round to the South West, and became strong. That afternoon we caught 11, but Frank, lost four in the home pool and retired with an injured knee and feelings. The Wellingtons, on the same beat lost 6. A total of nine had been lost in the home pool and only one caught.

Wednesday, and now the weather had really broken. There was a strong upstream wind, and heavy showers. That morning we caught 28 salmon, 25 of them were caught by three of us. On the top beat, Dennis had lost two, and caught his limit of ten. The other rod on that beat was Bill with 8, and Caroline with one. Frank, Agnes and the Duke had nothing from the bottom beat. On the middle beat I caught 8, and lost 7! One of my fish had an appalling wound from a seal, right through to its stomach cavity, it had sea lice, and had run half way up the river in this condition. Two of my fish had a Red Francis in their mouths as well as my fly.

Frank and Agnes Godchaux.

That afternoon the river rose about six to ten inches, and, in parts, became slightly coloured. Frank lost two in the pots, another in the bridge pool on the top beat, and another in Svartfoss, where he also caught one. He also fell over three times! His disaster period had lasted nearly two days, but it had now nearly ended. The Duke fell twice and lost four on the top beat and Agnes lost another. The Duchess caught two with sea lice with white tails in the bridge pool on the top beat. I started at the top of the bottom beat, and fished it all the way down, when I reached the main road, I found Charles landing a fish of 18 lbs in Papi. Dennis and the Hornes had exceeded their limit, I decided not to count my fish with the seal bite, in order to keep within my limit. I found the sea pool to be full of fish. We had caught another seventeen, making 45 for the day.

The Wellingtons and Frank, and Agnes had been having a difficult time and much more than their share of bad luck, but it was now to end. On biological advice we were asked to lift the daily limit on our catch of ten fish. We wanted to keep a limit, Helgi suggested that it should be twenty, but we settled for an agreed limit to kill of 15! This was before the days of Russian salmon fishing being opened to foreigners, and before catch and release for salmon was practiced outside North America. Such a serious discussion as we had been having is now virtually unimaginable.

Thursday, was overcast with light showers, water clear, river falling very slowly, and the river full of fish. This seemed like conditions to dream about. When would we wake up! But we were awake, and caught 37 that morning. The excitement shows in my notes, using the old pool numbers. 'I caught one in the lip above 21, then nothing in the upper pots, I lost one in the head of 21, and caught three under the bridge, and lost one below. I lost one and caught two in the first pot, and then another in the second pot. In 24, I caught two off the ledge, it is holding fish again. Nine fish and three lost in the morning.'

Frank lost one in 14, then Agnes caught one and they alternated, catching eight in all. The Duke and Duchess caught eleven at the very scene of their previous disaster, and didn't lose a single fish. Dennis spent one and a half hours fighting a 21 lb old cock fish in pool 21. It was caught in the mouth, and this was a fight amongst the enormous rocks. To land it here was a triumph after an epic struggle. On the bottom beat Bill reported very many rises but that the fish were coming short.

Thursday afternoon, we again caught 37, exactly the same number as in the morning. The Wellingtons caught 14 in the day. Bill and Caroline made up for their difficult morning by catching 12 on the top beat. Dennis caught 10 and lost nothing, achieving 15. He caught four fish below the gorge at Sólheimafoss, beside a rock that we claimed had a resemblance to his nose. Henceforth we christened that lie 'Dennis's Nose'! It is only good in high water. When I had caught my limit, I stopped fishing, and concentrated on helping Patsy catch her first fish.

Friday, surely this cannot continue! We had a falling river, clear water, and a river full of fish. It turned cold and the air temperature dropped to 40F! The water temperature dropped from 62F to 42F, by the evening. During some of the day the water temperature was 10F warmer than the air. If pundits are to be believed, surely this would stop fish taking fly. However we caught 52 that morning, and lost 15! Charles and I were on the bottom beat again. The fish had been running so fast and so far that this beat was proving the most difficult, but I caught five and Charles three. In Þegjandi the fish were taking far down the pool, and right into the tail.

In the afternoon, we caught another 37. Like so many salmon fishermen, we have endured blank weeks, and been thrilled to catch just one fish. To have a week like this is a chance that is much less than once in a lifetime. So we must enjoy it while we can, the adrenaline was running high. Once again I will let my notes tell my tale! I was on the top beat, and started at Sólheimafoss, fishing at the tail of the gorge from the right bank.

'I caught two from the beach in my first two casts. There was nothing at Dennis's Nose. I then went up to the top of the gorge. The fish were congregated in the bottom half of the gorge, all were visible.' I sat behind a rock, and from there, 'I could see the fish and both my flies. I caught five, and lost 2 more. Then I saw two fish swim up to my flies and I saw a simultaneous double take. The bigger fish took the dropper, and soon I lost my BC Special from the tail. (BC = Benjamin Carpendale, my youngest son, his design, and it might now be called a yellow and black Francis). Every fly was inspected by fish, which rose short coming up about 5 feet to break the surface about a foot behind a fly. That fish would show no more interest until I changed my fly, to something that looked considerably different. At last they stopped inspecting the flies, so I tried a large Green Francis on a sinking line, it looked enormous in the water, but I caught three more fish on it. The biggest fish rose three times but always came short.' In all I caught five in the gorge, plus the two a few yards below. Every fight was difficult; I had to go to the end of the cliff; keeping out of sight, climb down the cliff onto the beach. From there I waded out into midstream, from this position I could attempt to control the fish that I was playing in the gorge above. There are holes deep under the cliffs, but they must be worn smooth. Eventually I would coax the fish downstream and beach it. These fish weighed 5, 7, 12, 8, 17, 7 and 7 lbs, and were a heavy weight to carry across the river back to the car.

There was now only one hour to go, in that hour I lost three in the bridge pool, rose one in the first pot, caught two, and lost one, in the second pot. This gave me my 15, with 8 more that I had lost. Over dinner with stilton, we re-fought our battles, and calculated that in the day we had caught 89 salmon, lost 31, and had 120 more 'interviews' with fish! We had one and a half days left of the week. 'and so to bed!'

Saturday morning was still as cold, but the water temperature was now also low, so conditions should in theory be better! We caught 24 in the morning. In the home pool, I lost four in succession, on a tiny Black and Yellow Tube Fly, with a size 18 treble. Having had such an incredible few days, I may have been a little cavalier in my treatment of the fish, but the hooks were so fine, that if only one was attached, it tended to bend straight. I changed to a stronger hook, and then caught four in that pool, and two elsewhere, all of 7, or 8 pounds, four on the tube fly and two on a single hooked Jeannie size 12. Once again the bottom beat was not fishing so well.

In the afternoon, I was on the bottom beat, and as luck would have it, more fish had come in. These were smaller grilse. It was my turn to start at the bottom and the tide was very low. In what we still called the lower sea pool, but is actually, Efra (= Upper) Sjávarfljót, there were a number of fish milling around. I caught two of them, and the only ones that I ever caught so far down towards the sea. Working upstream, I then caught one, and lost two, in Matarpollur, and another in Papi. The top half of the beat was as slow as before, and Charles only caught one.

However upstream the fishing was still exceptional. Unfortunately a French motor caravan arrived at the farm-bridge on the top beat. It was parked above the Bridge Pool, French students dismounted, and wandered onto the bridge, peering into the river, looking at the salmon stacked below, in what is a short, and sensitive pool. The Duke and Duchess, who had only just arrived, were starting to fish, looking forward to their last assault on the pool. The fish were now disturbed, so they quietly withdrew to fish elsewhere. After two hours, they returned. The motor caravan was still above the pool, but all seemed at peace. They started to fish with expectations renewed. The students, who had been enjoying their evening meal, now needed to clean up. They climbed down the rocks to the head of the run, and proceeded to wash themselves and their dishes. Again, discretely the Wellingtons left without a word, but this time they went back to the lodge.

That evening before dinner we had a party for the guides and staff; we had much to celebrate. We had worked hard all week, fishing long hours, and this was the first time that any of us changed for dinner out of our fishing clothes. Spirits were high after such an incredible week. Caroline half filled a J&B bottle with water, it was not until a second glass that Charles noticed that there was no Whisky in his ice! When the Duchess appeared, newly changed, Agnes, who was an old friend, was heard to say 'you clean up real good!' In a short speech thanking the Icelanders, I pointed out that our catch that week was more than 1% of the entire Icelandic rod catch of the previous year!

The Duke and Duchess of Wellington with Agnes Godchaux.

The record party fishing 6 rods July 1986.

Next morning, our last, Dennis and I were on the top beat, and as is customary our fishing stopped at noon. We left the lodge at our usual time, a little after 8.00, not rushing to get on the river when fishing was allowed to start at 7.00. It was the turn of Dennis to start at the foss, and for me to start near the Bridge. As I arrived there, I saw the dreaded motor caravan with its curtains tightly closed. I parked beside it but saw no sign of movement. So I started to fish, and to think how I should handle the student problem! Very soon I was into my first fish, which I landed. I found that I had run out of polythene tubing for the fish, so laid it on a rock, and continued fishing.

Shortly after that, I felt that I was being watched, and saw a brightly dressed young man, I reeled in, climbed up to him and said 'Good morning are you French?' He admitted that he was. So I asked 'Do you speak English?' He said 'A little!' So I told him, speaking slowly, 'Yesterday you revenged Napoleon!' This certainly gained his attention, but he looked a little surprised and said 'Comment? Je ne comprend pas!' Slowly I explained that the night before, from the top of the bridge, they had looked down at the river, and seen salmon and two fishermen, to which he agreed. I then said that, later they had washed up in the river, pointing to the top of the pool. Yes, he again agreed, looking perhaps, more than a little mystified. I explained that they had twice disturbed the salmon in the pool, and the fishermen had gone home. He looked apologetic. I started on a new tack, 'Napoleon was defeated at Waterloo by the Duke of Wellington!' Yes he said rather dubiously, as if there existed a theory, that this might be the case! Then I said 'Yesterday the elderly couple that had been trying to fish were the Duke and Duchess of Wellington, and you drove them off the river!!!' He was highly amused, returned to the caravan to tell the others. After that I had no trouble, they kept well away from the river, and even offered me coffee.

I caught two more as they watched, and then lost another two, one from the tail of the pool. We waved goodbye to each other, and I went down to the first pot, where I rose one fish and lost another, in the next pot I lost two more and landed one. At 11.55 I caught one in Helluhylur off the ledge, and for the last minute I tried the run below, where I had seen fish, but never caught anything. To my joy I found that Charles had tried this run and had caught one earlier that morning.

After the experience of the night before the Duke and Duchess had fished the middle beat before they had to leave, early, to catch a flight that day. They caught six fresh fish with sea lice with white tails still attached, from three pools on the middle beat, before leaving. Frank had also done well on that beat. Down on the bottom beat Dennis and the Hornes had also ended the week on a good note with six fish up to 15 lbs, plus a normal quota of losses. This amounted to 24 fish in little more than three hours between us.

So ended this incredible week. Dennis had caught 82, and lost 22 in the week. The lowest catch by a rod team was 39, plus 27 lost. Our total catch was 345, plus 146 lost, the total number of fish played was 511. The total weight of our catch was 2298 lbs, average weight 6.6 lbs. We caught them from 23 pools on 31 different flies. The catch from the top beat was 145, from the middle 135, and from the bottom 65. Do remember that this was not greed, we were fishing according to biological advice as to what was good for the river.

We were entitled to keep a total of 90 fish, the rest were left in the freezer for the farmers. This made them extremely happy, and we had done much to increase the value of their river, for which we paid dearly in subsequent years! Also we left them 255 salmon for their own consumption!!

When we got back to Reykjavík we went to Hardy's agent to restock after the depredations of the week. Paul O'Keefe, told us what a difficult year it was, and how depressing were the reports coming back from the rivers. He then asked us how we had got on, he almost seemed to say, how had we suffered! When we told him his jaw nearly fell off!

Fáskrúð

The Laxá í Dölum Veiðifélag bought the one farm that owned the Fáskrúð, and wished to operate this using the Laxá í Dölum lodge, 1988 would be the first season. As we wanted exclusive use of this lodge for our party we agreed somewhat reluctantly to include this river in our contract only as an experiment. It is licenced as a three rod river. A fourth guide was promised who would know the Fáskrúð, and we would fish it with two rods.

The mouth of the Fáskrúð is a few miles North of Búðardalur, and not more than 30 minutes drive from the Laxá í Dölum lodge. It is a very attractive little river with 25 named, and numbered pools. It is suitable for fly-fishing, and access is good. It is a spate river and a rather late river. The highest point that salmon can reach is Katlafoss, and below this the only significant burn entering the river is a small one that enters the river just above pool 8, Hellufljót. We learned that the river had been stocked for the previous three or four years by putting 10,000 fry into three trout lochs up that burn.

We rented it for three weeks, the first week was to be fished by Billy Dunavant and his party. Their wives spent a little time at the lodge before going on to London in Billy's plane. As it had to return to Iceland to take the husbands to join their wives, it would be returning empty. With great generosity we were offered the free use of it. As the plane was a new Gulfstream, this was an excitement for all of those of us that were coming from England. It flew faster than the commercial jet, and landed us at the city airport, in high spirits, having enjoyed on board the most delicious white wine that I can ever remember; it was Californian.

We were eight fishermen fishing as four pairs, for two weeks, with most of the team changing at half time. Each pair fished Fáskrúð for one full day, and then six half days were fished in the rotation. Fishing a full day was the most satisfactory arrangement, and the very old self-catering hut on the Fáskrúð was used for a picnic and siesta. This was most welcome because the weather was cold, with water and air temperature about 45F much of the time.

The farmers had forgotten to arrange for seals to be shot, and now the legal season for shooting was nearly over. There were 16 seals visible on the bar at the mouth of the river. At low tide access to the river was not good, so altogether the fresh fish were very vulnerable. They not only intercepted the salmon as they entered the river, but even followed them up river as far as pool 8. This pool proved to be the main holding pool, possibly because of stocked parr returning after surviving the trout in the lakes, and the perils of the sea. A little stream ran from the lakes, entering the river just above this pool.

The special guide changed after the first week, Jón, and Björssi were a joy to have with us, and knew the river well. One guide that I have not named was a commercial fisherman, and he loved his brown vodka. We had not heard before of brown vodka, and it was sometime before its secret was divulged. It seems that it was brought into the country clandestinely in the mast of a fishing vessel. It was rust that caused the colour!

In our two weeks two rods caught 29 salmon from the Fáskrúð, from seven pools, numbered 4, 6, 8, 21, 26, 30, and 35. During the same time six rods caught 272 from the Laxá í Dölum. I had been let down for two rod weeks that I had to absorb myself. I invited family and friends to fill the gap, it was a joy to have them, but it did take me well over my fishing budget for the year, and I was not best pleased. I could not allow this to happen again.

If one divides the annual average catch on both rivers by the number of rods, the Fáskrúð does not show up badly in the comparison. However, as it is a later river, it is not comparable, until perhaps mid July. The farmers were hoping to sell the Fáskrúð at the same price as the Dölum, which is one of the prime rivers of the country. The Fáskrúð is a lovely river, and I would be happy to fish it later in the season, on a self-catering basis, and at a reasonable price. It would be fun for a family party with young. The old self-catering hut was very primitive, but a new self-catering lodge may have been built. I would wish to hear that an enhancement plan is in operation.

Culling seals, and stocking the river above the foss, possibly by transporting a few salmon above the foss to spawn, would improve the river considerably, and at minimal cost.

As it was, my friends had two wonderful weeks on the Laxá í Dölum and against that competition, they did not want to take the Fáskrúð again, unless it was comparable. Also we found six rods to be the ideal number, and we were reluctant to change. Another factor was that it is much more difficult to collect the larger party. The cost of being left with a spare rod was unacceptably high and very, very, occasionally someone let me down, leaving me to pay the farmers. This was not acceptable and they did not come again.

Chapter Seven
The North-West Fjords

It was not until 1999 that I was able to visit this part of Iceland, thanks to Árni Baldurson. Our party consisted of three 'White Knights' and one son and a nephew. On arrival in Reykjavík we were told that our river was suffering from a prolonged drought, with no rain for eight weeks and a shortage of fish in the river. We were asked if we would like an adventure. Of course, our answer was that we would!

On the map, the North-West fjords look dramatically beautiful and remote. The reality lives up to the anticipation. After a 30 minute flight we began our descent to Ísafjörður, flying over mountains and fjords, with a final tight circle within a mountain basin, to land beside the Fjord. Ísafjörður is an attractive little port, threatened by avalanches from the surrounding mountains. We were met by Steingrímur, ('Steini'), who was to be our guide. After meeting his family, having lunch in his house, and shopping, we were taken to a tiny fishing port of Bolungarvík, where we boarded a fishing boat. We were taken almost due North for 35 km to a bay called Fljótavík, where we transferred into an inflatable, and were landed on the beach, to be collected two days later. This place is within 2 km of the most extreme North-West tip of Iceland and is part of a large area that is no longer permanently inhabited. There was a refuge hut and three summer-houses. We carried everything up to our 'A frame' house, and settled in.

This was the last place that a polar bear was seen in Iceland. It landed from an ice flow, in 1975. Some people were in the refuge hut, and the bear was hungry, and investigating their packs, and rifle which were outside. Two children were expected at any moment. They were grandchildren of the last resident farmer. The bear tried to get into the hut. A man got out of the other side of the hut, got his rifle, and shot the bear! This was sad but necessary.

Reiðá

Below us was a narrow outflow from a tidal lake. Arctic char came in and out on the tide. At its head is a small river, called Reiðá, which runs down from the mountains, and into the lake. The char run up this, and there can be good fishing both in this river and at its mouth in the lake. It is about 10 km walk to this river. There were five of us, we went there next day with Steini, and caught, about 100 char of between one and two pounds, keeping just enough for our supper.

The weather was idylic, the scenery wild and beautiful, with a mass of wild flowers and birds that had no fear of man. Their enemy was the arctic foxes that were numerous, and also fearless of man. This is a nature reserve and all wildlife, other than the fish, are protected. Looking like a rocky outcrop on a hilltop was the remains of a Radar station that used to keep a watch on the Denmark Channel during the cold war. It was superseded by satellite observation soon after completion.

There had been a total eclipse of the sun in mainland Europe, while we had been the most North-Westerly people in Europe. All too soon the time came for us to leave, and we sat above the beach in the hope of 'rescue'. The boat did come but two hours late. In Ísafjörður we shopped for supplies, hired a second car, and drove to our river.

Laugardalsá and Langadalsá

There are twelve rivers in the North-West fjords listed in the statistics of 100 salmon rivers. These account for only 2% of the rod catch of salmon. Only two rivers are of significance. The Laugardalsá has a ladder close to the sea, and flows through a gorge. The average annual catch is about 348, there is self-catering accommodation, but we were advised that much of this river is barely suitable for fly-fishing. However this may prove to be interesting and challenging fly-fishing.

Laugardalsá.

Our destination was the Langadalsá. This was only 40 km as the crow flies, but about 180 km by road, to the mouth of our river. The road was very good, but it followed the shoreline of almost every side Fjord.

The self-catering lodge was clean and comfortable, with a big living room, a well equipped kitchen, four small twin bunk cabins, good washing facilities, and an outside store for deep freezers, cleaning fish etc.

There were five of us sharing three rods. The river flows North, and is divided into three beats of about 5 km each, with a total of 50 named pools. There is no gorge or foss, and if only it had not been so droughted, the river would have been inviting to fish. We met people who had fished it at the same time the year before, and they were most positive. Steini was a joy to have with us, and most encouraging. The two young men of our party, William Savage and Daniel Monro caught their first salmon, so our main object was achieved. There was a shortage of grilse this year. We only caught five salmon, the biggest 13 lbs, and only one was a grilse. In Iceland a first salmon is called a 'Mariu Lax', (Hail Mary salmon!).

We also had been given fishing on the Bjarnarfjarðará, this was about 50 km further, flowing East to the other coast, a little North of Hólmavík. This is reputed to be one of the very best Arctic Char rivers of Iceland for relatively big char. Certainly the river had some wonderful pools, and a good flow of water from springs, and melting snow. The upper section, known as Góðdalsá, was not included in our water, and it was even more beautiful. There had been a farm in this upper valley, but seven people were killed in an avalanche, and it was abandoned. An old man who is still living, and is now over 90, remembers picking berries in this valley. He saw what he took to be a cow, on the hillside above him, where no cow should have been. He told his father, who found no cow to be missing, so he went out to investigate, and found a polar bear, which he shot. This must have been in about 1920. I believe that only three bears, at the most have landed in Iceland in the twentieth century.

Chapter Eight
The Rivers of the North

There are 25 rivers listed in the national statistics for the North Coast region, and, on average, they account for 24.1% of the total rod catch of Salmon. Of these rivers 7 are of real significance. My personal experience in this area is very limited. From time to time, these Northern rivers used to suffer from the ocean temperatures being too cold, and there were big fluctuations in the catches. Now these rivers should benefit from global warming, and may have a very good period.

Continuing round the coast, clockwise:-

Hrútafjarðará

This river, together with its tributary Síká, (meaning boggy), was rented for many seasons by General Stewart, and it figures largely in his book, 'The Rivers of Iceland'. The present tenants are enforcing a rule of Fly-fishing only. Excluding the Siká, there is 14 km of fishable water, and this river is rated as a three rod river. In recent years the average catch has been 179 Salmon.

General Stewart, certainly found this to be an interesting river to fish. And it was dearly loved by him.

Miðfjarðará, with its tributaries Vesturá, Núpsá, and Austurá

This is a cyclical river that had recently shown an upward tendency, but surprisingly the year 2000 was most disappointing and 2001 was even worse. Catches in the last four years have declined from 1820 to 434. This is an exceptionally fine river, and I have no doubt that it will bounce back, if it is fished by experienced fishermen.

This is an astonishing river system, which I have greatly enjoyed; it has an almost infinite variety of pools. From the Road bridge down, the river is subject to a separate let for Sea Trout.

There is over 100 km of fishable water restricted to 12 rods, fishing five beats. From the Bridge over the main road, to the junction with the Vesturá is about 15 km, with 35 named pools. Then there is another 8 km to the place where the Austurá, and the Núpsá join to form the Miðfjarðará, this section has a further 18 named pools.

The Austurá flows through a deep gorge for about 14 km, from the junction with the Núpsá, to Kambsfoss. This foss was impassable to Salmon, but now there is a ladder. There are 46 named pools. This is a strenuous beat to fish, but the hard work is getting in and out of the gorge. The stretch immediately below the foss was particularly exciting to fish, with many Salmon visible to the fisherman. I have not been there since the ladder has been installed, and I don´t know the effect, on the fishing in the gorge. It has, undoubtedly, opened up about 10 km more river to fish, another 33 pools, for the Salmon to spawn, and the parr to live, before an impassable foss is reached.

Miðfjarðará - The Austurá.

The Núpsá has much the smallest flow of the three tributaries, but it has at least 20 km of stream to fish with 34 named pools, many of these are very small. With a good guide, and the right conditions, this little river can be fun to fish, but compared with the rest of this river system it is very lightly fished. The fishermen are spoiled for choice! When I have been there, there was a fish counter, and in the low water conditions very few fish were going up the Núpsá. It was obvious that it was more rewarding to concentrate elsewhere at that particular time.

The Vesturá, as the name suggests, is the western tributary. At first there is a stretch with of a shallow gorge, and then it flows through open country. The road, becomes a track, and then eventually peters out. There are 47 named pools over a distance of 27 km, before an impassable Foss is reached.

With so much river to fish, good guides are needed, and experience is at a premium.

Altogether the watershed is very large. The river flows from an area of heath, bog, and lakes. This adjoins the upper watersheds of Norðurá, and Kjarrá. The lakes in this whole area are famous for their Brown Trout.

The lodge has ten double bedrooms, is comfortable, and has an excellent sauna. It is run, and is largely staffed by the farmers that own it. For many years this river has been very well managed, and they have had an enhancement programme.

Einar Sigfusson and Anna with a fresh fish.

Myself on the Miðfjarðará with a beautiful salmon.

In recent years the average catch has been over 1000, and the best year of the 20th century was 1977, with 2581 Salmon caught, and the catch for the next two years was also over 2000. There was once a problem as a result of a large deposit of volcanic ash. The Miðfjarðará, usually has a run of big, and well shaped fish in the early part of the season.

Víðidalsá

This river has a great reputation. The name means the wide valley river. It has about 50 km of fishable water, with over 100 named pools, and is fished by eight rods. The average catch over the last 25 years has been 1276, virtually the same as that of its neighbour, the Miðfjarðará, which is fished by 2/4 more rods than Víðidalsá. It has only one minor tributary, the Fitjá, the river is, a decent sized river that normally has a good flow. The last two years 2000/2001 have been disappointing.

The lodge has recently been improved, and it has 10 double rooms, with a good sized dining room, sitting room, and the 'obligatory' sauna.

Sadly I have no personal experience of fishing this outstanding river, or the next three rivers. This is a big hole in my experience.

Vatnsdalsá

This is the river that was rented for many years by John Ashley-Cooper. The name means the lake valley river. It flows into a big tidal lagoon, which it shares with the Laxá á Ásum. By all accounts it is an exceptionally good river, but I do not have personal experience of it. The 28 year average catch to 2000 is 885, with the best year in 1986 of 1582. The worst year was 2000 with a catch of only 323. Many of the rivers in this area have had a bad patch, but not all. 2001 showed a marked improvement to 520. For the last four years their river has been totally catch and release from which it should benefit greatly.

Laxá á Ásum (see also page 2)

This little river flows out of two lakes, down to the same big tidal lake into which the Vatnsdalsá also flows. This river is only fished by two rods, and is the most expensive fishing in Iceland. The reason for this is that over the last 28 years, the average catch in a 90 day season, has been 1137, this equals an average daily catch per rod of 6.5 fish. In the last six years this average has declined to 3.7 fish. The run is predominately of small grilse, but John Ashley-Cooper records an exceptional fish of 18 lbs. One of the lakes has a dam, enabling an artificial spate to be created, in case of need.

One point of interest is that the name is 'á Ásum', not 'í Ásum', this means 'at', not 'in' the district of Ásum.

This river appeals greatly to some, but not to all. A very high proportion of the catch is taken from one long pool, Langhylur. This is a prime spawning area, and the river may be suffering from too heavy fishing.

The Svartá.

From a photograph by Håkon Steulund.

Blanda, and Svartá

Bland means whitish, and Svart means Black. The Svartá joins the Blanda 30 km from the sea.

There are 27 km of fishable water on the Blanda, the water is glacial, but is below the dam, which is used to power a turbine to generate electricity. Four rods fish below the dam, and four more fish below the ladder. This river, and its tributary, the Svartá, are fished from self-catering lodges. The Svartá has 30 km of fishable clear water. The Blanda is much more productive than the Svartá. The 28-year record year for the Blanda was 2363 fish, whereas the same for the Svartá was 619 fish. The 28-year averages are 1008, and 291, respectively, which shows a big difference, between these two rivers. They flow out of high mountains, and the temperature variations may well have a big influence on these catch records.

The Blanda is now expected to flow almost clear from early June to about the 10th of August. The river is being fished by four rods on the lower river in the early part of the season, and a further four rods above the ladder as the fish spread upstream. This river is greatly improved and is the earliest river in the North. It is a big river with an even greater average annual flow than the Laxá í Aðaldal.

The Blanda is not fished above the Svartá junction. This junction is fished by the Svartá rods where many fish are caught.

Fljótaá, Fnjóská and Skjálfandafljót are the next three rivers, which are not of significance to foreign fishermen, so I will pass over them rapidly.

Fljótaá is only fishable for 7 km, it is fished by 4 rods, and the average catch in the last 5 years is 128 salmon. The fishermen stay in a farmhouse.

Fnjóská is a relatively big river, with an average flow of 37 cubic metres per second, and is fishable for 40 km. It is fished by 6 rods from a self-catering lodge. The average catch in recent years has only been 155 fish, as compared with the 28 year average of 236. An Englishman, a Mr. Fortescue rented this river in the 1950s; he tried to improve it, but he was not successful. It is a decent sized river but the water is very cold, flowing out of high mountains. It is good for char.

Skálfandafljót, is fishable for 28 km, and is fished by 6 rods, from a self-catering lodge. There is still netting on this river, which is glacial. In the best year the catch was 907. The 28 year average is 372 salmon.

Laxá í Aðaldal (see also page 3)

This is the famous 'Big Laxá', which flows out of Lake Mývatn. The average annual flow is 36 cubic metres per second, but because the river is spring fed, and from such a large lake, the flow is relatively constant. This is a big, powerful river, and of the Icelandic salmon rivers, only the Sog in the South has a bigger flow. Surprisingly, the Laxá í Aðaldal is not controlled by a Veiðifélag. Even the names of this river are confusing! Its common name in English, is 'The Big Laxá', translated into Icelandic this becomes 'Stóra Laxá', this is the name of a salmon river in South Iceland. It is also called **'Laxá í Þingeyjarsýslu'**, which refers to the name of the district. Another familiar name is **Laxamýri**, which is the name of the lodge, and the bottom beat. This is the home of an Icelandic club that celebrated 60 years in 2000, and a total catch in its existence of over 66,000 salmon! It fishes ten rods on the river, controlling the lowest and upper salmon water. In between is **Árnes**. This has been controlled for many years by 'Frontiers', the American Company of sporting agents, and is a famous fishery for six rods which has a strong following. Both Laxamýri, and Árnes have excellent lodges. Part of this river is called the Laxá í Laxárdal, and the upper reaches are called the Laxá í Mývatnssveit.

In Chapter One I have written about Lake Mývatn, and the trout fishing on the river below the lake. This section ends at a dam that provides water for turbines to generate electricity. Here there is a salmon ladder that salmon have never found to be attractive. Below this is a wide stretch with islands that is not favourable for salmon to spawn. Some salmon are caught in this part of the river, but it is considered to be primarily trout fishing. There are four very simple small self-catering lodges. Below this is the salmon fishing that has made this river so famous.

The Salmon fishing is only 25 km, and is licenced for 20 salmon fishermen and further rods that fish for trout, and catch an occasional salmon. These are accommodated in 6 self-catering lodges, and 2 lodges with full board. There are two tributaries that can provide good sport. These are the **Reykjadalsá**, which is fished by four rods from a self-catering lodge, and the **Mýrarkvísl**, which is fished by three rods from a self-catering lodge. The 25 year averages are respectively 309, and 234.

In recent years the average catch of the Laxá í Aðaldal has been 1171 salmon for the entire river, which is down from the 27 year average, of 1812. In its best year 3063 salmon were caught.

This river is very fertile, so there is plenty of food for parr. Unfortunately the other side of the coin is that the river suffers from blanket weed for most of the season, and is occasionally subject to an algae bloom, which does not last long. At times the blanket weed catches on the fly almost every cast, and gets caught on the line while playing a fish. Nevertheless it is undoubtedly an extremely good river. So many Icelanders who know this river well consider it to be the best salmon river in Iceland. It is extremely interesting to fish, and there is much to learn. Some parts are fished from opposite banks by rods fishing different beats, and in some places it is necessary to fish from a boat.

A wonderful, and famous book was written about the Laxá í Aðaldal by Jakob Hafstein, which was published in Icelandic, in 1965. There is one chapter in English. It was his son who coached my three sons on the Fróðá in that same year for three days, and got them to catch their first eight salmon.

This is an important world class river.

Chapter Nine
The Rivers of the North East

Roads and internal flights are now so good that the North East and East are no longer regarded as being remote. The cost of salmon fishing in this part of Iceland used to be modest, compared with other parts, but the cost has now caught up with the rest of the country, according to the merits of the various rivers. This area is close to the limit for salmon habitat, and it is sensitive to the effects of annual variations in ocean currents. The sea temperature, at the time that smolt go to sea, and also the temperature after eggs hatch, are critical. 1981 to 1984 was a disastrous period for all these rivers from Deildará to Hofsá. The recovery was rapid after four years of virtual washout. This has brought down all the average catches. The catches in the worst of these years was reduced to about $1/8$ of the average of the rivers affected. There was a similar period that was a disaster in the late sixties. This is now history, and perhaps with global warming the chance of another similar disaster is greatly diminished. The average annual catch in this region is only 3.3% of the total rod catch.

This part of the country has always had a very great appeal to me, and I particularly look forward to fishing these rivers. The season starts later than in the South West, and it can suddenly turn cold in September, but in the high summer it is often warmer, and the weather is usually very different to that which is current in the West.

To get there, options include flying to Húsavik, or to Egilsstaðir, and hiring a car there, or flying to Þórshöfn, but there one must be met, as there is no facility to hire a car. The most western river in this region is Deildará, close to the little fishing village of Raufarhöfn.

Deildará

This river is fished with three rods, and 100 yards from the river's mouth there is a comfortable self-catering lodge. Inga, the farmer's daughter-in-law was most helpful and friendly. I had taken the river for a week, in order to introduce to fishing my new wife Joanna, and her two children, Edward and Angela, who were still of school age. In order to teach and inspire them we were joined by my son Ben, and Siggi Gunnarsson, the son of the chef at Laxá í Dölum. The plan was to fish as three couples, changing partners, also to ride. Siggi enjoyed riding and worm fishing. With us he would learn to fish with a fly, help with the horses, and we would all enjoy his company. This was an ideal place for such a family fishing holiday, the only problem was that we arrived in the middle of a drought, so we didn't see the river at its best. The water had been 22C or 72F. The self-catering worked well but it was difficult to persuade Joanna to let us share the chores. In Raufarhöfn, as the fishing boats returned, we tried to buy fish; the fishermen refused to accept payment, but we were told to take our pick from the catch.

My wife Joanna and my son Ben and her daughter Angela Temple.

The river flows out of a small lake, and it is only 7 km from there to the sea. There are about 27 pools, 19 are named, of these, 10 are the best. The run had been improved with an enhancement programme. In an average year it produces 165 salmon, and 391 has been its best. The season is from the 20th of June, until the 13th of September, The best period is usually from mid July to Mid August, over a 12 year period the catch has averaged 40% salmon, and 60% grilse,

The river runs through relatively flat land, many of the pools are like ponds with a run in, and a run out. These ponds provide refuges for the fish, have pond weed, and some have reeded edges. The best pools, in average order of catch are, 10, 5, 16, 17, 6, 13, 14 and 3.

Edward caught his first two salmon, on his own. Siggi, a worm fisherman caught his first salmon on fly, and Angela, who hooked fish and lost them, was given fish to play, and landed them. One fish that I hooked in pool 6 proved to be very strong and fresh. It jumped repeatedly, disturbing other fish, which scattered, jumping. I was certain that it was foul hooked, but it wasn't. It went round a rock downstream, then up to the very top round several rocks, well out on the backing. There was a big bay that was necessary to go round, to get to the top where Ben and I found my tired fish anchored to a rock, we eventually beached it on the far bank. It was 12 pounds, with sea lice. It was caught on a tiny tube fly with a size 14 treble. I call the fly a Toby, named after my grandson, and tied with a wisp of his red hair!

The week was coming to an end, and Angela had not yet caught a salmon. In the North East the drought continued, whereas on the Dölum it had broken, and

Edward Temple with his first salmon.

34 fish were caught in the morning. During the week we caught 11 salmon, and lost 12, with the six of us fishing three rods. We also caught 15 char, 3 brown trout and 1 sea trout.

But before the week finished, Ben was determined that Angela would catch the Salmon that she so greatly deserved. I quote from my fishing diary:-
'The young went out at 7.30 after changing rods and reels. They started at pool 10 Edward cast near the rock at the top of the lie, and saw a fish rise. He cast again, and saw two fish come, one to each fly. He hooked the smaller fish on the tail fly.

Deildará - Pool 6.

They played it upstream so as not to disturb the pool, and Ben netted it. Ben and Angela left Edward and Siggi there, and went down to pool 6, arriving there at 10.10.'

'Wading out a long way, to a depth of only 18 inches, Ben put Angela in position. The wind was behind her and there was a good ripple on the pool. Angela cast to the far bank at a gap in the reeds that had been formed by water fowl. This was nine feet above the lie formed by a rock. She pulled in the line a little and paused to talk, letting her fly sink. She brought it in slowly and cast again; a fish took her fly very gently, then it went wild, and after 3 minutes she lost the fish with both flies. They retied the cast, with only one fly, and cast again, with much to talk about. Again her fly was taken quietly, She played this fish gently, trying to tire it in clear water away from the lie, but it took control, and went off upstream round a rock. Giving slack line it reappeared below them going between two more rocks, and came off. They started again, with 20 lb nylon, and again were broken after 10 minutes.'

'Almost in despair they tried again and almost at once, again in exactly the same place, doing the same thing, she hooked her fourth. It jumped three times while still in the lie, and shot off upstream with Angela hanging on. After 30 yards the hook seemed to come out, but when they examined the line they found that the leader and the spliced loop were lost, also stripping three inches of the "Monocore" line. This is translucent, and was originally called a slime line. This doesn't cast a shadow on the bottom of the river, so it tends not to frighten the fish, particularly in low water and clear conditions, but at that time it couldn't be made as a floating line.'

Angela had lost two fish the day before and had now lost four more, and had never caught a salmon. There had not been a single grilse amongst them. They then tried a brown Akroyd size 6, going for a bigger fly. Once again Angela hooked another. It ran to the refuge hole in dead water near the head of the pool, went round a rock, and after 3 minutes, another fish was lost. This fly is named after Charles H. Akroyd from Brora, Scotland who was the pioneer of British fishing for salmon in Iceland first coming in 1877. He arrived by sea at Húsavík, and made his way to Laxamýri where he fished, coming back to fish for several years. He wrote a book about salmon fishing in Iceland called 'A Veteran Sportsman's Diary' published in 1926.

The day before I had seen bubbles coming from the bottom in the 'refuge' hole, where salmon went in this pool when disturbed. I climbed onto a rock and sat on the bottom two big salmon lying, as if asleep, half covered by soft mud, with bubbles occasionally coming from their gills. I stroked one with my rod point, then tilted it to 20 degrees before it woke up they took fright!

Ben and Angela re-equipped, making doubly certain of everything, waded out to the same spot, cast to the same gap in the reeds. The chatter must have been considerable! Then very quietly another fish took hold, it jumped twice and then ran downstream, then back straight at Angela and Ben. The soft bottom caused the water to become very cloudy; it milled about for 15 minutes before taking off upstream. Angela stayed where she was, and Ben gave chase, untangling the line from rocks two or three times before the fish reached the refuge. They thought that it was lost in weed, but it moved out together with five other big fish!! It then hid under a rock away from the refuge; Ben waded in deep and did more disentangling from amongst the rocks. By now Angela was at the refuge with the net, and the fish returned there. The fish was tired, and Angela netted it most skilfully. The fish was a fresh 11 pounder with a fly of mine in its mouth, and her Jeannie size 8 hooked into the base of the pectoral fin on the far side.

Angela with her fish.

After celebrating, we discussed what had happened, and came up with an alternative to the fashionable Pheromone theory as to why women attract so many fish. Could it be that Angela, a fizzy young girl, was excited to be looked after so attentively by her new and older step-brother, and she talked a lot? While talking, her fly may have sunk to the bottom in the slow current, at the precise place where a pod of 10, to 15, pound salmon were lying side by side? In total innocence the fish may all have been hooked while sleeping. Whatever the explanation, five were lost, and one was caught by Angela in the space of 2 $^1/_2$ hours, 6 fish, out of the 23, that the six of us hooked in seven days!!

There can be no doubt that the Deildará is an interesting river, which we greatly enjoyed, in spite of being droughted.

Ormarsá

The mouth of the Ormarsá is within 3 km of the mouth of the Deildará. This river has a bigger flow, and about 20 km is fishable. It is also a self-catering river and is fished by 4 rods. It has benefited from an enhancement programme. The average catch over 28 years has been 181 salmon, and the best year was 366 fish caught.

For some years Jim Edwards fished several of the North Eastern rivers, he has a particularly soft spot for the Ormarsá, but I haven't fished it. I hope that I will be able to do so one day. Access from a road is good. To the West of the river is an old lava flow.

Svalbarðsá

This is a pleasant river for fly-fishing, with about 15 km of fishable water, and 34 named pools. It is fished by three rods from a self-catering lodge. If help is wanted, it is often possible to come to an arrangement with the wife of one of the farmers.

The average catch over 28 years is 164, and the record catch was 396 in 1993. In that year fish were caught in 28 pools. Over three years for which I have statistics the percentages of grilse were 44%, 89%, and 52.5%. In 1994 seven fish were caught of over 20 lbs, the biggest being 24 lbs. The average weight varying from 5.74 lbs to 10.4 lbs. August is likely to be the best month. The best pools are usually:-

Svalbarðsselhylur

This is a long and productive holding pool on the middle beat where fish usually show. It is in a mini canyon that opens out at the bottom of the pool.

Stórifoss

Svarlbadsá - Stórifoss, I beached my fish under the dark cliff.

This is the furthest point that a fish can reach. To reach this pool involves a walk for almost the whole length of the beat, starting just below Rauður, pool 16, and walking to pool number 1. The foss is high, and the pool turns at 90 degrees to the right. One day I was fishing from the edge of the river inside the corner on the left bank, I played a salmon, and I beached it with a high cliff close behind me, this over-stressed my rod which exploded into six pieces. This proved that it was well designed, because there was not one weak place that would snap before the whole rod collapsed!

Svarlbadsá - My rod!

Laxahylur

This is pool 10, on the top beat, and is about 30 minutes walk from the end of the track. From top to bottom I find this a pleasant pool to fish.

Of the four best pools over a five-year period, three were on the top beat.

Whether fish are caught on flies, worms, or spinners depends on who may be fishing. Usually, on this river more fish are caught on a worm, but this doesn't detract from it being a charming fly-fishing river. There was one period when it was over advertised, and made to sound as if it was one of the prime rivers of Iceland; this it is not. When I have fished it, I have found the bottom beat to be disappointing, although I fish there with great conviction. I am certain that in suitable conditions it must be excellent. In the middle beat I have had little success except in Svarlbarðsselhylur. Before doing an analysis of the statistics, I was always drawn to the top beat, being ready to do the walk twice a day, if given the opportunity.

I feel that in this river, as in the Laxá í Dölum, the fish have no refuge, and are vulnerable to over fishing. This river has a modest run of salmon, and I believe that it would benefit from catch and release, and from some seeding of the river above the foss with parr.

Sandá

The Sandá is operated by a private club. I have not yet been lucky enough to fish this river, which I have been told is arguably the most enjoyable of all the North East Rivers. It is fished by four rods from a self-catering lodge; the fishermen are lucky to be there. The average river flow is double Vatnsdalsá, and over $1/3$ of Laxá í Aðaldal. This is a lot of water for a three rod river. The average of the last five

Hafralónsá.

From a photograph taken by Árni Baldursson.

years to 2000 is 152, and for the last 28 years is 233, the 1993 catch was 434, and the record 474 in 1977. At the height of the disaster period of 1981 to 1984 the catch dropped to 35!

Hölkná

This is fished as a three rod river. By repute it is a decent river but not up to the standard of its neighbours Sandá, and Hafralónsá, or others. The average catch over 28 years is only 86, and the record year 219 in 1977.

The road then crosses a very little Laxá, which would not be seen if it were not for its name. 'All that glitters is not gold!'

Hafralónsá (see also page 9)

The Hafralónsá has a good strong flow, and a fishable length of 25 km. Until recent years access in a vehicle was only possible during the fishing season for a short distance up the left bank. When we first came here it was necessary to bring tents, or to stay in a village. A self-catering lodge was built, which has now been upgraded to full board, for the six rods and sharers.

With difficult access, and long walking, the reaches above the lower foss were seldom fished. This river has a deserved reputation for holding a number of bigger salmon, in the high 'teens', with a few over twenty pounds. When walking such a long way it was essential to bear in mind what could be carried back. This was good for conservation, of what is not a large run of fish. Now the long walk is not required.

Bait fishing in rivers for salmon is illegal in Iceland. However this river went through a period when there were some excessively large bags of salmon killed by fishing with natural shrimp. Shrimp flies of many kinds are very effective in Iceland, and the real thing proved to be even more effective.

Fortunately, after that period, the river was leased by the Doppler family from Switzerland, who are also part of the SWICE group, that has leased several other rivers. They used this river for heavenly family holidays. The river was not fished intensively, and it became something of a 'sleeper', as did the Laxá í Dölum during the Pepsi tenancy. This gave it a chance to recover from previous over fishing. The Dopplers were succeeded by the present regime.

During the 1981-84 disaster the catch fell to only 25 in the worst year. The 28-year average catch is 228, but in the last five years to 2001, with more intense fishing, it has picked up to an average of 271. The best year was 402. The number of fish caught in a season on average per rod is low, but the season is short, and the quality of the fishing is high, and fish are of a good size.

A hut was taken one winter to the upper part of Hafralónsá, by driving across country from Hölkná. Now a track has been constructed all the way up the right bank.

The Hafralónsá has a small tributary, the Kverká, that is not let with the main river, this can provide some good sport during the last month of the season.

Robin Savage.

Miðfjarðará í Bakkaflóa

This little river may sometimes be known as the Finnafjarðará; it has a surprisingly strong flow. A tributary joins it about 1 km from the mouth, that is also called Kverká, but fish can only go up that for a few hundred yards. The main stream enters a gorge which is blocked by one foss, and then another not far above. Neither are formidable barriers, but attempts have been made to blow the first have failed. This river has a short season, it is fished by two rods that stay in a small, but adequate 'A' frame. The fishable length is little over 3 km, and yet the

Miðfjarðará í Bakkaflóa - Outside the 'A' frame.

average catch is 133 over 27 years, including the disaster period of 1981-84. The highest recorded catch is 248. To enhance the run some fish are being transported from where they are caught and reintroduced above the foss so that they can spawn naturally in otherwise unreachable water.

When we were invited to fish this river we saw a killer whale mopping up the salmon in the small bay, just outside the mouth. At first the river was very low, but then it rained enough for the river to rise, enabling fish to come in. I have particularly happy memories of this little gem of an unknown river.

Bakkaá

This is not a salmon river in fact it is a very tiny burn, even that is a compliment which it does not deserve. However, about ten years ago a man saw a monster salmon in this piddling little stream. It is surprising that it could find enough water to cover its back. He went to the petrol station in Bakkafjörður, and bought a small spinning rod, and a spoon. He retuned to the salmon and caught it. The fish weighed 43 lbs (of 500 gr). I do not know of a bigger salmon that has ever been

Robin with his three fish and Kristján Edwards who is now a part owner of this Miðfjarðará.

caught in Iceland! This wanderer may illustrate the natural way that gene pools are subject to out breeding! It is more probable that this fish was a wanderer from a fish farm East of Husavík, which may use salmon of Norwegian origin.

Miðfjarðará í Bakkaflóa - The upper river.

The Selá Lodge.

From a photograph by Árni Baldursson.

Chapter Ten
The Rivers of the East Coast

This part of Iceland accounts for 7.2% of the average annual rod catch. There are the three rivers of Vopnafjörður, and Breiðdalsá, which is near the South East corner of Iceland. Two of the rivers of Vopnafjörður, Selá and Hofsá, are exceptionally beautiful salmon rivers. It is difficult to say which is the better. It is like choosing between two beautiful women. Sigurður Helgason, for one, has lost his heart to both.

Selá

This is a seriously good river with about 26 km of fishable water. It is usually let for three or four days at a time, as is the Icelandic custom; this is for two or three full days and two half days. There is a comfortable lodge close to where the road crosses the river, where the 4 to 5 rods of the lower beats are well cared for. They fish the first 14 km. On the south bank 13 km up the valley from the main road, there is another lodge that is self-catering, this houses three more rods which fish the rest of the river. Sometimes the whole river is fished from the main lodge. The number of rods fishing increases as the season progresses and fish move through the ladder and up river.

Starting from the top, there is an impassable foss, at the head of a long gorge section of the river. This is accessible either from the road that goes up the valley of the Vesturdalsá, and then a walk across the moor to the river, or it is necessary to drive up as far as is possible on the left bank of the Selá, and then to walk on. Most of this gorge section can be fished, followed beside the river, crossing it when necessary. From the length that I have seen, there is much water that looks idylic for fishing the fly. This is well populated with gyr falcon. When I fished it the road stopped close to a sheep bridge, that led to the uppermost of the deserted farms. Now this road has been extended for another three or four kilometres. Once the salmon have got up the salmon ladder this upper water looks most enjoyable. From the foot bridge down to the end of the beat there is more good water but it is not a great distance. One more rod may be grafted into the rotation to fish the very top and bottom most sections of the river on alternate days. To fish the uppermost beat for a half day is very hard for an elderly fisherman.

The next stretch is 5 $^1/_2$ km to the Foss, which has a shear drop of about 20 feet. There is a well designed, and constructed salmon ladder that is most effective. The salmon run through the ladder freely, once the river reaches an adequate temperature. After that many of the pools above provide good fishing. Bear pool (Bjarnarhylur) is an exceptional holding pool. It is long, with the run close to the right bank, which is relatively high. Fish lie from very high up in this run to a long way down. When the river is high the tail is also excellent. The next pool below, Snagi, often holds good fish. Above Bear Pool, three pools are particularly interesting, Bryggjur, Stekkur, and Rauðhylur. In fact this ladder has transformed the river by opening up the upper water and the average catch is now more than 3 times what it was before it was built!

Selá - The Foss with ladder.

The Foss beat is always exciting. In Fosshylur fish can be seen at the tail of the white water, and all the way down into the tail, which can be fished from both sides. It is important to try not to spook the fish when getting into position to fish. Playing a fish can also be interesting here, as they will often try to go out of the pool. This is particularly awkward when fishing from the left bank, and they go down the main current close to the right bank. The next pool is Dammur, which is very short; fish seem to lie mostly in the tail, to the left of the current. Then there is a longer pool, Fossbreiða, this is quite wide with good runs, channels and many lies. It is mostly quite shallow. Often fish are showing here.

Selá - Fossbreiða.

There is also a road up the right bank, as far as the foss. About 600 yards below is a public swimming pool heated from a natural hot spring. The 100 yards above the swimming pool is particularly good fishing, and consists of a series of fast flowing rock pools, where fish rest when running. Below this is a gorge section that gradually broadens, and opens up. The pools that fish well in this section seem to vary considerably from year to year.

Selá - The swimming pool.

Selá - Árni Baldursson with a salmon.

Below that, there is a former road bridge that is still passable. Just above this can be good, and also the pool below, where a tributary comes in from the left bank at right angles to the main stream. Fresh fish often pause where the currents join. All the way from there to the sea varies from year to year, but I always fish the pool immediately below the lodge with high hopes, from the right bank.

The average catch in the last six years to 2001 is 1004 salmon. 2000 has been a particularly good year for the Selá, and a poor one for most other rivers in Iceland, largely due to very low water conditions. Considering that the season has a slow start, the average catch per rod, over the whole season is high. This river is far from easy to fish, several pools respond well to being fished with 'the hitch', and it usually has a good proportion of relatively big salmon. In the 28 year record year the catch was 1523.

A fine salmon from the Selá.

Vesturdalsá

This is a small river that meanders gently in its lower part until it runs into a tidal lagoon that is crossed at its mouth by the road to the North from Vopnafjörður. The river is fished by three rods, and the average catch of the last five years to 1999 is 193 salmon. Over a 28-year period the average was 228, in spite of this including the four disaster years when the catch fell to 34 in one year. 513 is the remarkable record, and was in 1977. The last four years have been a little disappointing but 329 were caught in 1995. In addition to the salmon it has a reasonable run of Sea trout. This river might be fun to take for a family party, particularly if it is possible to arrange to stay with a local family. I was hoping to do this, and stay with Garðar Svavarsson, and his wife. I was very sad to hear that he died, he knew the Selá, and the Vesturdalsá exceptionally well, and I have the happiest memories of fishing with him. This river is now controlled by the Vopnafjörður fishing club.

Garður Svararsson with a salmon of mine from the upper Selá.

Hofsá (see also pages 10 to 15)

This river has an enthusiastic following, in England, also in France, and one regular party from America. Brian Booth was the British pioneer of the Hofsá, and the Prince of Wales had a number of happy weeks fishing here. Now it has been leased by the Hofsá Fishing Club. The tenants take a close interest in the management, and improvement of the river. It is normally let for one week at a time with the changeover being at night.

Much damage can be done to the middle, and lower parts of this river by the spring flood. Earth works have to be done to conserve the river. Also much is being done to enhance the salmon run, by stocking, and by transporting the bigger fish that are caught above the foss, so that the nursery area for fish is extended. In summer the flow is considerably stabilised by spring water, and the river is particularly clear.

The access to the river by car is exceptionally good, and where wading is necessary, it is usually relatively easy. The only walking that is required for any distance is on the top beat, but even on that beat it is now possible to penetrate quite a long way by car driving slowly along a cliff face.

Hofsá - Sigurður Helgason fishing the Wood Pool.

The river is fished by seven rods, on seven single rod beats. The bottom beat was not quite as good as the other beats, so the farmers agreed to include the Sunnudalsá tributary with the let of the main river. This was then added to the bottom beat, which promptly improved! The Sunnudalsá, is a most attractive river to fish. To the south of Hofsá, is a fine range of mountains that retain some snow all summer. Streams coming out of these mountains are too cold for salmon, and are inhabited by Char. The Sunnudalsá has quite a long valley that just misses the coldest sources but is thought to be marginal for salmon. They run up through rock pools, into a gorge, where a number can be seen, and often they tease the fisherman. The salmon can surmount the first foss, but usually the water above is retained as a refuge, and at present is not fished. There are another 8 kms of river below the junction with the Sunnudalsá; this is let separately for sea trout fishing, and these fishermen stay in a farm.

Graham Ferguson playing a salmon on the Sunnudalsá.

The Hofsá Lodge.

The lodge is most comfortable, and is well run. The fishermen take a picnic lunch out onto the river, and don't change their beat at midday. The river is rested for only one hour for lunch, but the total time fished per day is less than on other rivers. This only applies to the British three-week period. The salmon fishing on the Hofsá is about 20 km, plus about another 5 km on the Sunnudalsá. The average catch of the last six years to 2001 has been 860 salmon. Over 28 years the average has been 984, and the record year, in 1992 was a remarkable 2238. During the disaster period of the four years 1981 to 1984, a total of only 729 salmon were caught. From 1985 to 1996 was an exceptionally good period. The river looks set for further improvement, now that it is being so well managed.

Hofsá - On the Top Beat.

West Rangá.

Chapter Eleven
The Rivers of the South Coast

Twelve Salmon rivers are listed, and they account for 13.3% of the total rod catch. In addition there has been a netting catch in the Ölfusá. 13.3% is far more than the historic average, because it includes the success of the Rangá operation. There are only two river systems of any significance as Salmon fisheries, and the importance of the catch from these is likely to increase.

Rangá

Two rivers, the East, and the West Rangá join near the sea. Their source is close to Hekla, which is the most active volcano in Iceland. The East Rangá is slightly glacial, and the West Rangá is largely spring fed. In their natural state these rivers had a very small run of salmon, because conditions are not suitable for spawning. There is a huge amount of volcanic ash in the river bed and these rivers are very cold.

Since 1990 there has been an extraordinarily successful Salmon ranching operation. An artificial salmon run has been established, and fish are collected for stripping for the hatchery. Parr, ready to smolt are placed in several holding pools beside the two rivers and then introduced into the rivers themselves. In the statistics the catch of these two rivers are often added together. In the best year so far 2001, the published rod catch was, an astonishing 5300, greater than the catch of any river in the country. This is an incredible achievement. Previously as a wild river, its 28-year low was a catch for the season of 10 salmon! This compares with an annual average catch in the last six years of 3223!! Much of the credit for this goes to Þröstur Elliðason.

The average flow of the East Rangá is 19 cubic metres per second, and the fishable length is 22 km, it has been fished by 16 rods. The water of the East Rangá becomes milky when there is an increase in water from the glacial sources that may be due to heavy rainfall or unusually hot weather.

The West Rangá has an average flow of 44 cubic metres per second. This is more than that of the Laxá í Aðaldal and it is fishable for 40 km. The West Rangá was fished by 12 rods, increased to 16 rods. There can be a natural run of large of Sea Trout in both rivers. There are fully equipped lodges on each river.

This is an artificial commercial operation, that provides outstanding fly fishing for many visiting anglers, many of whom have not fished before in Iceland. This is a very good introduction to the country, and may encourage the fishermen to discover the delights of rivers elsewhere in Iceland.

In Iceland fly fishing is predominately with very small flies and using a floating line. On the Rangá large flies, and sinking lines are widely used, and often are essential.

There are some remarkable brown trout in the Rangá system, in particular in a very short tributary of the West Rangá called the Galtalækur. It is only about 3 km long with 20 pools of superlative trout fishing.

View down Beat One from above the Foss, River Hofsá.

Taken from a painting by William Garfit.

The fly fishing period has now been extended to the fall season, and each year more salmon are being released and the number of rods is kept down. In 2002 the catch was 1912 with about 700 released.

The furthest that a salmon can swim up the Hofsá is to the foss. Below this is a shallow gorge, in a deep valley. There is about one mile to walk beyond the end of the road up to the foss. This upper beat from the foss down is outstandingly beautiful, and exhilarating to fish. A day on this beat is one to remember and treasure. The rock pools of this stretch, gradually have more and smaller boulders. Then the valley widens, and the river is predominately gravel as it meanders through the valley.

The Hofsá valley.

One of the Hofsá farms, Burstafell, is a magnificent example of an old Icelandic farm house. It was in family occupation when we first fished the Hosá, but is now a museum.

Certainly the Hofsá, and its neighbour, the Selá are two of the most desirable rivers to fish for Atlantic salmon, and lucky are those that fish there!

Hofsá - Burstarfell, the old farmhouse.

Hofsá - Burstarfell, the old farmhouse.

The next 150 kilometres!

Between Hofsá, and Breiðdalsá there many good rivers for char, and some sea trout. There are also some rivers flowing North from glaciers of Vatnajökull. There are many small streams, and clear water tributaries of the glacial rivers that are known and enjoyed by the residents of that part of Iceland, with sea trout, char, and occasional salmon. There is even one big lake that is reputed to hold a monster, similar to the Loch Ness monster!

South of the last of these glacial rivers, there are many short rivers with char that flow out of the steep mountains that are between Vatnajökull and the coast. This part of the coast has a number of fjords, and fishing towns, and villages. There is a considerable threat to this area from proposals for three vast salmon farms in cages by Norwegian interests, with at present a planned capacity for a total of 22,000 tons of salmon. In cold seasons these fjords have been known to freeze over. Already one such plant is operating using Norwegian stock, with risks of introducing disease, and parasites, also of escapees mixing the genetic strains of the Icelandic stock. This is causing great concern, only time will tell what will happen.

Iceland has had an exceptional record for conservation and management of its rescources of fish that are so vital to its economy. The fear is that a most careful environmental impact report has not been considered before a decision is taken.

Breiðdalsá

South of Vopnafjörður, the only river for a great distance that has a sufficient watershed for a river of a decent size that is not glacial, is Breiðdalsá. It is about 150 km swimming distance around the coast from Vopnafjörður to Breiðdalsvík, and a further 425 km to the next salmon river of consequence. This has been a good river for char, and an attempt is being made to augment the run by ranching salmon for sport fishing. The natural run has averaged a catch of 141 salmon over 25 years, and 1000 to 2000 char. This is a project of Þröstur Elliðason, who has been so successful with the Rangá operation. There is about 40 km of fishing, on the main river and its tributary Tinnudalsá, with 60 named pools. 1999 was the first year that was expected to benefit from the stocking programme. First there was a serious, and prolonged drought, which was followed by a big flood. In spite of the weather, the season ended with 128 salmon. This was a big increase on the last three years, but not what was expected. Hopes were high for 200, the catch was larger at 233 and 335 in 2002, but not yet what is anticipated. This is an exciting project, and is an effort to repeat the success of the Rangá operation, on a more modest scale.

This is a spate river that flows out of steep mountains; the snow melt has finished before the salmon are expected. An exceptionally comfortable fishing lodge, with ten bedrooms, has been grafted on to the village hotel. Eight rods are allowed. The plan is that the first 20 days of August should be restricted exclusively for fly-fishing.

This river is in a most beautiful and remote corner of Iceland, and I hope this operation achieves the success that it deserves. There is plenty of suitable river bed for spawning, but the river is too cold for parr to thrive. It will be most interesting to learn what percentage rate of return is achieved from the smolt in the release pens.

The Breiðdalsá also has good fishing for arctic char and brown trout.

The Breiðdalsá.

Laxá í Nesjum

This little river is about 90 minutes drive South West of Breiðdalsá and is also subject to another smolt release project of Þröstur Elliðason. It is fished by two rods. Several salmon of over 20 lbs have been caught, it is looking promising, but these are early days. It is at present being started as an add-on to the Breiðdalsá operation. This river also has a run of sea trout.

The local farmers Veiðifélag has now taken over the running of the Eastern Rangá, and Þröstur Elliðason, who developed this remarkable fishery, is continuing to operate on the Western Rangá for a part of the season.

Ölfusá

This is a great glacial river, which has tributaries that include, Hvítá , Brúará, Stóra Laxá, Litla Laxá, and Sog, or Sogið. The Ölfusá was still extensively netted for three days per week up to the end of the season of the year 2002. It seems possible that this might be the last year that these nets will have been operated. If at some time this netting does cease it will have considerable beneficial results throughout the whole watershed.

Hvítá

The Hvítá, (White water river), carries less volcanic ash than some other glacial rivers. The Hvítá has an astonishing average annual flow of 360 Cu. Metres per second, 10 times that of the big Laxá. It is fishable for 25 km, and is fished by about 18 Icelandic fishermen. Its average for the last 5 years has been 203, and the record catch in the last 25 years, 825. Salmon can spawn, and parr can live, either in this river, or its various feeder streams, in addition to those tributaries that rate as salmon rivers. A part of the Hvítá is separately listed, and is above the junction with the Sog. The 27-year average is 687 salmon, and there is a self-catering lodge. This is called the Hvítá í Árnessýslu.

Other tributaries are the Litla Laxá, and the Brúará. Judging only by what I have seen of the Litla Laxá, it looks delectable, but I believe that it is kept as a spawning reserve and the salmon come into it extremely late. I believe that the Brúará is another river that is too cold for salmon to thrive and may have ranching potential, however the biggest opportunity for this is believed to be the Tungufljót.

Tungufljót

This is not yet a salmon river, so perhaps it should not be included in this chapter. However it seems that this is a spectacularly beautiful river for salmon fishing, if only there were salmon in it. It has a large flow, without an obstruction for a considerable distance. Where this river flows through a gorge, it is considered to be relatively accessible. There is now a plan for a major ranching operation, as on the Rangá, but for this to be successful the nets on the Ölfusá must be bought out. If this has been achieved there is a very good chance that the Tungufljót will become a new Mecca for salmon fishermen. There should also be considerable knock-on benefits for all rivers of this watershed.

Stóra Laxá

This means big Salmon river, however when someone refers to the 'Big Laxá', they are invariably referring to the Laxá í Aðaldal, in the North. The Stóra Laxá is fishable for 32 km, before it becomes impossible to fish, running through a very long and deep gorge. This river has a long narrow watershed, flowing out of the middle of Iceland, between two big glacial rivers. This is a cold river for the fish,

Stóra Laxá gorge.

and is therefore somewhat marginal. The fish are of a high quality, big and strong; as they must be to get up the river. There are three self-catering lodges, being fished by 3, 2, and 5 rods respectively. The upper lodge is the only one that I know, and it was excellent.

For many years this river has been controlled by the Reykjavík Angling Club. Not many foreigners have fished it. I enjoyed four days in the uppermost lodge in 1985, alone with my ex-wife, hoping that we could get back together. Except for the first night, we had the lodge to ourselves. It seemed a rather weird river and a weird situation. It was spectacularly beautiful, very remote and difficult to fish. In view of the circumstances, we did not want a guide, although one would have been very useful for the fishing. We contacted one salmon each, but landed nothing, not even a parr. The fishing is strenuous, the pools, and the gorge are deep.

The average catch in recent years has been about 305 salmon.

Sog, or Sogið

This river flows out of Þingvallavatn, which is an enormous, 83 sq. km, spring-fed lake. A little below the lake is a dam, and a big power station. The river is only 14 km long, but it has consistently a very big flow, averaging 98 cubic metres per second, nearly three times that of the Laxá í Aðaldal. It is fished by 13 rods staying in 5 self-catering lodges.

This is a big river, unlike any other in Iceland. I do not have statistics, but I doubt if the percentage of fish caught on a fly is high. In recent years the average catch for the river has been 332 salmon. The river is only a short drive from Reykjavík, so the fishing pressure on it is great, people usually only fish it for one, two or three days at a time. This river would be greatly improved by closure of the Ölfusá nets.

Mike Savage in a hot pool at Landmannalaugur.

Chapter Twelve
Sea Trout and Migratory Char

Salmon fishing in Iceland is fashionable, and expensive. Fishing for Sea Trout or for Char is altogether in a different category; much of it need not be expensive, but it can also provide excellent sport.

I had heard of wonderful Sea Trout fishing in Iceland, and of rivers with large runs of migratory Char. On the whole, and until recently, the Icelanders have kept this fishing for themselves. It seems that rivers tend to have a good run of one, or of the other. Some salmon rivers, such as the Laxá í Kjós also have a modest run of sizeable sea trout. Other rivers have a numerous run of Char, and a modest run of salmon. The table at the back of this book, gives a fair indication of some such rivers. Other rivers may have a considerable run of Sea Trout , or of Char, and have an occasional stray salmon.

My first attempt at fishing specifically for Sea Trout in Iceland was in 1977, when we fished the Ólafsfjarðará, early in September this was not a success (see pages 4 to 5). This river runs into the Akureyri fjord well to the North of the town. It did have a good run of smallish Sea Trout, but they were running into a lagoon, just up from the sea, no doubt, they would have run up the river later; it also produced an occasional salmon.

My next attempt was in 1983, when I had gathered more information, but not enough. We were booked to stay at the Edda Hotel at Kirkjubæjarklaustur, and had fishing on two rivers to the East, one of the many rivers called Laxá, and a Brúará. We were fishing in early September, all of which could have been good, but the Sea Trout were not yet coming in. The manageress was most kind, and

Brúará with an old sea cliff to the left. This is now some miles from the present coast line.

helpful. She even took us at midnight, without any appointment, to the farmhouse of a local farmer. I learned later that he was not only a Member of Parliament, but was the Speaker of the Althing (Parliament). He offered to rent us his own stretch of river another year, I now know that this would have been very good. It was part of Grænilækur. While exploring we stumbled on a private fishing lodge on a wonderful looking river, that was made to look even better, in our eyes, because we saw two large sea trout that had been caught that very day, of 6 to 8 pounds. This fishing was never let, the owner was at that time searching for a Dutch treasure ship that was lost on the Icelandic coast about 300 years before, and was excavating a 'find', which proved to be disappointing. Deposits of silt extend the coastline, as a result this ship must now be buried quite far inland.

Our two little rivers were fresh water tributaries of glacial rivers, and were crystal clear, every fish, and every rock could be seen. I caught one salmon, the only one seen, and I picked up a decent sized Sea Trout that had just come through the glacial river and died.

From this trial fishing, we learned a lot. The best Sea Trout fishing is on rivers in the middle of the South Coast, centred on Kirkjubæjarklaustur. The best fishing is in late August, September, and into October, (these rivers are also fished for Sea Trout in May, but this is for stale fish that are returning to the sea). In warm weather, the glacial rivers are big, and they bring down huge quantities of volcanic ash, which is eventually deposited on the coast. This is most abrasive, and cannot be tolerated by the Sea Trout. Many of these Sea Trout rivers are tributaries of these glacial rivers, and the fish run up when the weather turns cold, and the glacial melt is greatly reduced.

Kit Savage on a glacier covered with volcanic ash.

Eldvatn at dusk.

From a photograph by Árni Baldursson.

Other rivers in this area are spring-fed rivers, which are crystal clear, and run directly into the sea. The biggest of these is Eldvatn, (Fire Water), which has three main tributaries. A branch of a glacial river is lost in an enormous lava flow. This resulted from an eruption of Laki in 1783. It was one of the biggest eruptions in recorded history, with an effect like a nuclear winter; it caused a famine in Iceland, and bad crops throughout Europe. The water from this lava flow emerges as clear water from springs, which feed Eldvatn, Grænilækur, and other rivers. These have a wonderful run of big sea trout. Vast glacial rivers pour into the sea, to the East, and West of this area of clear water rivers. If there is heavy rain during summer months these glacial rivers so pollute the sea with volcanic ash that the Sea Trout even keep away from the clear water rivers. This was our experience in September 1998. We arrived in torrential rain. Before we arrived, and after we left, the fishing was excellent.

An Icelander in Reykjavík, may be telephoned by a friendly farmer, and he can be told 'Come quickly, conditions are perfect'. For a foreigner it is not so easy, plans are made months in advance and it is chancy. If it is hit right, the fishing is comparable with the Rio Grande, in Tierra Del Fuego, and the Icelandic rivers have more variety and interest, but it is unpredictable, a guide is needed, and a good 4WD car. That is fishing! Now there is a lodge available specialising in Sea Trout fishing in this area. When we fished there one of our guides had a very large, and rather unsuitable car. It seemed that the reason for this was that his Thai 'wifelet' was housed in the back of the car. She had become a good fly fisherman.

I have been stuck in mud, wading in a small tributary of Eldvatn, and when wading, in Eldvatn, itself, it is necessary to take the utmost care because there are sudden, deep, holes in the lava of the river bottom. Some of these holes are only large enough for one leg! When the river was high we once drove through water that was about two feet deep for over half a mile. Our guide drove as if his car was a speed boat. It was not surprising that next day his car was 'kaput'.

Don't be put off! There is really good fishing to be had, and for wonderful fish, in rivers that are a pleasure to fish. There are many 'secret' places for sea trout in other parts of Iceland. If one is lucky one can hear of them and one can always hope to be lucky enough to try one. There are also quite big sea trout in some of the salmon rivers such as the Laxá í Kjós.

There is also good fishing for Sea Trout in the lower parts of some rivers, which may be let separately with a self-catering lodge, or a farmhouse where one can stay. For example there are such beats on the Miðfjarðará, and the Hofsá. The lower sections of many North Coast rivers, particularly where there are fresh water, or brackish lakes near the estuaries, may have excellent Sea Trout in May, June, and July, (for example, the Víðidalsá, the Vatnsdalsá, and the Laxá á Ásum). Personally this does not appeal to me as interesting fishing, whereas the South Coast Sea Trout rivers do have great appeal to me.

It is easy to be confused as to whether fishing is for Sea Trout, or Char, (Bleikja). There are very many small rivers that have large runs of Char, which are either very minor Salmon Rivers, or not even Salmon Rivers at all. This is usually because

Eldvatn Lodge in Winter.

From a photograph by Árni Baldursson.

the river is too cold for salmon. Char are more tolerant of cold, white glacial water, and also ordinary river water that has its source in high, cold mountains, with too steep a river course to give the water time to warm up. The North West Fjords, and the East Coast have many rivers of this sort.

In other parts of this book, and in the table of statistics, there is more information about places where there may be good fishing for Sea Trout and for Char. The size of Char in Iceland normally average one to two pounds, some weigh up to about four pounds. Some of the Sea Trout particularly on the South Coast, can be as large as a big salmon.

Biologically there is no difference between a Brown Trout and a Sea Trout, other than the sea trout has developed an instinct to go to the sea in order to find more food. It seems that in some rivers only females go to sea, so Brown Trout and Sea Trout interbreed. It is similar with Char. No biological difference has been found between Migratory Char and Lake Char. The situation is also similar, as regards the relationship between Rainbow Trout and Steelhead.

Tables 6-8 give more information.

Chapter Thirteen
Brown Trout and Lake Char

My imagination was fired by a photograph, shown to me in 1964, by Brian Booth, of a catch of four huge Brown Trout. It had been caught by him in a lake in North East Iceland. The owner's farm was a long way away. Brian had been told by the farmer, that there were no fish in this lake. However Brian had seen divers living on the lake, and deduced, 'No fish! No divers!'

From this, three lessons can be learned. Firstly, all fishing rights are privately owned, and however remote the water is from human habitation, permission must be obtained. Secondly, there is wonderful fishing in Iceland for wild Brown Trout. Thirdly, not everything is known, even by the local people, so it pays to be observant, and to experiment. This is of interest to someone camping, and has time to experiment, and is of little interest to those in the middle of their working lives, to whom time is of the utmost value.

In Iceland there are three outstanding areas for Brown Trout fishing.

A Brown Trout fighting.

The most accessible is the Laxá í Aðaldal, below Mývatn, already mentioned in the first chapter of this book. For fishing here a fly net is essential. This is really top class river fishing for fine wild fighting fish. There are two lodges, or hostels for the Trout fishing on this river. In the lake there is a big population of Lake Char. I have found the Lake Char to be very bad fighters, but they are good to eat.

In the centre of the South of the country, quite a way inland in an absolute wilderness not far from the Western end of Vatnajökull, is an area of lakes. These are known as Veiðivötn, the Fishing Lakes. They hold a remarkable number of good Trout. These lakes are fished in a rotation so that each is rested for some years before being fished again. Few holds are barred as to fishing methods in the

Galtalaekur.

From a photograph by Árni Baldursson.

places open for fishing. I believe that a favourite method here is to fish with herring strip!

The third area is in the West. It is on the moor, which forms the source of the Kjarrá, Norðurá and the Miðfjarðará, and consists of many lakes with some interconnecting streams. The summer track that gives access was among the worst in Iceland, and only suitable for good 4WD vehicles; I understand that the access has been greatly improved. Camping is necessary, and it was advisable to go as a party with two such vehicles. Access is both from the upper valley of the Hvitá, and from the North. The weather can be wild and the ground can be boggy. One night, a party with small children were fishing there; they had a Land Rover badly bogged, the camp was blown down in the night, and their boat was blown onto an island. They did have three cars, and managed to sort themselves out the next day.

Brown Trout.

There are many other remarkable rivers, streams and lakes with good brown trout fishing. Some are absolutely exceptional and are being made available for foreign fishermen. Two examples are Galtalækur, which I have mentioned as a tributary of the West Rangá. Another is the Minnivallalækur, which is only one hour's drive South of Reykjavík, and in which a 20 lb brown trout might be caught. It is to be hoped that catch and release is practiced in such rivers or the fishing could deteriorate fast if fishing pressure increases.

Fishermen coming from the British Isles, are aware of Char, but usually have never seen one. They are known as having been left behind by the ice age, and the populations have been separated for so long that each population in Britain is slightly different. In Iceland there are thought to be two different char, the Migratory Char and, the Lake, or non-migratory char. Biologists affirm that they are the same. The Migratory Char is similar in habit to the Sea Trout and is

An Arctic Char.

covered in that chapter. The Lake Char occurs in many lakes and in parts of some rivers. They are usually caught when fishing for Trout, but Mývatn has a commercial fishery for Char. Some of these are smoked using sheep's dung as fuel. This is a traditional Icelandic method, and they are sold as a speciality, having a very strong flavour.

Trout fishing is available informally from many farms, upon payment of a reasonable fee. Visitors can stay in hotels, or in farmhouses or camp. In some places it would be fun to stay on a farm, and to gain access to less accessible places to fish, by hiring horses. There are two good little books available from Icelandic tourist offices, one lists farm houses, with accommodation available, and their facilities, and the other lists trout fishing areas, with maps, and where to obtain permission to fish.

Tables 6-8 give more information.

Chapter Fourteen
Greenland

In a book about Iceland, it may seem illogical to include even a brief chapter about Greenland. A glance at a map shows the enormous size of Greenland, and its proximity to Iceland. There are many flights between the two Islands. Greenland is considered to be part of North America, and Iceland to be part of Europe. The climates, and geology, are vastly different, although they are so close, and Greenland extends much further South than Iceland. The Greenland icecap is vast, and the climate is much colder. Yet the early Viking marketing men called the one Iceland, and the other Greenland, apparently the wrong way round. That part of Greenland that the Vikings settled was the South West. In this part, there are many identified remains of Viking farms, today some of these are farmed by Eskimos.

My wife, Gina, I, and my brother Robin, who was then a farmer in Kenya, jumped at an opportunity to fish in this part of Greenland in 1963. We were told by the Danish travel company that the fishing would be for 'salmons' and that we would stay at the Arctic Hotel at Narsarsuaq. We soon realised that the fishing was for arctic char, there were no salmon. We flew in a chartered plane, most of the other passengers were tourists who would have a cruise for one week up the coast: this was in the last week of August, and we were the last visitors of the season. I suspect that our main function was to fill the surplus seats on the plane.

As we flew in we saw many icebergs, and pack ice. We learned that the airport was built during World War II, and there is a huge hospital built on the perma frost. We were told that the hospital was used at the time of the Korean war for American wounded, so that they would not return to the US until they were fit to be seen! True or not, I do not know! The Arctic Hotel was converted service accommodation. The male and female ablutions were next to each other, and a slight movement to a tap in one, would result in the shower in the other either become scalding or freezing! A sense of humour was needed, but the staff were charming and nothing was too much trouble.

We fished three glacial rivers, and three non-glacial streams, the latter were necessarily very small, as they had no glacier in their watershed. In the glacial rivers, it was extraordinarily difficult to tell whether the stream had any depth, as the water was so opaque. About two miles up the 'home river' there was a small fresh water tributary, with a congregation of char. As we cast, they would move aside from the line. The walk up river on the flood plain was like walking on a field of stone footballs! One mile further was the foot of the glacier.

There were two rowing boats with outboard motors. Often there was fog, and the pack ice flowed in and out on the tide. This was the last week, and the staff had run out of sheering pins, which were needed if a propeller touched the pack ice. At the head of the fjord was a river that had wonderful char of 5 to 6 lbs, that fought like demons. According to an excellent Danish map this river was not

Migratory Char in Greenland.

From a photograph by Árni Baldursson.

glacial, but it most certainly was! The furthest upstream that I went was to a place where the river was steep, and in a scrubby gorge. There I saw a large char rising out of the milky water to fly on the surface.

One day we went down the fjord, by ourselves in thick fog. Our idea was to branch left into a side fjord, which had at its head a calving glacier. This could be dangerous when a new berg brakes off, rotten bergs are also dangerous because they can explod, or turn over. The sun above the fog disappeared, and we discovered that it had gone behind a mountain, and we had in front of us a cliff, with a grounded iceberg. I was navigating, and turned left, and drove the boat through the fog, the next thing that we saw was the calving glacier immediately in front of us, we had passed two rivers! So we turned back, and soon found the first, a small clear stream, pouring down a steep watercourse. I walked steeply up about half a mile, and found a small pool on a bend. Here my fly was taken by the biggest char, which I have ever seen, probably of about 10 lbs. This I lost!

We went down the fjord to the next river. A glacier calved into a glacial lake, out of which this river ran. There was an Eskimo fishing vessel at the mouth, and the river was being netted for winter supplies.

Next day we were taken down the fjord, in an ancient motor yacht that had seen different days, we learned that it had been Göering's yacht! We passed Igaliko, which had its bishop during the Viking period, and landed at the mouth of a clear water stream that flowed out of a lake. We didn't catch anything worthwhile. We made another visit to this wonderful river at the head of the fjord; this time there was an Eskimo boat, and this river was also being netted, for winter supplies. They had caught a number of very fine Char. These are slow growing, and return to the rivers every year to spawn. On our way back, we met the pack ice coming in on the tide, so we had to turn into the mouth of our home river, rather than go on down to the little harbour.

We had arranged a two-day expedition, crossing the fjord, to Qargssiarsuk, on the other side. This was Eirík the Red's settlement of Brattahlíð, where he lived after leaving his farm on the Haukadalsá, which we knew so well. All was as it should have been according to the Saga. Here at Busahlíð there was a small Royal Greenland Company store. About 300 sheep had been rounded up and driven here by Eskimos on Icelandic horses. The sheep were forced off a natural rock quay, leaping into two barges that were to take them to slaughter. It did not require much imagination to see a boat of similar size belonging to Leifur Eiríksson moored at this spot before his historic voyage to Vinland, and his discovery of mainland America. Close by were the remains of Eirík's own house, and out of sight from it, over a knoll the little Christian church of his wife, Þjoáhildur. He allowed her to be Christian but he didn't wish to see her church from his house. Since our visit replicas have been built nearby, leaving even less to the imagination.

The tug sailed towing the two barges full of sheep. The tug and barges were soon dwarfed by an iceberg that they sailed past. We were given the horses that we had arranged to rent. They were tired and with saddle sores. We rode bareback, with a snaffle bit, with one rope that went behind the ears, and another as reins. We slung our fishing tackle, and food, and bedding, over our horses' withers.

In addition to the Savages there was Don Archbold, the owner of a big fleet of heavy transport from Leeds, and a Glaswegian dentist called Arthur. Neither of them had ridden before. We rode over a saddle to the next fjord to the North, which we were told had been the farm of an Irish freed slave, who had settled here with Eirík. As we neared the farm, we passed some small barley fields, to be harvested green, as hay. They can only make enough hay to feed the sheep in a very cold winter. Otherwise they are left out to fend for themselves, browsing in the scrub. The present farm was set near the shore of the fjord with another older house nearby. We stopped to admire the view, and from far behind, we were overtaken by Arthur, saying 'woe, woe,' hoping that this would stop his horse! It didn't stop until it came up against the door of the farmhouse! We were made welcome in the older house. The farmer's daughter, aged about twelve, led us on her horse for another two miles, or so, to a small clear water river where we were to fish. She slipped off her horse, leaving her rope reins dangling, so we did the same. We were fully equipped with fly rods, waders etc, etc. From her tight, form-fitting trousers the girl produced a reel of nylon, and a small spoon, soon she had a cord full of fish. We did catch a very few small char, and quite soon we made our way back on the horses that had enjoyed their grazing, and were waiting for us.

When we got back to the farm, we left our horses as we had learned to do on the river, and cooked a meal, before going to bed after a long and interesting day. Poor Arthur was very over-tired, he was sharing a room with Don. Through the thin partition we heard him say to Don 'I am not long for this worrrld!' Meanwhile our horses had decided to return home for the night, but luckily the young Eskimo girl came to our rescue as we slept. She recovered them for us, and tethered them to a fence.

Next day quite early we had to leave on our return journey. Don, as inexperienced as Arthur, but rather more dashing, decided that he would be more comfortable with stirrups. His horse was held. With his bedding slung across his horse's withers, wearing his waders, and carrying his rod and tackle, he mounted his horse. He had a rope with a loop at each end. He put his feet in the loops, to use as stirrups, however he had no girth. He reined back off a rock shelf, and dashed off at a canter - for about ten yards before coming to grief! Luckily no harm was done, and we all proceeded together at more sedate pace, back to Qarssiarssuk, and in our boat, home to Narsarsuaq.

Our conclusion was that there is wonderful fishing for Char in Greenland, and it would be a dream to be based in a privately owned, or chartered, boat. This would enable the party to map-read, and to explore, looking for suitable rivers, and try them. These Char are most sporting fish, and are terrific fighters. This was altogether a most interesting experience that we did not regret in any way.

When we were ready to leave, we all gathered on the tarmac of the airport. The hotel was closing for the winter, so the staff joined the tourists and the fishermen. The captain walked up and down, looking doubtfully at the number of passengers, and their mountain of baggage. He must have decided to hope for the best, as we were all loaded. There was not much alternative, as we were the last scheduled flight out before winter. The plane started up, using the whole runway; which was at right angles to the fjord, with a mountain ahead on the other side. Close to the mountain, the captain turned the plane left, down the fjord, labouring to make height. When we were over the sea, he turned East, giving us a wonderful low level view of the surrounding mountains, rivers, lakes, glaciers and the icecap itself.

Table 1 1860 farms that receive an income from Sport Fishing.

Table 2 - Table of Salmon Rivers - as at 2001

See notes on page 202

District	River	Tributaries	Category	Fishable	Flow	No. of rods	5 Yr. Av.	Av. per rod	28 Yr. Av.	28 Yr. High	28 Yr. Low	Comments
South West	Elliðaár		from lakes		5cm	6 now 4	498	125	1226	2071	414	a, in Reykjavík
	Úlvarsá			7Km	1.2cm	2	207	103	315	709	110	b, in Reykjavík
	Leirvogsá			12Km		2	467	234	458	1057	136	b, guest house
	Laxá í Kjós	Bugða	from lakes	25Km		12 now 10	1177	117	1522	3883	719	b, i, f/b
	Brynjudalsá			2Km		2	106	53	113	247	20	b
	Laxá í Leirársveit	Leirá	from lakes	13Km		6-8	890	111	1021	1887	545	b, f/b & between lakes
TOTAL	7 rivers 14.1%								4807			
Borgarfjörður	Andakílsá		from lake	10Km		2	120	60	143	331	63	c, s/c
	Hvítá		Glacial	2Km		7	481	69	466	788	213	c, s/c
		Grímsá og Tungá	from lake	32Km	4.75cm	10	1488	149	1364	2116	717	c, i, f/b
		Flókadalsá		14Km		3	351	118	333	613	181	c, s/c
		Reykjadalsá	hot springs	20Km		2	73	36	89	275	25	hotel?
		Þverá og Kjarrá	from lakes	84Km	36cm	7+7=14	1688	121	1867	3558	1082	c, I, 2 f/b
		Norðurá		45Km	21cm	12+2=14	1332	95	1560	2132	856	c, f/b, & s/c
		Gljúðará	from lake	15Km		2	146	73	221	522	73	c, s/c
TOTAL	8 rivers 17.7%								6033			
North to Saæfell	Langá		from lake	21Km		now 13	1397	107	1305	2405	610	d 2 f/b
	Álftá	Veitá		30Km		2	210	105	283	485	132	s/c, I
	Hítará	Grjótá	from lake	29Km		6	358	60	326	649	151	2 f/b, J
	Haffjarðará		fly only, ex lakes	8Km		8 now 6	662	110	663	1131	465	f/c
	Straumfjarðará		fly only, ex lake	11Km	3cm	3	234	92	336	755	161	f/c
TOTAL	9 rivers 9.1%								3115			
Breiðafjörður	Fróðá			4Km		3	21	7	92	254	13	s/c
	Setbergsá					2	39	20	124	296	0	s/c
	Laxá á Skógarströnd					2	84	42	129	277	33	s/c
	Miðá í Dölum	Tungá				3	69	23	113	245	31	J, s/c
	Haukadalsá	Þverá		6Km	7cm	5+2=7	563	112	679	1232	331	e, f/b, upper s/c
	Laxá í Dölum		from lake	23Km		8 now 6	924	220	933	2385	324	f/b
	Fáskrúð			17Km		3	183	61	225	464	96	s/c
	Flekkudalsá					3	148	49	239	509	100	s/c
	Krossá á Skarðsströnd			12Km		2	55	28	98	208	27	s/c
	Hvolsá	Starðahólsá		12Km		4	35	9	176	768	18	f, J, s/c
TOTAL	15 rivers 8.5%								2912			
North West Fjords	Laugardalsá		from lakes	6Km		2 then 3	208	69	303	703	111	s/c
	Langadalsá			16Km		3	114		144	292	31	s/c
TOTAL	13 rivers 3.4%								1164			

Table 2 cont. - Table of Salmon Rivers - as at 2001

See notes on page 202

District	River	Tributaries	Category	Fishable	Flow	No. of rods	5 Yr. Av.	Av. per rod	28 Yr. Av.	28 Yr. High	28 Yr. Low	Comments
North Coast	Hrútafjarðará	Síká	fly only	14Km		3	185	62	280	536	126	J, f/b, fly only
	Miðfjarðará og Vesturá	Nupsá og Austurá		90Km		10+ st	924	92	1236	2581	433	J, f/b
	Víðidalsá	Fitjá		50Km		8	817	102	1141	2023	580	J, f/b
	Vatnsdalsá		Catch & release	40Km	9cm	6+1 above	691	99	885	1582	323	J, f/b
	Laxá á Ásum		Lakes			2	722	361	1137	1881	430	f/b
	Blanda		Glacial & Hydro	27Km	26cm	4+4 above	1168	146	1009	2363	375	s/c
		Svartá		30Km	23cm	4	364	91	291	619	46	
	Fljótaá			7Km		4	123	31	160	388	49	J, farm house
	Fnjóská			40Km	37cm	6	188	31	233	554	60	s/c
	Skjálfandafljót		Netted	28Km		6	330	55	372	907	67	s/c
	Laxá í Aðaldal		Lake & Springs	25Km	36cm	20	1922	43	1752	3063	845	g, l, m, 6 s/c &, 2 f/b
		Reykjadalsá				4	73	18	246	657	39	s/c
		Mýrarkvísl		31Km		4	147	37	221	490	49	s/c
TOTAL	25 rivers 28.8%								9837			
North East	Ormarsá			17Km		4	138	34	181	366	45	h, s/c
	Deildará		Through lake	6Km		3	139	46	165	391	27	h, s/c
	Svalbarðsá			22Km		3	154	51	164	384	29	h, s/c
	Sandá				13cm	4	146	36	233	474	35	h, s/c
	Hólkná					3	54	18	86	219	11	h, s/c
	Hafralónsá	Kverká	Spring fed	25Km		6	270	45	228	402	25	h, s/c
	Miðfjarðará	Kverká	from lakes	4Km		2	114	57	133	248	15	h, s/c
TOTAL	7 rivers 3.5%								1190			
East Coast	Selá		Spring fed	40Km		7	1057	151	863	1523	123	h, f/b & upper s/c
	Vesturdalsá			28Km		3	140	47	224	513	34	h, hotel, or house
	Hofsá	Sunnudalsá	Spring fed	22Km+J		7+st	868	124	980	2238	141	h, f/b & s/c for J
	Breiðdalsá	Tinnudalsá		30Km		6-8	133	17	137	412	4	f, J, f/b
TOTAL	6 rivers 6%								2043			
South Coast	Rangá	East Rangá	slightly glacial	22Km	19cm	16	3710	232	982	5466	10	k, l, f/b
		West Rangá	Spring fed	40Km	44cm	12	Incl.	with	East	Rangá	above	k, l, f/b
	Ölfusá	Hvítá	Glacial	25Km	360cm	About 18	199	11	337	825	6	s/c
		Stora Laxá	Spring fed	32Km		3+2+5=10	271	27	293	707	76	3 s/c
		Litla Laxá	nursery	25Km								
		Hvítá í Árnessýlu	Glacial	70Km		About 25	293	12	689	1175	190	s/c
		Sog	Lake & spring	14Km	98cm	13	344	26	402	714	223	5 s/c
TOTAL	12 rivers 8.8%								2991			
GRAND TOTAL	100 rivers 100%								34092			

Notes for Table of Salmon Rivers

General Notes
  i. The time and length of the season varies from river to river. The length of the season needs to be known to calculate an average daily catch per rod.
  ii. An increasing number of rivers are being fished as Fly only for all or part of the season. This may decrease the total catch.
  iii. Catch and release began in 1996 on a voluntary basis and is increasing.
  iv. The catch on a river varies considerably according to the skill of the fisherman and their knowledge.
  v. The relative importance of the South coast is understated in the 28 year average because of the success of the Rangá project.

Abbreviations
  f/b = Full Board
  s/c = Self-Catering (cleaning and cooking may be arrangeable)

Table 1 Footnotes
  a. Disease in 1999. Rod number reduced to 4, and only fly-fishing above the foss from 2000.
  b. 1988 catch statistics considerably inflated by very small farm escapees.
  c. Nets in Hvítá ceased operating from 1991.
  d. From 1999 the Langá is being fished in one rotation, instead of divided in two.
  e. The upper Haukadalsá and the Þverá can also be fished with two rods, but are seldom fished.
  f. Salmon supplemented by ranching for sport. i.e. This is more intense than the river being 'enhanced'.
  g. The Laxá í Áðaldal, has two large lodges for brown trout fishing, above the Hydro Electric dam.
  h. North East, and East Coast rivers, from Örmarsá to Hofsá, suffered a natural disaster in the years 1981 to 1984, which reduced catches dramatically. They recovered fully, and very quickly.
  i. These rivers also have a significant number of Sea Trout.
  j. These rivers have a considerable number of migratory Char.
  k. The Rangá, East, and West, has been transformed since 1990 from being a large river with very few salmon, into a most successful salmon ranching operation for sport fishing.
  l. 1992 Faroese nets bought off.
  m. Below the Foss 8 more rods fish predominately for trout but catching a few salmon. Above the Foss all the way to Myvatn there is superlative trout fishing.

Table 3 - Salmon catch in Icelandic rivers in 1974-2001. Average, maximum and minimum catch in the period is calculated.

River	1974	1975	1976	1977	1978	1979	1980	1981	1982	1983	1984	1985	1986	1987	1988	1989	1990	1991	1992	1993	1994	1995	1996	1997	1998	1999	2000	2001	Av. catch	Max. catch	Min. catch
Elliðaár	2033	2071	1692	1328	1383	1336	938	1074	1219	1508	1331	1157	1083	1175	2006	1773	1384	1127	1393	1390	1132	1088	1211	568	492	424	592	414	1226	2071	414
Úlvarsá (Korpa)	357	438	406	361	327	215	110	166	158	450	225	303	376	245	709	440	306	238	517	457	338	316	339	217	248	162	223	185	315	709	110
Leirvogsá	332	739	544	474	463	386	136	213	322	514	320	438	324	291	1057	458	489	435	556	428	490	520	552	411	540	467	487	434	458	1057	136
Laxá í Kjós	1270	1901	1973	1677	1648	1508	950	1290	927	1545	1273	871	1043	933	3422	1819	1370	1328	1053	1103	683	866	629	985	1192	1171	940	916	1296	3422	629
Bugða	158	269	410	263	136	125	212	260	232	450	461	283	201	230	389	314	226	265	191	163	100	154	143	162	173	126	132	90	226	461	90
Brynjudalsá	205	271	185	173	98	100	11	24	120	177	68	29	44	59	287	118	385	235	154	118	88	597	186	76	102	120	136	95	152	597	11
Botnsá	247	194	158	146	171	242	121	77	92	100	70	54	117	33	209	80	105	148	97	61	58	127	65	20	92	73	124	94	113	247	20
Laxá í Leirársveit	1116	1654	1288	1154	1252	899	707	670	545	708	742	860	1610	914	1887	1186	1052	850	652	747	853	1425	1368	697	816	1065	925	948	1021	1887	545
Andakílsá	235	331	262	187	237	138	69	104	89	108	106	101	145	136	203	122	97	134	85	109	125	118	15	184	63	177	79	95	143	331	63
Hvítá	393	521	388	401	788	573	555	364	348	213	326	597	469	514	439	301	263	572	520	622	560	407	502	213	692	504	425	571	466	788	213
Grímsá og Tunguá	1419	2116	1439	1103	1952	1527	869	845	717	1382	1061	1463	1836	825	1963	1200	756	1294	1864	1228	1485	1123	1484	1613	1705	1872	1048	1005	1364	2116	717
Flókadalsá	411	613	432	263	547	377	266	181	234	281	303	351	384	282	293	182	241	350	322	387	341	288	233	319	360	347	380	362	333	613	181
Reykjadalsá	156	275	185	112	120	105	56	80	100	91	58	42	69	42	33	75	77	157	107	40	25	97	36	94	95	73	72	33	89	275	25
Þverá og Kjarrá	1748	2690	2330	2368	3132	3558	1938	1245	1616	1901	1082	1550	2127	1703	1567	1327	1485	1979	2314	1554	1605	1638	1381	1633	2181	2136	1281	1210	1867	3558	1082
Norðurá	1428	2132	1675	1470	2089	1995	1583	1185	1455	1643	856	1121	1523	1034	1359	867	1070	1267	1965	2117	1625	1697	1964	1899	2001	1676	1650	1337	1560	2132	856
Gljúfurá	150	522	356	400	461	286	130	101	184	225	110	138	280	73	181	133	97	171	286	192	150	356	209	240	152	134	104	99	211	522	73
Langá	1379	2131	1568	1720	2405	1893	1049	735	1090	960	610	1155	1765	1023	1409	748	1000	951	1290	777	978	1400	1517	1366	1560	1641	1011	1407	1305	2405	610
Urriðaá				84	112	202	102	65	151	162	142	103	55	16	105	63	34	13	19	54	15	37	47	29	42	62	22	24	70	202	13
Álftá	154	341	204	300	386	255	265	267	396	485	268	333	399	202	443	283	245	274	333	242	247	263	283	266	191	275	132	187	283	485	132
Hítará	383	525	351	346	649	314	167	252	202	201	151	203	506	273	428	225	257	393	255	279	206	424	355	217	311	443	404	418	326	649	151
Haffjarðará	613	559	595	624	950	701	494	465	562	625	549	562	1131	521	875	661	599	711	818	617	672	735	602	560	752	793	672	532	663	1131	465
Straumfjarðará	451	755	433	466	648	391	320	437	350	360	215	327	378	161	334	300	267	308	233	260	253	315	269	226	297	260	198	191	336	755	161
Vatnsholtsós og vötn					290	325	112	175	140	171	135	200	143		183	126	101	88	107	105	98	119	108	68	63	69	88	25	132	325	25
Fróðá		182	199	254	225	234	130	94	75	100	60	27	58	61	71	51	50	51	52	105	29	26	13	13			29	23	92	254	13
Grísholtsá og Bakká	60	55	75	70	125	61	24	48	37	64			38																57	125	24
Setbergsá					244	167	81	192	170	173	147	215	233	100	296	134	203	117	120	76	40	0	80	44	63	44	39	7	124	296	0
Laxá á Skógarströnd	99	167	114	190	179	177	109	183	121	201	189	277	218	117	242	103	106	101	72	68	33	41	94	46	121	98	75	81	129	277	33
Dunká				83	76	142	58	138	85	129	52	135	124	68	126	71	96	104	125	103	50	76	150	62	39	47	45	96	91	150	39
Skrauma	6	10		22	23	18	10			32	16	16	23				0	3	6	10	4	0	16			0	0		11	32	0
Hörðudalsá	74	55	55	51			51	55	27	87	50	79	43	18	116	78	62	77	68		17	17	23	17	13	5		17	48	116	5
Miðá og Tunguá	117	245	121	146	135	203	85	182	132	161	128	46	101	35	200	118	90	88	214	112	42	58	48	31	103	93	40	80	113	245	31
Haukadalsá	810	914	904	862	926	643	408	814	598	886	633	499	817	650	1232	511	540	703	776	632	407	394	626	331	916	646	348	577	679	1232	331
Laxá í Dölum	341	547	488	419	533	630	324	671	650	947	903	1600	1907	1408	2385	1006	1049	1227	1124	929	625	764	1032	764	1432	938	607	877	933	2385	324
Fáskrúð	202	298	136	242	226	261	140	190	154	214	165	257	449	381	464	203	226	183	330	212	96	157	187	144	265	145	143	221	225	464	96

205

Table 3 cont. - Salmon catch in Icelandic rivers in 1974-2001. Average, maximum and minimum catch in the period is calculated.

River	1974	1975	1976	1977	1978	1979	1980	1981	1982	1983	1984	1985	1986	1987	1988	1989	1990	1991	1992	1993	1994	1995	1996	1997	1998	1999	2000	2001	Av. catch	Max. catch	Min. catch
Flekkudalsá	300	462	343	342	467	509	293	255	237	249	189	133	244	129	360	140	145	241	262	247	100	109	192	148	226	131	108	131	239	509	100
Krossá á Skarðsströnd	106	120	109	81	106	156	115	157	126	203	93	27	117	51	208	99	30	100	125	114	44	100	72	28	50	71	76	52	98	208	27
Búðardalsá	35				100	120	131	71	54	71	32	51	55	56	111	81	106	146	131	56	41	31	45	59	42	43	45	105	73	146	31
Hvolsá og Staðarhólsá	126	136	185	163	180	90	18	140	111	100	144	137	323	101	768	163	331	327	306	274	243	313	83	25	61	18	26	46	176	768	18
Fjarðarhornsá				8	0	38	8	18	34	60	31		29	12	16	4	8	33	24	12	4	2	2	2		0		1	16	60	0
Laugardalsá	309	601	245	681	703	596	276	288	250	181	125	421	386	190	501	280	161	284	220	265	157	223	111	135	343	149	156	257	303	703	111
Ísafjarðará	10	27		52	29	25	12	12	9		5	6	14	3	23	16	14	55	15	12	3	8	5	4	13	4	4	7	15	55	3
Langadalsá	78	172	170	189	203	277	206	111	101	98	31	54	112	67	95	130	88	217	292	241	72	251	192	133	186	82	76	94	144	292	31
Hvannadalsá	57		56		120	101	47	30	45	27	24	71			110	23	42	304	71	51	41								72	304	23
Selá í Steingrímsfirði	34	22		27	17	17	23	6	7	0	7	44	22	18	60		66	95	81	8	64	20	49	45	4	11	0	19	29	95	0
Staðará í Steingrímsf	44	100	108	124	101	95	72	46	41	26	25	28	64	40	71	62	118	82	169	43	26	101	57	32	29	6	14	41	64	169	6
Víðidalsá í Steingrímsf	182	49	54	61	93	104	98	34	54	12	16		56					29	29	8		59	23	25	47	39	20	0	50	182	0
Hrófá		20		22	56	74	48	41	29	14	21	54	62	23	85	41	32	94	93	64	23	57	61	25	93	23	25	17	46	94	14
Krossá í Bitru				49	140	125	151	153	109	90	41	109	180	121	88	79	39	19	63	65	52	61	37	45	85	114	76	47	86	180	19
Víkurá	5	38	92	68	121	219	125	174	61	75	45	70	100	40	89	40	38	28	77	70	20	98	43	54	119	90	81	78	77	219	5
Prestbakkaá	44			66	93	105	21	40		57	39	85	115	43	123			51	73	45	12	38	33	33	13	37	17	19	52	123	12
Laxá í Hrútafirði	9	32	18	23	17	39	43	61	45	126	165	133	98	69	69	11	47	96	84	47	12	33	16	51	75	48	14	17	54	165	9
Hrútafjarðará og Síká	194	291	228	262	346	312	253	288	220	287	195	345	536	259	532	252	200	359	459	411	176	288	205	201	243	218	141	126	280	536	126
Miðfjarðará	837	1414	1601	2581	2337	2132	1714	1213	926	882	583	1059	1719	1073	2081	1175	774	1112	1401	1023	668	1032	714	602	1772	1203	612	433	1238	2581	433
Tjarnará á Vatnsnesi			34		112	82	53	56	36	53	23	55	25	0		40	18	51	23	40	9	30	0	37	61	32	10	6	37	112	0
Víðidalsá og Fitjá	1051	1140	1238	1792	1851	1948	1423	1392	1132	1082	625	713	1541	1563	2023	924	604	667	1473	1342	580	981	783	691	1081	1089	644	581	1141	2023	580
Vatnsdalsá	706	832	571	1203	1466	1413	1033	985	721	879	699	856	1582	1496	1243	660	604	683	998	853	516	601	723	769	1149	629	323	584	885	1582	323
Laxá á Ásum	1439	1881	1270	1439	1854	1650	956	1413	1036	1050	625	1440	1857	1157	1617	749	651	833	861	1458	805	1549	627	715	1136	430	770	562	1137	1881	430
Blanda	1173	2363	1485	1367	2147	906	778	1412	861	511	495	766	1814	1243	1217	375	607	568	432	404	357	519	600	877	1984	1191	706	1086	1009	2363	357
Svartá	420	232	96	46	295	469	444	125	73	147	132	330	391	462	275	118	105	108	363	495	400	547	244	532	619	213	170	283	291	619	46
Laxá á Refasveit	79	58	41	71	94	146	153	71	39	57	70	111	144	132	140	96	156	117	297	227	144	143	104	139	179	105	69	88	117	297	39
Hallá				171	185	197	138	96	57	111	86	109	55	62	62	50	30	45	56	53	28	48	57	38	38	31	8	22	73	197	8
Fossá á Skaga	5	6		34	62	98	94	26	14	25	8	22	32	20	22	24	12	22	20	25	10	16	14	17	17	13	15	16	26	98	5
Laxá á Skaga	120	134	73	140	200	220	245	161	113	93	74	134	138	176	137	70	103	70	144	106	26	30	38	41	79	10	0	0	103	245	0
Sæmundará	115	116	160	212	303	112	70	52	29	75		139	94									62	25	54	103	43	25	59	97	303	25
Húseyjarkvísl	112	118	141	158	194	84	107	52	54	90	77	105	104	101	73	113	89	103	245	160	80	73	71	70	94	39	32	47	100	245	32
Hofsá í Vesturdal	23	2		15			12	16	23														0						13	23	0
Kolka							12	12	7			24	15	24	10	18	16	18	16	55			4	1	58	5	10	27	18	58	5
Hrolleifsdalsá	20	24	28	41	41	65	17	4	4	7	4	25									7				13	1	4	11	18	65	1

Table 3 cont. - Salmon catch in Icelandic rivers in 1974-2001. Average, maximum and minimum catch in the period is calculated.

River	1974	1975	1976	1977	1978	1979	1980	1981	1982	1983	1984	1985	1986	1987	1988	1989	1990	1991	1992	1993	1994	1995	1996	1997	1998	1999	2000	2001	Av. catch	Max. catch	Min. catch
Flókadalsá í Fljótum						40	22	54	2	10		22	68	38	64	119	135	44	164	136	15	2	21	15	40	30	12	22	50	164	2
Fljótaá	204	189	173	269	316	199	165	125	71	60	68	83	150	112	93	323	388	135	282	203	78	102	73	119	284	51	49	114	160	388	49
Eyjafjarðará						27	71	21	14	7	11	11	13	13	10	6	40	22	54	33	15	17	10	15	27	8	3	10	20	71	3
Fnjóská	386	268	250	273	554	446	527	257	323	98	107	120	144	93	124	112	121	135	554	411	128	60	95	156	286	157	197	146	233	554	60
Skjálfandafljót	92	67	412	288	336	317	426	108	169	100	165	679	721	503	379	431	493	318	862	907	379	273	353	277	263	520	379	208	372	907	67
Laxá í Aðaldal	1817	2326	1777	2699	3063	2372	2324	1455	1304	1109	1256	1911	2730	2422	2255	1619	1543	1439	2295	1983	1226	1116	1047	1227	1928	845	916	1042	1752	3063	845
Reykjadalsá og Eyvindarl	337	264	133	593	657	492	321	271	114	210	155	344	373	241	435	241	272	191	280	249	110	119	132	109	65	64	39	87	246	657	39
Mýrarkvísl	210	201	121	181	221	197	169	242	179	248	215	388	490	252	287	239	188	243	390	266	139	234	160	270	212	122	49	83	221	490	49
Ormarsá	123	117	147	275	286	119	124	54	45	87	73	203	350	275	278	264	187	156	335	366	169	163	181	141	134	108	163	143	181	366	45
Deildará	158	189	168	224	357	164	111	393	27	55	69	234	253	178	173	145	142	88	281	391	173	206	82	141	192	65	144	122	165	391	27
Svalbarðsá	234	172	155	240	257	158	167	51	36	41	29	161	171	176	198	238	135	136	289	384	145	215	177	98	159	124	92	143	164	384	29
Sandá	288	238	315	474	418	3411	380	138	53	47	35	257	340	403	290	182	81	100	354	434	204	209	152	91	177	190	143	128	233	474	35
Hölkná	135	118	92	219	130	66	73	26	26	25	11	109	121	131	144	105	91	55	150	130	45	78	44	36	53	47	59	77	86	219	11
Hafralónsá	343	302	227	312	276	264	180	36	60	52	25	132	223	296	361	313	223	123	266	402	147	1234	222	221	260	254	315	303	228	402	25
Miðfjarðará við Bakkafj	147	144	183	248	242	135	80	39	15	39	32	116	168	206	186	235	136	101	192	172	60	170	96	101	145	116	108	98	133	248	15
Selá í Vopnafirði	589	711	845	1463	1394	767	637	192	168	229	123	627	1258	1523	1102	895	634	772	1318	1092	631	1160	737	685	1140	991	1360	1108	863	1523	123
Vesturdalsá	391	329	326	513	498	268	141	42	34	61	47	280	197	380	231	226	163	116	264	321	218	329	201	216	159	71	129	124	224	513	34
Hofsá	1277	1117	1253	1273	1336	599	615	145	141	258	185	1219	1631	1710	1210	809	552	642	2238	2028	1012	1028	826	607	1008	1020	804	903	980	2238	141
Selfljót og Gilsá				77	32	19	7		6	15	16	65	70	32	12	5	26	42	90	98	16	32	8	18	25	20	22	41	33	98	5
Fjarðará í Borgarf.eystri				44	27	13	5	1																		12	5	8	13	44	1
Breiðdalsá	126	123	76	248	412	248	153	41	20	21	4	78	158	257	185	104	91	116	226	130	72	180	92	63	85	128	171	233	137	412	4
Geirlandsá í V-Skaft.	56	162	59	99	91	88	65	59	42	51	46	49	26	32	62	47	74	93	66	27	20	38	52	47	30	12	14	31	55	162	12
Eldvatn, Meðall	24	51	13	43	33	45	12	17	11	17	3	9	11	11	37	14	15	13	24	18	5	17	8	11	6	3	2	1	17	51	1
Tungufljót			14	34	43	74	46	16	20	36	28	23	36	20	25	9	11	21	49	63	35	22	28	10	30	8	7	11	28	74	7
Kerlingardalsá og Vastnsá					28	33	16	57	48	90	49	47			144	78	107	107	169	130	95	73	75	80	98	65	41	32	76	169	16
Rangárnar	29	57	95	46	82	98	65	80	65	22	10	17	78	32	53	80	1622	453	521	1041	1576	1523	1298	2960	3848	2536	3744	5466	982	5466	10
Stóralaxá í Hreppum	157	340	293	266	571	272	76	242	218	481	707	183	166	113	115	188	200	286	420	384	278	440	456	359	336	194	183	282	293	707	76
Brúará	88	84	57	49	64	49	19	57	32	63	92	48	58	76	37	34	44	72	43	80	49	54	44	42	76	14	20	15	52	92	14
Sog		593	589	537	620	439	223	329	343	248	361	424	497	490	714	325	397	396	341	429	283	300	254	252	413	491	249	317	402	714	223
Hvítá í Árnessýslu		1175	1159		1169	1028	299	762	634	846	941	550	990	965	788	680	486	456	687	938	723	580	596	405	418	190	204	250	689	1175	190
Ölfusá		298	549		825	503	6	102	368	237	381	254	405	393	535	616	315	249	293	515	375	366	192	185	224	155	258	172	337	825	6
Kálfá í Gnúpverjahr			69	42	4	4	8	10			19		11	15	66	104	87	37	2	14	40	30	54	39	60	87	56	61	40	104	2
Vatnas. Baugstaðaós									59	20	20	9	14	11	21	8	16	36	20	23	16	16	21	26	23	8	14	16	20	59	8

207

Table 4

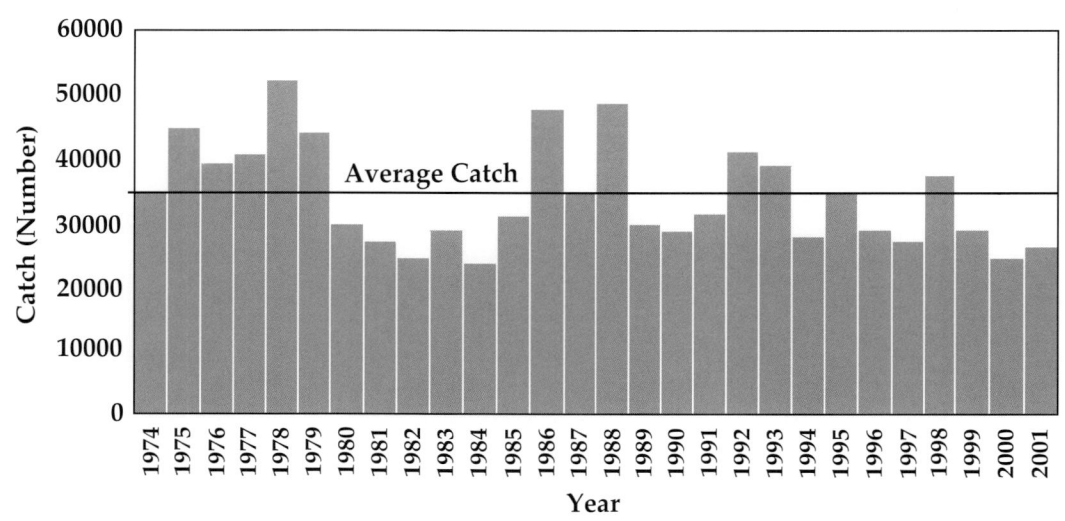

Figure 2 - Total number of salmon in the rod fishery in Iceland 1974-2001.

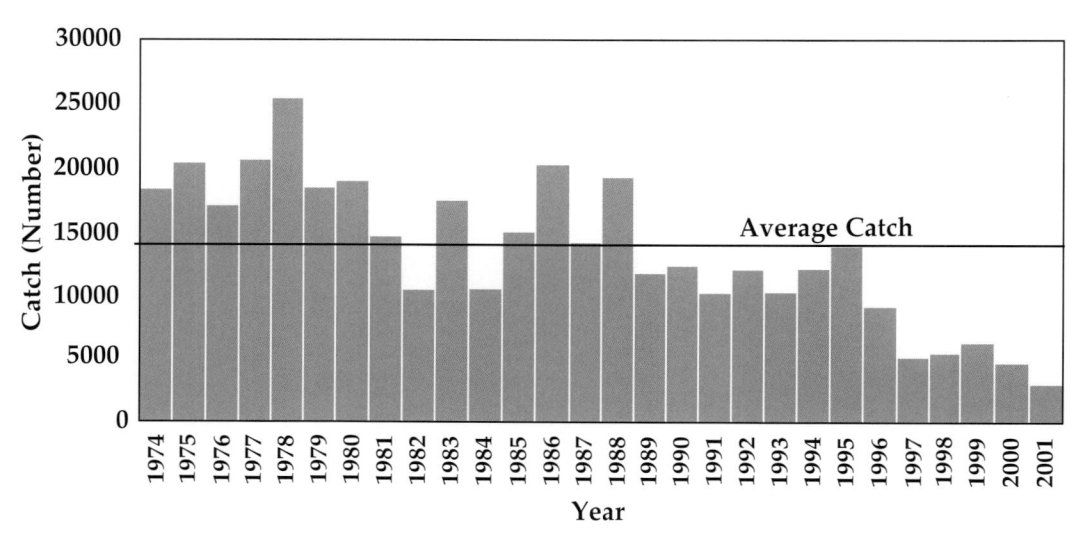

Figure 3 - Total number of salmon in the net fishery in Iceland 1974-2001.

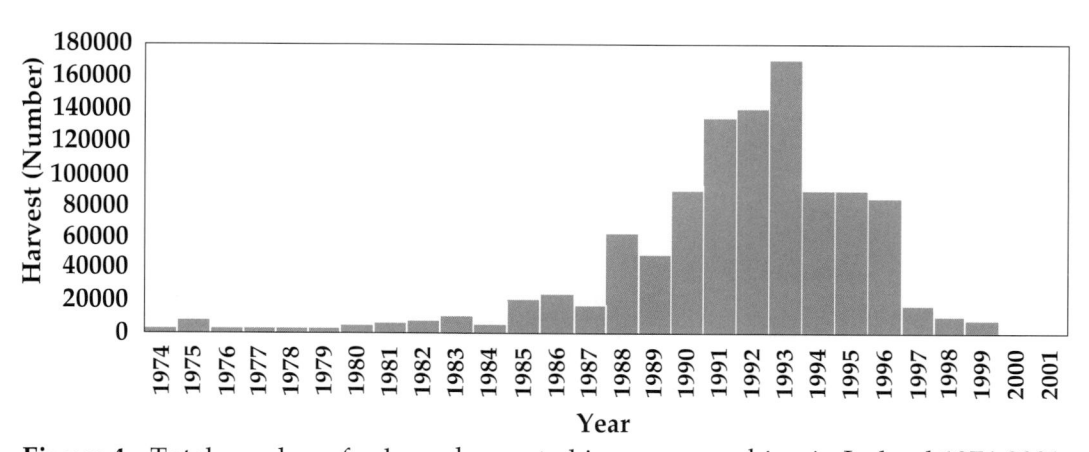

Figure 4 - Total number of salmon harvested in ocean ranching in Iceland 1974-2001.

Table 5 - Rod catch, number of released salmon in the rod fisheries, net catch and harvest in ocean ranching of salmon in Iceland 1974-2001.

Year	Rod catch	Released	Killed	Net catch	Catch rod and net	Ocean ranching	Total number	Wild salmon %
1974	34107		34107	18044	52151	3765	66916	93.3
1975	45882		45882	20402	66284	7720	74004	89.6
1976	39249		39249	17130	56379	3247	59626	94.6
1977	41302		41302	20864	62166	2405	64571	96.3
1978	52679		52679	25946	78625	1953	80578	97.6
1979	43955		43955	18306	62261	1967	64228	96.9
1980	30007		30007	18992	48999	3138	52137	94.0
1981	27777		27777	14478	42255	4626	46881	90.1
1982	24671		24671	11107	35778	5340	41118	87.0
1983	29267		29267	17761	47028	11194	58222	80.8
1984	23582		23582	10912	34494	6595	41089	83.9
1985	31621		31621	14942	46563	19750	66313	70.2
1986	46671		46671	20437	67108	24100	91208	73.6
1987	33907		33907	13960	47867	14140	62007	77.2
1988	47979		47979	18781	66760	64017	130777	51.0
1989	30082		30082	11738	41820	48617	90437	46.2
1990	29443		29443	12339	41782	90726	132508	31.5
1991	31492		31492	10454	41946	133203	175149	23.9
1992	42309		42309	12062	54371	140763	195134	27.9
1993	39025		39025	10197	49222	168427	217649	22.6
1994	28042		28042	11846	39888	89225	129113	30.9
1995	34241		34241	13185	47426	88527	135953	34.9
1996	29436	669	28767	8668	37435	84365	121800	30.7
1997	28640	1558	27082	5735	32817	15248	48065	68.3
1998	40286	2826	37460	5939	43399	11223	54622	79.5
1999	31438	3055	28383	6657	35040	9648	44688	78.4
2000	27257	2918	24432	4170	28602	375	28977	98.7
2001	29943	3611	26332	3043	29375	0	29375	100.0
Average 1974-2000	34976	2205 6 yr. Av.	34571	13891	48462	39048	87510	55.4

Table 6 -
Top 10 list of salmon rivers in Iceland 2001.

No.	River	Salmon catch
1	Eystri-Rangá	2976
2	Ytri-Rangá	2342
3	Langá	1407
4	Norðurá	1337
5	Þverá og Kjarrá	1210
6	Selá í Vopnafirði	1108
7	Blanda	1086
8	Laxá í Aðaldal	1042
9	Laxá í Kjós og Bugðá	1006
10	Grímsá og Tunguá	1005

Top 10 list of brown trout rivers and lakes in Iceland 2001.

No.	River or Lake	Brown Trout catch
1	Veiðivötn	8928
2	Laxá í Mývatnssveit	4015
3	Fremri-Laxá á Ásum	3278
4	Laxá í Laxárdal	1848
5	Laxá í Aðaldal	1796
6	Litlaá	1662
7	Þórisvatn	1505
8	Elliðavatn	1134
9	Hróarsholtslækur	931
10	Ölfusá	911

Top 10 list of arctic char rivers and lakes in Iceland 2001.

No.	River or Lake	Char catch
1	Hlíðarvatn í Selvogi	3880
2	Eyjafjarðará	2931
3	Skógaá	2489
4	Arnarvatn-Stóra	2361
5	Vatnsdalsá	1919
6	Víðidalsá og Fitjá	1903
7	Flókadalsá	1539
8	Hörgá	1373
9	Breiðdalsá	1121
10	Vesturdalsá	1079

Table 7 - Catch of brown trout, the rod fishery in some Icelandic rivers in 1987-2001.

River	1987	1988	1989	1990	1991	1992	1993	1994	1995	1996	1997	1998	1999	2000	2001	Av. catch	Max. catch	Min. catch
Laxá í Leirársveit	157	1448	194	219	221	223	180	183	153	157	116	189	239	176	209	271	1448	116
Andakílsá	4	6	1	5	0	2	1	0	3	1	7	3	4	8	4	3	8	0
Hvítá í Borgarfirði	152	190	99	192	0	149	155	364	305	722	264	583	358	924	663	314	924	0
Grímsá og Tunguá	71	49	49	74	4	216	108	357	188	30	136	213	189	250	291	148	357	4
Þverá og Kjarrá	35	80	36	99	0	121	98	109	152	247	101	247	263	463	266	154	463	0
Álftá	29	46	57	108	184	191	156	220	251	261	298	332	324	443	338	216	443	29
Hítará	5	17	14	30	23	23	39	0	34	61	33	25	30	29	28	26	61	0
Hörðudalsá	7	0	5	8	0	0		0	0	0	0	0	0		0	2	8	0
Miðá og Tunguá		0	0	1	0	4	0	1	0	0		0	0	2	2	1	4	0
Haukadalsá	0	0	78	3	1	2	1		0	14	0	2	0	0	2	7	78	0
Staðarhólsá og Hvolsá	3	2	3	2	6	3	1	2	1	2	4	2	2	2	3	3	6	1
Fjarðarhornsá	0	2	1	0	0	0	0	0	0	0			0		0	0	2	0
Selá í Steingrímsfirði	0	0		0	0	0	0	0	0	0		0	0	0	0	0	0	0
Stöðará í Steingrímsfirði	0	0	0	0	1	0	0	0	0	0	0	0	0	14	0	1	14	0
Hrútafjarðará og Síká	1	1	0	2	7	1	0	0	2	1	2	0	1	0	1	1	7	0
Miðfjarðará	20	16	7	58	41	6	10	7	9	3	2	2	15	6	9	14	58	2
Víðidalsá og Fitjá	0	3	26	13	41	34	23	14	16	42	52	316	80	151	143	64	316	0
Vatnsdalsá	366	685	245	667	571	506	335	388	450	318	300	617	520	695	807	498	807	245
Fremri Laxá á Ásum	1069	2352	338	2965	4121	3911	2709	2744	2011	1301	2379	2567	2496	2980	3278	2481	4121	338
Húseyjarkvísl	60	7	12	426	476	483	369	540	373	349	407	373	349	397	277	327	540	7
Hrollleifsdalsá		0	13	7	34	102	59	53		113	32	126	86	73	81	60	126	0
Flókadalsá		87	27	93	111	109	54	82	0	81	29	36	169	244	263	99	263	0
Fljótaá		0	3	0	10	0	0	0	0	0	1	1	0	0	0	1	10	0
Svarfaðardalsá				24		44	23	40	18	44	26	39	30	52	156	45	156	18
Hörgá				23	79	25	24	38	11	46	43	26	36	39	31	35	79	11
Eyjafjarðará	34	49	26	67	165	86	100	153	130	146	138	142	169	241	202	123	241	26
Fnjóská	20	8	14	14	31	25	12	45	27	31	53	25	44	22	28	27	53	8
Skjálfandafljót	591	99	150	119	79	88	44	53	6	18	25	89	69	17	70	101	591	6
Laxá í Aðaldal	835	894	1079	1275	1465	1286	1307	705	900	594	929	1068	1232	1647	1796	1134	1796	594
Laxá í Laxárdal		807	1075	1012	606	708	508	679	723	713	1020	1981	2099	2111	1848	1135	2111	508
Laxá í Mývatnssveit		2351	3786	3235	2186	1905	1808	1263	1558	1765	2680	5966	4214	4411	4015	2939	5966	1263
Litluárvötn		710	610	422	784	684	730	583	464	416	269	427	466	512	1662	624	1662	269
Ormarsá	35	50	21	20	31	28	15	42	9	33	17	11	18	35	44	27	50	9
Selá í Vopnaf.	3	8	10	14	9	2	4	2	8	9	6	5	14	8	5	7	14	2
Vesturdalsá	3	1	9	5	4	4	0	6	1	1	0	0	19	2	0	4	19	0
Hofsá og Sunnudalsá	11	8	53	31	50	43	54	22	24	30	49	32	29	39	27	33	54	8
Gilsá og Selfljót	33	12	15	72	70	53	39	20	27	45	77	67	34	88	54	47	88	12
Breiðdalsá	197	31	15	148	169	245	117	307	242	306	375	214	146	143	315	198	375	15
Geirlandsá	362	303	356	193	88	109	108	118	251	235	389	274	151	237	159	222	389	88
Skaftá	422	1286	483	192	424	354	464	405	388	813	969	458	456	610	836	572	1286	192
Eldvatn í Meðallandi	84	170	92	35	27	38	112	129	171	192	161	215	57	53	58	106	215	27
Grænlækur		700	894	1425	1648	2640	2338	3311	3638	2730	2493	1679	1293	1264	864	1923	3638	700
Tungufljót	62	67	148	84	134	134	249	156	174	239	384	224	273	286	286	193	384	62
Heiðarvatn			215	399	301	373	284	255	116	102	212	269	277	326	609	288	609	102
Rangár og Fiská				179	163	527	359	337	230	393	635	468	487	494	547	402	635	163
Ölfusá og Fiská		60	29	44	70	52	58	366	53	103	161	513	399	301	911	223	911	29
Sogið	2	6	8	6	10	7	6	11	15	29	23	37	40	28	27	17	40	2
Hróarholtslækur	403	550	465	322	391	449	301	580	374	326	492	1011	680	765	931	536	1011	301

Table 8 -
Catch of arctic char in the rod fishery in some Icelandic rivers in 1987-2001.

River	1987	1988	1989	1990	1991	1992	1993	1994	1995	1996	1997	1998	1999	2000	2001	Av. catch	Max. catch	Min. catch
Laxá í Leirársveit	0	7	7	1	4	6	18	14	21	4	35	62	42	43	124	26	124	0
Andakílsá	10	231	284	479	3	341	0	3	218	189	238	116	84	131	294	175	479	0
Hvítá í Borgarfirði	27	9	15	19	613	88	106	14	12	4	4	78	11	2	886	126	886	2
Grímsá og Tunguá	1	2	2	24	250	12	3	6	1	1	0	4	4	1	7	21	250	0
Þverá og Kjarrá	3	9	111	76	113	14	35	25	9	7	63	2	5	8	19	33	113	2
Álftá	0	1	2	1	4	6	10	9	2	3	6	6	0	7	0	4	10	0
Hítará	193	134	132	234	518	396	184	0	259	131	426	7	344	146	136	216	518	0
Hörðudalsá	18	291	231	614	451	340		271	423	361	1021	1003	453		907	491	1021	18
Miðá og Tunguá		73	70	470	478	650	530	441	674	350	396	825	925	591	1009	532	1009	70
Haukadalsá	679	22	11	237	919	149	267		661	747	629	904	1011	775	952	569	1011	11
Staðarhólsá og Hvolsá	401	224	338	941	882	397	616	733	934	1490	1316	1469	1016	949	583	819	1490	224
Fjarðarhornsá	20	107	306	562	536	233	73	80	135	165			47		93	196	562	20
Selá í Steingrímsfirði	261	12		229	334	259	77	404	145	356		171	246	529	0	233	529	0
Stðará í Steingrímsfirði	584	35	13	183	385	265	254	163	201	92	164	288	76	297	275	218	584	13
Hrútafjarðará og Síká	269	59	68	221	532	192	135	129	221	499	363	564	346	610	358	304	610	59
Miðfjarðará	236	167	89	221	273	152	97	123	144	47	267	304	277	97	316	187	316	47
Víðidalsá og Fitjá	1325	366	26	377	547	467	676	1214	3485	2782	1551	5568	3824	3138	1903	1817	5568	26
Vatnsdalsá	727	1182	270	1642	1851	1112	1427	1058	812	2498	1861	1438	2755	2712	1919	1551	2755	270
Fremri Laxá á Ásum	137	236	15	34	52	35	6	26	41	61	52	64	27	153	53	66	236	6
Húseyjarkvísl	7	2	8	64	28	17	32	44	48	45	30	46	17	8	18	28	64	2
Hrollleifsdalsá		47	45	221	401	410	381	628		218	198	377	325	311	281	296	628	45
Flókadalsá	110	1028	280	2134	2198	1144	1040	1673	489	265	1135	655	2405	775	1539	1125	2405	110
Fljótaá		1	44	627	643	881	1242	7071	6928	6931	1648	893	792	944	298	2067	7071	1
Svarfaðardalsá			873		1049	668	1691	358	417	475	526	704	560	842	742	1691	358
Hörgá			1692	1394	1238	1783	1590	1063	1245	1293	1229	856	1216	1373	1331	1783	856
Eyjafjarðará	1557	1467	127	2123	2836	3095	3080	3319	2151	2098	3625	3137	2900	2620	2931	2471	3625	127
Fnjóská	496	217	238	390	469	239	251	550	391	339	409	579	700	612	695	438	700	217
Skjálfandafljót	275	338	561	391	331	160	173	198	151	214	506	403	658	1034	356	383	1034	151
Laxá í Aðaldal	35	187	114	137	86	48	114	57	52	29	64	52	48	115	121	84	187	29
Laxá í Laxárdal		18	0	13	8	1	4	1	2	6	18	83	3	13	3	12	83	0
Laxá í Mývatnssveit		1	63	3	2	2	1	0	1	1	24	329	142	28	2	43	329	0
Litluárvötn		297	307	310	368	684	259	220	193	131	104	97	123	117	388	248	551	97
Ormarsá	245	114	141	181	175	127	131	126	103	101	68	93	129	128	56	128	245	56
Selá í Vopnaf.	249	56	52	211	105	103	51	106	84	164	115	37	55	72	53	101	249	37
Vesturdalsá	506	51	78	513	1402	726	321	383	474	872	1080	457	815	864	1079	641	1402	51
Hofsá og Sunnudalsá	357	32	143	67	357	471	268	261	183	344	250	246	557	744	30	287	744	30
Gilsá og Selfljót	230	61	71	455	382	368	242	381	261	532	421	221	340	375	469	321	532	61
Breiðdalsá	453	74	70	600	22	23	410	369	977	396	197	235	415	601	1121	398	1121	22
Geirlandsá	60	69	48	29	50	43	40	39	48	43	28	26	27	54	44	43	69	26
Skaftá	14	28	12	23	5	7	19	28	14	21	16	56	27	107	130	34	130	5
Eldvatn í Meðallandi	21	22	3	21	3	27	19	6	60	114	61	29	27	16	50	32	114	3
Grænlækur		78	12	151	247	177	288	273	403	290	294	223	114	128	212	206	403	12
Tungufljót	63	37	28	107	65	46	43	85	67	60	53	52	52	40	66	58	107	28
Heiðarvatn			106	203	213	319	159	296	131	89	498	616	385	331	1021	336	1021	89
Rangár og Fiská				75	65	106	90	83	94	165	150	72	54	95	88	95	165	54
Ölfusá og Fiská		8	7	12	17	12	10	72	40	20	30	21	11	16	26	22	72	7
Sogið	255	312	227	426	558	173	130	209	316	914	754	860	455	451	765	454	914	130
Hróarholtslækur	13	134	110	144	384	172	92	136	169	360	80	113	96	55	52	121	360	13

Index

A
Akroyd, Charles H., *ix, 160*
Akranes, *49, 69*
Akureyri, *2, 3, 4, 10, 26, 38, 111, 186*
Álftá, *viii, xii, xiv, 81, 202, 205, 211, 212*
Andakílsá, *205, 211, 212*
Angling Clubs, *25, 28, 48, 81, 185*
Arctic Char, *10, 16, 25, 27, 137, 147, 149, 180, 195, 196, 210, 212*
Árni Baldursson, *xvi, 10, 62, 65, 67, 77, 129, 164, 169, 172, 188*
Árni Magnusson, *116*
Ashley-Cooper, John, *12, 153*
Austurá, *vi*
Avon, Hampshire, *15*

B
Bakkaá, *167*
Balmoral Estate, *35*
Barrows Golden Eye, *3*
Biologist, *30, 45, 115, 194*
Bird List, *100*
Birkbeck, Mark, *58*
Bjarnafjarðará, *xx, 149*
Blanda, *vii, xx, 29, 155, 203, 206, 210*
Block, Jack, *89*
Boote, Paul, *58*
Booth, Brian, *10, 12, 174, 192*
Borgarnes, *7, 8, 19, 66, 69*
Borgarfjörður, *v, xii, 5, 16, 31, 48, 66, 81, 202*
Brattahlíð, Qagssiarssuk, *22, 92, 198*
Breiðdalsá, *170, 179, 180, 203, 207, 210, 211, 212*
Breiðafjörður, *28, 88, 91, 202*
Brig O'Dee, *37*
Brown trout, *viii, xv, xvii, 4, 5, 25, 27, 151, 159, 180, 182, 191, 192, 194, 204, 210, 211*
Brúará, *183, 186, 207*
Brynjudalsá, *v, xx, 62, 64, 202, 205*
Búðardalsá, *91, 206*
Bugða, *19, 20, 31, 49, 51, 54, 55, 57, 58, 59, 60, 61, 202, 205, 210*
Bush, Vice President, *70*

C
Campbell, Hugh, *34, 45*
Catch and release, *7, 12, 14, 30, 37, 43, 44, 53, 68, 71, 81, 100, 140, 153, 163, 194, 203, 204*
Cauveri, River, *132*

Char, *vii, viii, ix, xii, xiv, xv, 4, 10, 81, 82, 91, 103, 147, 148, 155, 159, 175, 179, 180, 186, 189, 191, 192, 194, 195, 196, 197, 198, 199, 204, 210, 212*
Charles, The Prince of Wales, *174*
Chilcott, Simon, *57, 58*
Cod War, *2, 4*
Constantine, Loudie, *xv, 12*
Cormorant, *42*

D
Deildará, *vi, xx, 157 to 161, 203, 207*
Desmond, Dennis, *120, 127, 137, 138, 139, 140, 141, 142, 144*
Dettifoss, *9, 24*
Dionard, *34, 45, 46*
Doppler, The Family, *165*
Dunká, *91, 205*
Dunnavant, Billy, *109, 137*
Durness, *16*

E
East coast, *vii, 29, 33, 92, 170, 191, 203, 204*
Edda Hotel, *27, 186*
Edwards, Belinda (née Fuchs), *112, 114, 120*
Edwards, Jim, *19, 57, 58, 88, 89, 112, 114, 122, 123, 132, 162*
Eider, *2, 25, 100*
Einar Pétursson, *6, 7*
Einarsfljót, *6, 75*
Einar Sigfusson, *79*
Erik the Red, or Eiríkur Raudi, *i, x, xvi, 21, 22, 92*
Eldvatn, *xx, 188, 189, 190, 207, 211, 212*
Elliðaár, *v, xx, 8, 16, 48, 73, 202, 205, 210*
Enderby, Dominic, *112*
European Union, *26*
Eyed ova, *45, 46*

F
Falcon, Gyr, *14, 24, 170*
Faroes, *21*
Fáskrúð, *vi, xx, 91, 110, 133, 145, 146, 205*
Ferguson, Alys, *5, 8, 12*
Ferguson, Graham, *5, 8, 35, 58, 59, 79, 98, 123, 175*
Ferguson, Julian, *15, 71, 79, 82*
Finnur Guðmundsson, Doctor, *1, 2*
Fjóla Edwards, *19*
Flekkudalsá, *91, 202, 206*

Index - cont.

Flies,
    Bomber, *40*
    Jeannie, *19, 20, 39, 113, 135, 141, 161*
    Red Francis, *39, 114, 135, 139, 165*
    Shrimp, *39, 90, 114, 135, 165*
    Black and Yellow, *39, 135, 141*
Fljótaá, *vii, 155, 203, 207, 211, 212*
Flókadalsá, *v, xx, 5, 66, 69, 202, 205, 207, 210, 211, 212*
Fnjóská, *vii, 155, 207, 211, 212*
Forte, Sir Charles, *82*
Fróðá, *v, xx, 16, 91, 156, 202, 205*
Frontiers, Sporting Agents, *156*

G

Garfit, William, *xv*
Gilchrist, Sir Andrew, *4*
Gljúfurá, *vi, xx, 5, 66, 80, 81*
Godchaux III, Frank, *59, 137, 139*
Godchaux, Agnes, *139, 142*
Godchaux, Charles, *127, 137*
Goðdalsá, *149*
Golden Plover, *24, 46, 94, 96, 100*
Grænilækur, *xx, 3, 187, 189, 211, 212*
Grant, Gardner L., *68*
Gravlaks, *47*
Greenland, *viii, xv, 21, 22, 76, 91, 110, 196, 197, 199*
Grétar Halldórsson, *112, 113*
Greylag, *2, 3, 100, 104*
Grímsá, *v, xx, 5, 6, 66, 68, 202, 205, 210, 211, 212*
Grísholtsá, *91, 205*
Guillemots, *46*
Gunnar Björnsson, *112, 134, 137*

H

Haffjarðará, *vi, xii, xx, 5, 82 to 90*
Hafralónsá, *v, vii, xx, 5, 9, 10, 164, 165, 203, 207*
Halldór Vilhjálmsson, *68*
Harlequin duck, *ix, 1, 2, 3, 4, 96, 100*
Haukadalsá, *vi, xx, 2, 22, 91, 92, 94, 96, 97, 100 to 108, 110, 137, 198, 202, 204, 205, 211, 212*
    The Þverá, *v, vi, xx, 7, 71, 72, 96, 103, 104, 105, 106, 107, 202, 204*
    The Upper, *vi, 103, 204*
Helgi Jakobsson, *xvi, 108, 109, 137*
Helgi Sigurðsson, *xii, 58, 74, 83*
Helgi Tómasson, *63*
Helgi-mobiles, *74, 83*

Helluvað, *3*
Hítará, *vi, xx, 81, 202, 205, 211, 212*
    Grjótá, *202*
    Tálmi, *82*
Hof, *10, 12*
Hofsá, *v, vii, xvi, xx, xxii, 5, 11, 12, 13, 14, 92, 157, 170, 174, 175, 176, 177, 178, 179, 189, 203, 204, 206, 207, 211, 212*
    Sunnudalsá, *175, 203, 211, 212*
Hofsjökull, *1*
Hölkná, *vii, xx, 165, 203, 207*
Holt, Brian, *1, 7*
Hörðudalsá, *92, 205, 211*
Horne, Bill, *137, 139, 144*
Horne, Caroline, *137, 139, 144*
Höskuldur, *110, 126, 131*
Hrútafjarðará, *vi, ix, xx, 150, 203, 206, 211, 212*
    Siká, *150*
Húsavík, *160*
Hvalfjörður, *49*
Hvítá, *v, vii, xx, 5, 6, 16, 28, 31, 65, 66, 68, 69, 71, 73, 80, 183, 202, 203, 204, 205, 207*
    Brennan, *66*
    Straumarnir, *66, 80*

I

Icelandair, *20*
Icelandic Horses, *6, 198*
Igaliko, *23, 198*
Ísafjörður, *111, 147, 148, 206*
Ivanovich, Bo, *59*

J

Jackson, John, *82*
Jakob Hafstein, *16, 156*
Jowitt, Lord, *46*
Júlíus Guðjónsson, *14, 15*
Justice, James Robertson, *41*

K

Kalli, *57*
Keflavík, *14, 23, 26, 27, 112*
Kendall, Donald, *108, 109*
Kirkjubæjarklaustur, *186, 187*
Kjarrá, *vi, xx, 5, 6, 19, 60, 69 to 79, 151, 194, 202, 205, 210, 211, 212*
Kollafjörður, *48*
Krafla, *39, 135*
Kristinn, *75, 76*
Kristján Geirmundsson, *2*
Krossá á Skarðsströnd, *91, 202, 206*
Kverká, *165, 167, 203*

Index - cont.

L
Lada, *59, 60*
Laki, *21, 189*
Lambá, *6, 70, 76, 78*
Land Rover, *1, 5, 16, 49, 60, 61, 70, 74, 193*
Langá, *vi, xii, xx, 80, 81, 202, 204, 205, 210*
Langadalsá, *vi, xx, 148, 202, 206*
Langjökull, *66*
Laugardalsá, *vi, xx, 148, 202, 206*
Laxá á Ásum, *vii, xx, 2, 30, 153, 189, 203, 206, 210, 211, 212*
Laxá á Skógarströnd, *91, 202, 205*
Laxá í Aðaldal, *vii, ix, xx, 3, 16, 24, 203, 204, 207, 210, 211, 212*
    Árnes, *156*
    Reykjadalsá, *v, xx, 66, 69, 156, 202, 203, 205, 207*
    Laxamýri, *156, 160*
Laxá í Dölum, *vi, ix, xvi, xx, 44, 69, 79, 91, 92, 93, 108 to 136, 145, 146, 157, 163, 165, 202, 205*
Laxá í Dölum, The Record Week, *vi, 137 to 145, 146*
Laxá í Kjós, *v, xx, 19, 31, 48 to 61, 63, 108, 186, 189, 202, 205, 210*
Laxá í Leirársveit, *v, xx, 64, 202, 205, 211, 212*
Laxá í Þingeyjarsýslu, *155*
Laxdæla Saga, *110*
Leifur Eiríksson, *22, 198*
Leirvogsá, *v, xx, 48, 202, 205*
Lindler, Larry, *57*
Litla Þverá, *v, 6, 38, 69, 70, 71, 74*
Long tailed duck, *ix, 1, 2, 3, 4*

M
Marlborough, Duke of, *89*
Mariu Lax, *149*
Massingbird-Mundy, Hugh, *124*
Mcleod, Bob, *45*
McPhail, Rodger, *xv,*
Merlin, *24, 100*
Miðá, *205, 211, 212*
Miðá í Dölum, *91, 110, 202*
Miðfjarðará, *vi, vii, xx, 150, 151, 152, 153, 154, 168, 189, 194, 203, 206, 207, 211, 212*
    Austurá, *vi, 150, 151, 203*
    Núpsá, *vi, 150, 151*
    Vesturá, *vi, 150, 151, 203*
Miðfjarðará í Bakkaflóa, *xx, 167, 168*

Mink, *3, 30, 41, 117*
Mosquitoes, *3, 24, 41*
Munro, Daniel, *149*
Mýrarkvísl, *156*
Mývatn, *3, 4, 5, 9, 21, 155, 156, 192, 195, 204*

N
Narsarsuaq, *196, 199*
Neve, Andrew, *96*
New Zealand, *33, 34, 105*
Newcastle, *61*
Nicklaus, Jack, *109*
Nonni Pálsson, *57, 58, 59*
Norðurá, *v, vi, xvi, xx, 5, 6, 16, 18, 19, 66, 79, 151, 194, 202, 205, 210*
North Atlantic Salmon Fund, *x, xv*
North Coast, *2, 9, 26, 90, 150, 189, 203*
North West Fjords, *vi, 91, 147, 148, 191, 202*
Nupsá, *vi*

O
Ok, *68*
Ólafsfjarðará, *xx, 4, 186*
Ölfusá, *vii, xx, 28, 43, 181, 183, 185, 203, 207, 210, 211, 212*
Ormarsá, *vii, xx, 161, 162, 203, 207, 211, 212*
Örn Friðriksson, *3, 5, 35*
Orri Vigfússon, *v, ix, x, xi, xv, 42, 47*
Owners' Beat, *82, 86*

P
Páll Jonsson, *xvi, 16, 19, 82*
Pepsi, *45, 108, 109, 112, 165*
Pink footed goose, *ix, 1*
Polar Bear, *147, 149*
Portland Hitch, *40, 81*
Pronounciation, Icelandic, *23*
Ptarmigan, *ix, 2, 47, 100*
Puffins, *46*

Q
Qagssiarssuk, Brattahlíð, *22, 92, 198*

R
Ragnar Guðmundsson, *13, 116, 118, 125, 137, 138*
Rangá, *vii, xvi, xx, 6, 31, 46, 180, 181, 182, 183, 194, 202, 203, 204, 210*
Raufarhöfn, *157*
Razor bills, *46*
Reed, Nathaniel, *68*
Reiðá, *vi, xx, 147*

Index - cont.

Restigouche, 43
Reykholt, 69
Reykjadalsá, *v, xx, 66, 69, 156, 202, 203, 205, 207*
Rio Grande, *189*
Robinson, Christopher, Roxton Bailey Robinson, Sporting Agents, *xv, xvi*
Roux, Michel, *15*
Rowcliffe, Lilla, *vi, 132*
Russia, *xii, 39, 43*

S

Saga, Laxdæla, *16, 110, 126, 130, 198*
Sandá, *vii, xx, 163, 165, 203, 207*
Savage, Ben, *16, 37, 38, 60, 61, 75, 82, 96, 112, 113, 157, 158, 159, 160, 161*
Savage, Caroline, *102*
Savage, Christopher or Kit, *1, 5, 187*
Savage, Gina, *8, 82, 112, 196*
Savage, Joanna, *xv, 17, 89, 108, 157, 158*
Savage, Nick, *16, 18, 49, 63*
Savage, Robin, *5, 9, 16, 38, 59, 61, 71, 72, 75, 79, 82, 90, 98, 112, 123, 124, 127, 166, 168, 196*
Savage, Sandy, *xii, xv, 9, 16, 18, 20, 37, 38, 72, 82, 83, 84, 102, 112, 114, 117,*
Savage, William, *149*
Schwerdt, Sue, *104*
Schwiebert, Ernest, *68*
Scoters, *ix, 1*
Scott, Sir Peter, *ix, 1, 2*
Sea trout, *vii, xvi, xx, 4, 24, 25, 43, 48, 51, 54, 60, 61, 68, 81, 90, 91, 150, 173, 175, 179, 180, 182, 186, 187, 189, 191, 194, 204*
Seals, *42, 43, 145, 146*
Selá, *vii, xvi, xx, 92, 169, 170, 171, 172, 173, 174, 178, 203, 206, 207, 210, 211, 212*
Self-catering, *ix, 16, 27, 32, 66, 69, 81, 91, 92, 145, 146, 148, 155, 156, 157, 161, 163, 165, 170, 183, 185, 189, 204*
Sellick, Christopher, *1, 5, 8, 14*
Setbergsá, *91, 202, 205*
Siggi Gunnarsson, *157*
Sigurður Helgason, *v, xii, xiii, xiv, xv, xvi, 12, 15, 58, 59, 69, 70, 75, 170, 175*
Sigurjón Einarsson, *6*
Skjálfandafljót, *vii, 155, 203, 207, 211, 212*
Skraumá, *91*
Skuas, *24, 96*
Skútustaðir, *5*

Smolt, *14, 26, 27, 30, 38, 45, 46, 65, 73, 91, 92, 157, 180, 182*
Snæfellsnes, *vi, 16, 29, 44, 81, 82, 87, 88, 91, 110*
Sog, *vii, xx, 155, 183, 185, 203, 207*
Spinner, *28, 37, 101, 133*
Stilton Cheese, *137, 141*
Stóra Laxá, *vii, xx, 32, 155, 183, 184, 210*
Stórikroppur, *69*
Surtsey, *21*
Svalbarðsá, *vii, xx, 162, 203, 207*
Svartá, *vii, xx, 154, 155, 203, 206*
Svartá Salman, *xiii*
Swice group, *92, 93, 103, 165*
Symonds, Peter, *xv,*

T

Temple, Angela, *157 to 161*
Temple, Edward, *157 to 160*
Thai 'wifelet', *189*
The Rivers of Iceland, *ix, xii, xvii, 2, 108, 150*
    General Stewart, *ix, xi, xii, xvii, 2, 108, 109, 111, 127, 150*
Þingvallavatn, *185*
Þröstur Elliðason, *179, 180, 182, 183*
Þverá, *v, vi, xx, 5 to 9, 12, 19, 38, 60, 66, 69 to 97, 103 to 107, 202, 204, 205, 210, 211, 212*
Tipping, *26*
Torfi Ásgeirson, *92, 93, 94, 101, 104, 105*
Tóti Tönn, *53, 56, 58, 77*
Tungufljót, *183*

U

Ulfarsá, *48*
Urriðaá, *xii*

V

Varmá, *v, xx, 48*
Varzuga, *43*
Vatnajökull, *21, 179, 192*
Vatnsdalsá, *vi, xx, 12, 31, 153, 163, 189, 203, 206, 210, 211, 212*
Veiðifélag, *12, 25, 28, 30, 66, 145, 155, 183*
Veiðihuis, *83*
Vesturá, *vi*
Vesturdalsá, *vii, 170, 173, 203, 206, 207, 210, 211, 212*
Veteran Sportsman's Diary by Charles H. Akroyd, *ix*
Viðidalsá, *vi, xx, 153, 189, 203, 206, 210, 211, 212*

Index - cont.

Vikings, *xvi, 8, 21, 22, 23, 45, 70, 74, 110, 125, 130, 196, 198*
Vopnafjörður, *14, 169, 173, 179*

W
Wading staff, *32, 41, 127*
Walker, James, *89, 90, 114*
Wellington, Duke and Duchess of, *137, 138, 140, 142, 144*
Whooper swans, *3, 33, 100*
Wildfowl Trust, *ix, xvii, 1, 4*
Wimbrel, *24, 99, 100*
Wright, Charlie, *35*